THE VAT AND PROPERTY GUIDE

2nd edition

Sean Finn of Lovells

LEGALEASE
PUBLISHING

ISBN: 1-903927-61-7

Published by Legalease Publishing, Kensington Square House, 12-14 Ansdell Street, London W8 5BN

The publisher and authors are not responsible for the results of any actions (or lack thereof) taken on the basis of information in this book. Readers should obtain advice from a qualified professional when dealing with specific situations.

Crown copyright material is reproduced with the permission of the Controller of HMSO and the Queen's Printer for Scotland.

Printed and bound in Great Britain by Latimer Trend, Plymouth.

www.legalease.co.uk

PREFACE

This book has been written as an introduction to the VAT treatment of commercial and non-commercial property transactions, and to the impact of VAT on the structure of property dealing and investment. No one concerned with the ownership, development, financing or management of property can afford to ignore VAT which, at 17.5%, is payable in addition to the cost of many sales and acquisitions of property, as well as on building and associated costs. This tax can be recovered in many transactions, but only if they are properly structured. Failure to consider the VAT implications of a transaction could, therefore, create a real cost of up to 17.5% of the total value of a property, plus penalties and interest in certain cases. Accordingly, it is worth spending time considering the VAT effects early on in a transaction, in case an alternative way of structuring it is available to provide a better VAT position (other tax and commercial issues being neutral). The book will be relevant to everyone who is concerned with property or construction, but those who should find it particularly useful include:

- builders;

- tenants of non-domestic buildings;

- property developers;

- charities and religious bodies;

- landowners of all kinds;

- private hospitals;

- banks and building societies; and

- private schools.

Since its introduction in the UK in 1973, VAT has become a significant factor in business transactions, and its importance increases with the passing of the years and each new Finance Act. The Finance Act 1989 introduced new provisions which made many property transactions subject to VAT for the first time. Since then, planning to mitigate the impact of VAT has become a major feature of all aspects of the ownership, development, financing or management of real property in the UK. This has been countered by anti-avoidance provisions, such as those introduced by the Finance Act 1997 (disapplication of the option to tax), which can apply whether or not there is any intention to avoid tax, and seem to have been designed as a trap for the unwary. More recently, the Finance Act 2004 introduced for the first time an obligation on taxpayers to disclose certain VAT schemes to the tax authorities, and many (although not all) of the schemes earmarked for disclosure involve property-related transactions.

Appendix 1 sets out the basic VAT treatment of some common transactions involving both commercial and non-commercial property.

We stress that this book is only intended as a general introduction to VAT in property transactions – individual circumstances may differ, and it is essential that specific advice is taken and the legislation itself is considered before entering into any particular transaction.

All references are to the Value Added Tax Act 1994, as amended, except where otherwise stated. Only the law of England and Wales, in force as at 1 August 2005, is considered.

On 18 April 2005, the Inland Revenue and HM Customs and Excise were integrated into a new single department, HM Revenue & Customs (referred to in this book as HMRC).

Sean Finn, London, September 2005

ABOUT THE AUTHOR

Sean is a partner in the London office of Lovells. He advises a wide range of clients on all aspects of corporate and business taxation.

He acts for a broad range of household names across a number of industrial and financial sectors, and has particular expertise in advising on tax aspects of private equity transactions, M&A, reconstructions, and property- and VAT-related transactions.

Sean is a member of the Chartered Institute of Taxation and a member of the European VAT Club.

Contents

Preface iii

Table of cases xi

Table of statutes xii

Table of statutory instruments xiii

Table of HMRC materials xiii

1. Key VAT concepts and terms 1
1.1 Scope of VAT 1
1.2 Taxable supply 1
1.3 Taxable person 1
1.4 Registration 2
1.5 Registration of a property business 2
1.6 Group registration 3
1.7 Charging VAT 3
1.8 Accounting periods 4
1.9 Paying VAT 4
1.10 Recovery of VAT 4
1.11 Place of supply 5
1.12 Election to waive exemption 6

2. Basic principles – commercial and non-commercial buildings 7
2.1 Introduction 7
2.2 The distinction between commercial and non-commercial buildings and
works 7
2.3 Dwellings 8
2.4 Relevant residential purpose 9
2.5 Relevant charitable purpose 9

3. Construction, conversion, alteration, demolition and civil engineering . . . 11
3.1 Introduction 11
3.2 Meaning of construction and conversion 11
3.3 Treatment of building services and building materials – general 13
3.4 Construction and alteration of commercial buildings 13
3.5 Construction, conversion and alteration of non-commercial buildings 13
3.6 Building materials 15
3.7 Services of architects, surveyors, etc 16
3.8 Apportionment 16
3.9 Demolition 16
3.10 Construction of civil engineering works 16
3.11 Undertakings under section 106 Town and Country Planning Act 1990 and
similar agreements 17

3.12 DIY housebuilders and self-build projects by voluntary bodies 17
3.13 Building regulation fees 18

4. Disposals of non-commercial property **19**
4.1 Disposals by the person constructing 19
4.2 VAT implications generally for developers of non-commercial buildings . . . 22
4.3 Disposals by persons other than the person constructing 24
4.4 Surrenders of leases of non-commercial buildings 24

5. Disposals of commercial property **25**
5.1 Introduction 25
5.2 Sales of freeholds of commercial property 25
5.3 The grant or assignment of leases of commercial property 27
5.4 Surrenders and assignments of leases of commercial property 27
5.5 Reverse premiums 30
5.6 Rent-free periods 32
5.7 Partnership interests 32
5.8 Licences to occupy 33
5.9 Miscellaneous standard-rated property transactions 34
5.10 Property exchanges 36
5.11 Lease break clauses 36
5.12 Statutory compensation 36
5.13 Dilapidations 36
5.14 Rent apportionments 37

6. The election to waive exemption **39**
6.1 What is the election to waive exemption? 39
6.2 Why elect? 39
6.3 Extent of the election 40
6.4 When the election does not apply 41
6.5 The anti-avoidance provisions 42
6.6 Who may elect? 43
6.7 Agreements (not) to elect 43
6.8 What does the election cover? 43
6.9 Effect of the election 44
6.10 Who does the election bind? 45
6.11 Revoking the election 45
6.12 Cessation of the election 45
6.13 Example of the operation of the election 46
6.14 Does the election add VAT to the rent? 47
6.15 The timing of the election 47
6.16 How is the election made? 48
6.17 Electing where exempt supplies have been made 49
6.18 The recovery of input tax 50
6.19 Recovery of input tax incurred before an election 52
6.20 Elections by members of VAT groups 53
6.21 Agricultural land 53
6.22 Disadvantages of the election for purchasers and tenants 53
6.23 Landlords of commercial buildings and land 55

6.24 Vendors of commercial buildings and land 56
6.25 Residential developers who are vendors 57
6.26 Commercial property lenders 57

7. When is VAT payable in property transactions? 59
7.1 Introduction 59
7.2 Construction work 59
7.3 Sales of freeholds 60
7.4 Grants or assignments of leases, etc for premiums 62
7.5 Grants of leases and licences for rent 62
7.6 Surrenders of leases, etc 62
7.7 Variations of leases 63

8. Self-supplies 65
8.1 What is a self-supply? 65
8.2 Who is affected by a self-supply? 65
8.3 Self supply of in-house construction services 66
8.4 The value of the self-supply of in-house construction services 66
8.5 The impact of the self-supply of construction services 66
8.6 Self-supply on change of use of non-commercial building 67

9. The capital goods scheme 69
9.1 Introduction 69
9.2 What land and buildings are affected? 69
9.3 How is the tax adjusted? 70
9.4 How the adjustment works 71
9.5 Short leases 72
9.6 Transfer of a business as a going concern 72
9.7 VAT groups 73

10. Legal and beneficial owners 75
10.1 Elections by beneficial owners 75
10.2 Transfer of a business as a going concern and nominees 76
10.3 Recent developments 76

11. Transfers of property as a going concern 79
11.1 Introduction 79
11.2 TOGCs of rental properties 80
11.3 Miscellaneous examples of property TOGCs 82
11.4 TOGCs and VAT groups 86
11.5 Input tax on transaction costs 87

12. Abuse of law and VAT disclosure rules 91
12.1 Introduction 91
12.2 Abuse of law principles 91
12.3 Which schemes must be disclosed? 93
12.4 Do all businesses have to disclose? 94
12.5 Designated and hallmarked schemes 95
12.6 How and when should disclosure be made? 97
12.7 Penalties for failing to comply with disclosure requirements 97

13. Transactions under planning agreements **99**
13.1 Introduction 99
13.2 Dedication of roads and sewers 99
13.3 Section 106 and similar agreements 99
13.4 Cash contributions made by developers 100
13.5 Transfers of roads, etc to management companies 100

14. Some other implications of VAT in property transactions **101**
14.1 Stamp duty land tax 101
14.2 Stamp duty land tax and VAT on leases 102
14.3 Stamp duty land tax and transfers of a going concern 102
14.4 Land Registry fees 103
14.5 Capital allowances 103
14.6 Capital gains tax 103
14.7 Service charges 104
14.8 Insurance premiums paid by tenants to landlord 104
14.9 Payments of landlords' costs by tenants 104
14.10 Fixtures and fittings 106
14.11 Covenants concerning land 106
14.12 Rights of light 106
14.13 Crane over-sailing licences 106
14.14 Default on rent by tenant 107

**Appendix 1: Summary of VAT in commercial and non-commercial property
transactions** **111**

**Appendix 2: Draft letter to HMRC notifying it of an election where no exempt
supplies have been made or will be made in relation to the relevant land
prior to the day on which the election takes effect** **113**

**Appendix 3: Draft letter to HMRC where an exempt supply has been or will be
made in relation to the relevant land prior to the day on which the election
takes effect** **114**

**Appendix 4: Pro forma notice of agreement for transfer of a going concern to
nominee purchaser** **115**

**Appendix 5: Standard VAT and transfer of a going concern wording for property
sale contract where vendor has elected to tax the land being sold** **116**

**Appendix 6: Additional VAT transfer of a going concern clauses where the
purchaser is buying land as nominee for another person** **118**

**Appendix 7: Draft letter notifying transfer of a going concern and asking to
return records** **119**

Appendix 8: HMRC Notice 742/02 – Land and property **120**

Appendix 9: HMRC Notice 742A/02 – Opting to tax land and buildings **142**

**Appendix 10: HMRC Notice 700/9/02 – Transfer of business as a going
concern** **159**

Appendix 11: HMRC Business Brief 10/96 (extract) 174

Appendix 12: HMRC Business Brief 5/97 (extract) 176

Appendix 13: HMRC Business Brief 26/98 (extract) 177

Appendix 14: HMRC Business Brief 16/99 (extract) 178

Appendix 15: HMRC Business Brief 8/01 (extract) 179

Appendix 16: HMRC Business Brief 11/01 (extract) 181

Appendix 17: HMRC Business Brief 14/04 (extract) 182

Appendix 18: HMRC Business Brief 21/04 (extract) 185

Appendix 19: HMRC Business Brief 30/04 189

Appendix 20: HMRC Business Brief 32/04 (extract) 192

Appendix 21: HMRC Business Brief 12/05 (extract) 194

Appendix 22: HMRC Business Brief 16/05 (extract) 196

Subject index 199

TABLE OF CASES

Abbey National Plc v Customs & Excise Commissioners [2001] STC 297 . . . . 11.5
Abbey National Plc v Customs & Excise Commissioners [2005] EWHC 831 (Ch) 5.4, 10.3
Re Abbotsley Golf & Squash Club Ltd 1997, VAT Tribunal decision 15042 . . . . 5.8
Beaverbank Properties Ltd v Customs & Excise Commissioners
2003, VAT Tribunal decision 18099. . . . . 6.9, 6.19
Belgian State v Temco Europe SA ECJ case C-284/03 . . . . 5.8
Blythe Limited Partnership v Customs & Excise Commissioners
1999, VAT Tribunal decision 16011 . . . . 6.16
British Telecommunications Plc v Customs & Excise Commissioners
1999, VAT Tribunal decision 16244 . . . . 5.8
BUPA Hospitals Ltd v Customs & Excise Commissioners ECJ case C-419/02. . . . . 12.2
Carter t/a Protheroe Carter & Eason v Customs & Excise Commissioners
1994, VAT Tribunal decision 12047 . . . . 14.13
Chalegrove Properties Ltd v Customs & Excise Commissioners
2001, VAT Tribunal decision 17151 . . . . 11.2
Customs & Excise Commissioners v Cantor Fitzgerald International [2001] STC 1453 . . . . 5.5
Customs & Excise Commissioners v Latchmere Properties Ltd [2005] STC 731 . . . . 10.3
Customs & Excise Commissioners v Link Housing Association Ltd [1992] STC 718 . . . . 4.1
Customs & Excise Commissioners v Redrow Group Plc [1999] STC 161 . . . . 14.9
Customs & Excise Commissioners v St Dunstan's Educational Foundation [1999] STC 381 . . . . 2.5
Daniels v Customs & Excise Commissioners 1993, VAT Tribunal decision 12014 . . . . 5.8
Fforestfach Medical Centre v Customs & Excise Commissioners
2000, VAT Tribunal decision 16587 . . . . 6.16
Re GW Green & Mrs JA Green 1991, VAT Tribunal decision 9016 . . . . 1.5
Halifax Plc v Customs & Excise Commissioners ECJ case C-255/02. . . . . 12.2
Higher Education Statistics Agency Ltd v Customs & Excise Commissioners
1999, VAT Tribunal decision 15917; [2000] STC 332 . . . . 7.3, 11.2
KapHag Renditefonds, 35 Spreecenter Berlin-Hellersdorf, 3. Tranche GbR v
Finanzamt Charlottenburg ECJ case C-442/01 . . . . 5.7
Lloyds Bank Plc v Customs & Excise Commissioners 1996, VAT Tribunal decision 14181. . . . . 5.11
Lubbock Fine & Co v Customs & Excise Commissioners [1994] STC 101. . . . . 14.12
Mirror Group Plc v Customs & Excise Commissioners [2001] STC 1453. . . . . 5.5
Nell Gwynn House Maintenance Fund Trustees v Customs & Excise Commissioners
[1999] STC 79 . . . . 14.7
Ridgeons Bulk Ltd v Customs & Excise Commissioners [1994] STC 427. . . . . 5.5, 5.6
Royal and Sun Alliance Insurance Group Plc v Customs & Excise Commissioners
[2003] STC 832. . . . . 6.9, 6.19
Sinclair Collis Ltd v Customs & Excise Commissioners [1999] STC 710; [2001] STC 989;
ECJ case C-275/01 . . . . 5.8
Skatteministeriet v Henriksen [1990] STC 768 . . . . 5.9
Swindon Masonic Association Ltd v Customs & Excise Commissioners [1978] VATTR 200 . . . . 5.8
Tameside Metropolitan Borough Council v Customs & Excise Commissioners 5.8
[1979] VATTR 93
University of Huddersfield Higher Education Corporation v Customs & Excise Commissioners
ECJ case C-223/03 . . . . 12.2

TABLE OF STATUTES

Agricultural Tenancies Act 1995 c8 . . . . 5.12
Capital Allowances Act 2001 c2
    s235 . . . . 14.5
    s238 . . . . 14.5
Companies Act 1985 c6 . . . . 12.2
    s259 . . . . 12.4
Finance Act 1997 c16
    s37(5)-(6) 6.5
Finance Act 2003 c14 . . . . 14.2
    Sch 2, para 2 . . . . 14.1
    Sch 4, para 2 . . . . 14.1
    Sch 10, para 6 . . . . 14.3
Finance Act 2004 c5
    s19 . . . . 12.1
    Sch 2 . . . . 12.1
Landlord and Tenant Act 1954 c56 . . . . 5.12
Landlord and Tenant (Covenants)
    Act 1995 c30 . . . . 14.14
Law of Distress Amendment Act 1908 c53
    s6 . . . . 14.14
Stamp Act 1891 c39
    s5 . . . . 14.3
Town and Country Planning Act 1990 c8
    s106 . . . . 5.11, 13.3
Value Added Tax Act 1994 c23
    s4(1) 1.1
    s4(2) 1.2
    s19(3) 5.10
    s24(1) 1.9
    s24(2) 1.7
    s26 . . . . 1.9
    s35 . . . . 3.12
    s43 . . . . 1.6
    s44 . . . . 11.4
    s45 . . . . 5.7
    s89 . . . . 6.14, 6.24
    s96(1) 4.1
    Sch 1, para 1(1) 1.4
    Sch 1, para 1(3) 1.4
    Sch 1, para 9 . . . . 1.4
    Sch 6, para 1 . . . . 1.7
    Sch 8, Group 5 Item 1(a) 4.1
    Sch 8, Group 5 Item 1(b) 4.1
    Sch 8, Group 5 Item 2 . . . . 3.5, 3.7
    Sch 8, Group 5 Item 3 . . . . 3.5
    Sch 8, Group 5 Item 4 . . . . 3.5
    Sch 8, Group 5 note (2) 2.3
    Sch 8, Group 5 note (3) 2.3
    Sch 8, Group 5 note (4) 2.4
    Sch 8, Group 5 note (6) 2.5
    Sch 8, Group 5 note (11) 3.8
    Sch 8, Group 5 note (12)(a) 3.5

Sch 8, Group 5 note (12)(b) 3.5, 4.1
Sch 8, Group 5 note (13) 4.1
Sch 8, Group 5 note (14) 4.1
Sch 8, Group 5 note (15) 3.2
Sch 8, Group 5 note (16) 3.2
Sch 8, Group 5 note (16)(b) 3.2
Sch 8, Group 5 note (17) 3.2
Sch 8, Group 5 note (18) 3.2
Sch 8, Group 5 note (19) 3.10
Sch 8, Group 5 note (22) 3.6
Sch 8, Group 6 Item 1 . . . . 4.1
Sch 8, Group 6 Item 2 . . . . 3.5
Sch 8, Group 6 note (4) 4.1
Sch 8, Group 6 note (6) 4.1
Sch 9 . . . . 1.2
Sch 9, Group 1 . . . . 5.8
Sch 9, Group 1 Item 1(a) 5.2
Sch 9, Group 1 Item 1(c)-(n) 5.3, 5.9
Sch 9, Group 1 note (1) 4.4, 5.4
Sch 9, Group 1 note (1A) 4.4, 5.4
Sch 9, Group 1 note (2) 5.2
Sch 9, Group 1 note (4) 5.2
Sch 9A 6.20
Sch 10, para 1(3) 8.6
Sch 10, para 1(5) 8.6
Sch 10, para 1(6)(b) 8.6
Sch 10, para 2(1) 5.2, 5.3, 6.1
Sch 10, para 2(2) 4.1, 4.3
Sch 10, para 2(2)(a) 6.4
Sch 10, para 2(2A)-(2B) 6.4
Sch 10, para 2(2)(b) 6.4
Sch 10, para 2(2)(c) 6.4
Sch 10, para 2(2)(d) 6.4
Sch 10, para 2(3)(a) 6.4
Sch 10, para 2(3)(b) 6.4
Sch 10, para 2(3AA) 6.4
Sch 10, para 2(8)-(9) 6.19
Sch 10, para 3(2) 6.3
Sch 10, para 3(3) 6.3
Sch 10, para 3(4) 6.11
Sch 10, para 3(5) 6.11
Sch 10, para 3(6)(b)(ii) 6.17
Sch 10, para 3(9) 6.17
Sch 10, para 3A 6.4
Sch 10, para 8 . . . . 5.4, 10.1, 10.2, 10.3
Sch 11A, para 2 . . . . 12.5
Sch 11A, para 5 . . . . 12.3
Sch 11A, para 6 . . . . 12.3
Sch 11A, para 7 . . . . 12.4
Sch 11A, para 8 . . . . 12.4
Sch 11A, para 9 . . . . 12.4
Sch 11A, para 11 . . . . 12.6

TABLE OF STATUTORY INSTRUMENTS

Value Added Tax Regulations 1995
(SI 1995/2518)
reg 58 . . . . 1.7
reg 84(1) 7.3
reg 84(2) 7.3
reg 93 . . . . 7.2
regs 99-111 . . . . 6.18
reg 101 . . . . 1.10
reg 113(b) 9.2
reg 113(c) 9.2
reg 113(d) 9.2
reg 113(e) 9.2
reg 113(f) 9.2
reg 113(g) 9.2
reg 113(h) 9.2
reg 115(3) 9.4

reg 115(3A)-(3B) 9.4
Value Added Tax (Disclosure of Avoidance
Schemes) Regulations 2004
(SI 2004/1929) 12.4
para 2 . . . . 12.6
Value Added Tax (Disclosure of Avoidance
Schemes) (Designations) Order 2004
(SI 2004/1933) 12.5
Sch 1 . . . . 12.5
Sch 2 . . . . 12.5
Value Added Tax (Self-Supply of
Construction Services) Order 1989
(SI 1989/472) 8.3
Value Added Tax (Special Provisions)
Order 1995 (SI 1995/1268)
Art 5 . . . . 11.1

TABLE OF HMRC MATERIALS

Budget Notes
Note 6 (2005) 12.5
Business Briefs
10/96 . . . . 10.2, A11
5/97 . . . . 3.13, A12
26/98 . . . . 11.3, A13
16/99 . . . . 7.3, A14
21/99 . . . . 5.8
8/01 . . . . 11.5, A15
11/01 . . . . 11.2, A16
14/04 . . . . 6.9, A17
21/04 . . . . 5.7, A18
30/04 . . . . 5.7, A19
32/04 . . . . 6.1, A20
12/05 . . . . 5.5, A21
13A/05 . . . . 6.16
16/05 . . . . 5.4, A22
Customs & Excise Manual
Vol 1, Pt 8, s2.19 . . . . 5.4
Vol 1, s3, para 7.8.2 . . . . 5.11
Vol 1, s10, Ch 2 para 3.2 . . . . 11.2
Vol 1, s10, Ch 2 para 4.8 . . . . 11.4
Vol 1, s10, Ch 2 para 5.4 . . . . 11.2
Notices
700
para 6.8 . . . . 1.5
700/8/04 . . . . 12.6

700/9/02 . . . . A10
paras 2.3-2.5 . . . . 11.2
para 2.3.3 . . . . 11.3
para 2.4.1 . . . . 11.2
para 2.7 . . . . 11.5
para 7.2 . . . . 11.13
para 7.3 . . . . 11.2
708/02 . . . . 3.5, 4.1, 4.2
para 3.3 . . . . 3.2
para 13.8 . . . . 3.6
742/02 . . . . A8
para 8.1 . . . . 3.11, 13.2
para 8.2 . . . . 13.5
para 8.3 . . . . 13.3
para 8.5 . . . . 13.4
para 10.6 . . . . 14.11
para 10.7 . . . . 5.12
para 10.9 . . . . 5.14
para 10.10 . . . . 5.13
s11 . . . . 14.7
para 13.5.2 . . . . 4.2
742A/02 . . . . A9
para 2.4 . . . . 6.12
para 4.2 . . . . 6.21
para 5.2 . . . . 6.17
Stamp Duty Land Tax Manual
para 3800 . . . . 14.3

1. Key VAT concepts and terms

Summary

- This chapter summarises the way VAT works, and explains some of the terms which need to be understood before looking at the specific details of the application of VAT to property transactions. Practitioners with a working knowledge of VAT can skip this part.

1.1 Scope of VAT

VAT is charged on any taxable supply of goods or services in the UK by a taxable person in the course or furtherance of any business he carries on.[1]

1.2 Taxable supply

1.2.1 A taxable supply is defined as being a supply of goods or services made in the UK, other than an exempt supply.[2] Exempt supplies are those which fall within the specific categories set out in Schedule 9. Accordingly, all other supplies are taxable supplies. This includes supplies on which VAT is charged at 0% (the zero rate), 4% (the farmer's flat rate), 5% (the lower rate applicable to domestic fuel and power) and 17.5% (the standard rate).

1.2.2 Certain supplies (eg those not made in the UK or not made in the course or furtherance of a business) are outside the scope of UK VAT altogether. A transfer of a business as a going concern is likewise outside the scope of VAT.

1.3 Taxable person

A taxable person is anyone who makes or intends to make taxable supplies, and is registered for VAT or is required to be registered (see **1.4** below). A person for these purposes may include:

(a) an individual;

(b) a company;

(c) a partnership;

---

1 Section 4(1).
2 Section 4(2).

(d) co-owners (eg joint tenants or tenants in common); and

(e) the trustees of a fund or charity.

1.4 REGISTRATION

1.4.1 A person must register for VAT if the value of the taxable supplies made by him exceeds or is likely to exceed a specified limit (which usually changes annually). From 1 April 2005, registration is required:[3]

(a) at the end of any month, if the value of taxable supplies made by a person has exceeded £60,000 in the 12 calendar months then ending; or

(b) at any time, if there are reasonable grounds for believing that the value of the taxable supplies made by a person in the next 30 days will exceed £60,000.

A person does not, however, become liable to be registered under the provisions referred to in (a) above if HMRC is satisfied that the value of the person's taxable supplies in the period of one year beginning at the time at which he would otherwise become liable to be registered will not exceed £58,000.[4]

1.4.2 Even if not required to do so, a person may choose to register for VAT if either:

(a) he makes taxable supplies, but the value of those supplies does not exceed the limits referred to above; or

(b) he is carrying on a business, intends to make taxable supplies and can satisfy certain evidential requirements.[5]

Registering voluntarily for VAT is often beneficial to a business, since it enables the recovery of input tax (see **1.10** below).

1.5 REGISTRATION OF A PROPERTY BUSINESS

1.5.1 HMRC has said that if persons intend to co-operate in making supplies as a joint venture, but have not formed a company or entered into a formal partnership agreement, this may nevertheless amount to a partnership, which should be registered as such for VAT purposes.[6]

---

3 Sch 1, para 1(1).

4 Sch 1, para 1(3).

5 Sch 1, para 9.

6 HMRC Notice 700, para 6.8.

1.5.2 Joint tenants are jointly registrable in respect of the total value of supplies made by them as joint owners, as there is no basis for dividing the value of the supply between them. The case of *GW Green and Mrs JA Green* [7] is an example of this. Briefly, the facts were that a married couple purchased garages and let them to tenants. The tribunal held that the letting of the garages was a business activity, carried on by the couple together, and they were liable to be registered together. The liability to register jointly arises even if the joint owners are not a partnership although, as there is no separate category of joint ownership for registration, HMRC will register them as a partnership.

1.6 GROUP REGISTRATION

Companies under common control may (but need not) register together as members of a VAT group, in which case they are treated much as a single company for VAT purposes. [8] In particular, supplies between companies in the VAT group are ignored for VAT purposes. Where there is a VAT group registration, supplies between members of the group and third parties are treated as made to or by a nominated company in the group, known as the 'representative member'. A VAT group registration need not include all companies in a corporation tax group.

1.7 CHARGING VAT

1.7.1 Where the standard rate applies, the supplier must charge his customer VAT at 17.5% of the value of the supply. [9] VAT charged in this way is called output tax (being the VAT on supplies and invoices going out of the business). The person charging output tax must account for it to HMRC at the end of the VAT accounting period in which it was charged, whether or not he has received payment from his customers. [10]

1.7.2 The value of a supply is the consideration obtained by the supplier from the purchaser or a third party for the supply.

1.7.3 Where a supply is made between connected persons (for example, if they are under common control but not in a VAT group) for a consideration

---

7 Unreported, 1991, VAT Tribunal decision 9016.

8 Section 43.

9 Section 24(2).

10 Unless the value of taxable supplies made by the person is less than £660,000, when he may be authorised to use a special scheme known as the cash accounting scheme: Value Added Tax Regulations 1995, SI 1995/2518 (VATR 1995), reg 58.

in money which is less than the open-market value, HMRC has the power to substitute the market value of the supply. Where the supply is taxable, HMRC can only substitute the market value if the person to whom the supply is made is not entitled to obtain credit for the VAT charged on the supply.[11]

1.8 ACCOUNTING PERIODS

VAT accounting periods may be either monthly or quarterly, and VAT is accounted for on a return submitted to HMRC by the supplier at the end of each period. VAT-registered persons whose annual liability for VAT exceeds £2m and who make quarterly returns are required to make payments of VAT on account monthly, rather than each quarter.

1.9 PAYING VAT

VAT on goods or services supplied to a person and used or to be used for the purpose of his business is called input tax (being the VAT on supplies and invoices coming in to the business).[12] If the person paying input tax is registered for VAT and the input tax is directly attributable to standard-rated or zero-rated supplies made or to be made by him, he can recover the input tax from HMRC.[13]

1.10 RECOVERY OF VAT

1.10.1 In property transactions, attribution of input tax is normally determined on a property-by-property basis. A person should recover all the input tax directly attributable to a building in relation to which taxable supplies are made or to be made if either:

(a) he makes taxable supplies of the building by selling or leasing it; or

(b) he occupies it to carry on a business which makes only taxable supplies.

A person will not recover any input tax directly attributable to a building in relation to which only exempt supplies are made or to be made. Where a property is used to make both taxable and exempt supplies, only a proportion of the input tax is recoverable.[14]

---

11 Sch 6, para 1.
12 Section 24(1).
13 Section 26.
14 VATR 1995, reg 101.

1.10.2 Where supplies are zero-rated, exempt or take place outside the UK, no VAT is charged by the supplier to his customer. Moreover, provided the person making the supplies is registered for VAT, he is able to obtain credit for (or repayment of) any input tax paid by him which is directly attributable to any supplies he makes which are zero-rated or treated as taking place outside the UK, provided they would be taxable if made in the UK. He cannot obtain credit for (or repayment of) any input tax paid by him which is directly attributable to any exempt supplies he makes, or to supplies which are made otherwise than in the course of business.

1.10.3 Consequently, zero-rating is the most favourable VAT treatment, as it does not require the supplier to charge VAT to his customers and does not restrict recovery of VAT input tax. The making of exempt supplies, however, will be less desirable because the input tax attributable to such supplies is not recoverable.

1.10.4 Where VAT is eligible for recovery from HMRC, this is done by setting it against the output tax which a taxpayer accounts for on his return or, if his input tax exceeds his output tax on that return, claiming a repayment. A credit or repayment may be obtained or claimed in full in the return for the period in which the VAT is incurred – there is no need to wait until there is sufficient output tax to set against the input tax. The maximum delay between paying VAT to a supplier and obtaining a credit or repayment (where the entitlement arises) should be about four months for a person with a quarterly accounting period.

1.11 PLACE OF SUPPLY

VAT is only payable on supplies made in the UK. The basic rule is that the place of supply of land is where the land is situated. Services connected with land are also treated as taking place where the land is situated. Services in connection with land include:

(a) leases for 21 years or less;

(b) licences to occupy;

(c) other rights over or in relation to land;

(d) construction services;

(e) demolition services; and

(f) services provided by others involved in matters relating to land (such as estate agents, auctioneers, architects, surveyors, engineers and lawyers involved in negotiating the sale and purchase of interests in land).

1.12 ELECTION TO WAIVE EXEMPTION

Also known as the option to tax, this allows a person to choose to make exempt supplies of property into taxable supplies (see **Chapter 6**).

2. BASIC PRINCIPLES – COMMERCIAL AND NON-COMMERCIAL BUILDINGS

Summary

- Supplies of 'commercial' property are usually exempt from VAT.
- Supplies of 'non-commercial' property are usually zero-rated for VAT purposes.
- Certain transactions are always standard-rated for VAT purposes.
- Special rules may vary the above treatments.

2.1 INTRODUCTION

In general terms, dealings in property are exempt from VAT, except for certain transactions in relation to non-commercial property (which are zero-rated)[1] and certain specified transactions which are always standard-rated (most notably the freehold sale of a 'new' building).[2] As explained above,[3] input tax attributable to exempt supplies cannot be recovered, so property owners are in most cases now permitted to elect to charge VAT on what would otherwise be exempt supplies of commercial property, thereby allowing recovery of input tax.[4] Supplies in connection with construction and demolition are standard-rated, with limited exceptions relating to non-commercial property.[5] Bear in mind, however, that a sale of property which amounts to a transfer of a business (or part of a business) as a going concern is not a supply for VAT purposes.[6]

2.2 THE DISTINCTION BETWEEN COMMERCIAL AND NON-COMMERCIAL BUILDINGS AND WORKS

The distinction between commercial and non-commercial buildings is important, because non-commercial buildings are treated differently (and

---

1 See **4.1** below.
2 See **5.2** and **5.9** below.
3 See **Chapter 1**.
4 See **Chapter 6**.
5 See **Chapter 3**.
6 See **Chapter 11**.

usually more favourably) for VAT purposes. Non-commercial buildings and works are:

(a) buildings designed as 'dwellings' (basically, domestic property) – see **2.3** below;

(b) buildings intended for use solely for a 'relevant residential purpose' – see **2.4** below;

(c) buildings intended for use solely for a 'relevant charitable purpose' – see **2.5** below;

(d) civil engineering works for permanent residential caravan parks;

(e) approved alterations to listed buildings within categories (a)-(c) above; and

(f) conversion of an existing non-residential building (or part of one) into a dwelling or number of dwellings or a building intended for use solely for a relevant residential purpose if the supplies are made to a housing association.

Buildings and works in the categories described above are referred to throughout this book as 'non-commercial'. All buildings and works not falling within the categories described above are referred to as 'commercial'.

2.3 DWELLINGS

2.3.1 To qualify as a 'building designed as a dwelling or a number of dwellings', each dwelling must satisfy the following conditions:

(a) each dwelling must consist of self-contained living accommodation;

(b) there must be no direct internal access between the dwellings;

(c) planning consent must have been granted for each dwelling; and

(d) the planning consent, and any covenants, must not prohibit separate use of the dwelling.[7]

2.3.2 Construction of a dwelling includes construction of a garage built at the same time and intended to be occupied with the dwelling.[8]

---

7 Sch 8, Group 5 note (2).
8 Sch 8, Group 5 note (3).

2.4 RELEVANT RESIDENTIAL PURPOSE

Use for a 'relevant residential purpose' means use as:

(a) a children's home;

(b) an old people's home or home for the physically or mentally disabled;

(c) a hospice;

(d) student accommodation or a school boarding house;

(e) accommodation for the armed forces;

(f) a monastery, nunnery or similar establishment; or

(g) any institution which is the sole or main residence of at least 90% of its residents.[9]

Hospitals, prisons, hotels, inns and similar establishments are expressly excluded.[10]

2.5 RELEVANT CHARITABLE PURPOSE

2.5.1 Use for a 'relevant charitable purpose' means use by a charity:

(a) otherwise than in the course or furtherance of a business; and/or

(b) as a village hall or similarly in providing social or recreational facilities for a local community.[11]

Business activity

2.5.2 For the purposes of **2.5.1(a)** above, HMRC has set out guidelines on what constitutes a business activity.[12] A business activity involves making supplies for a consideration, where the activity has a degree of frequency or scale and is continued over a reasonable period of time. An activity may still be regarded as a business activity if the amount charged does no more than cover the cost to the charity, or even if the amount charged is less than cost. However, HMRC accepts that business use not exceeding 10% of the time the building is available for use can be ignored.[13] For example, buildings used by sixth-form colleges with charitable status will qualify, provided no more than 10% of the students are fee-paying.

---

9 Sch 8, Group 5 note (4).

10 *Ibid.*

11 Sch 8, Group 5 note (6).

12 HMRC Notice 701/1/04, para 4.

13 *Hansard*, 16 May 1989 at 73, Standing Committee G.

2.5.3 In *Customs & Excise Commissioners v St Dunstan's Educational Foundation*,[14] the Court of Appeal held that a building was not 'used by a charity' for non-business purposes where the charity allowed another organisation (in this case a fee-paying school) to use the building free of charge. In such a case, the charity did not 'use' the building at all.

Village halls and local community facilities

2.5.4 For the purposes of **2.5.1(b)** above, there is no requirement that the use should be for non-business purposes. Therefore, the charity can charge a fee to individuals for use of the facilities, provided that the facilities benefit the local community.

---

14 [1999] STC 381.

3. Construction, conversion, alteration, demolition and civil engineering

Summary

- Supplies of goods and services in connection with construction, conversion, renovation and maintenance are usually standard-rated.

- Supplies of goods and services in connection with the construction of buildings designed as dwellings, or intended for use for a 'relevant residential purpose' or 'relevant charitable purpose' *may* be zero-rated.

- In the case of relevant residential or relevant charitable purpose buildings, zero-rating only applies to supplies made directly to the person who is to use the building.

- Additionally, in such cases the supplier will only qualify for zero-rating if he obtains a certificate of use from the user.

- Supplies by architects, surveyors, etc are always standard-rated unless subsumed in a 'design and build' contract.

3.1 Introduction

The meaning of 'construction' for VAT purposes is important. Construction and similar services, and building materials supplied for such services, are generally standard-rated. Zero-rating applies to construction of non-commercial buildings but not, generally, to other works relating to such buildings (except as detailed at **3.5** below).

3.2 Meaning of construction and conversion

Construction of a building

3.2.1 For VAT purposes, 'construction' means, broadly, only new construction. The definition of 'construction of a building'[1] does not include conversion, reconstruction, alteration, enlargement or extension of an existing building, or providing an annex to an existing building. However, there are two narrowly defined exceptions to these exclusions, so that 'construction of a building' does include:

---

1 Sch 8, Group 5 note (16).

(a) an enlargement or extension of an existing building which creates an additional dwelling or dwellings;[2] and

(b) the construction of an annex intended solely for use for a relevant charitable purpose which is capable of functioning independently of the existing building and which has separate access from the existing building.[3]

Construction of a civil engineering work

3.2.2 The definition of 'construction of a civil engineering work'[4] expressly does not include the conversion, reconstruction, alteration or enlargement of such a work.

Conversion

3.2.3 'Conversion' is a separate concept from construction, but is not defined in the VAT legislation.

Construction/reconstruction

3.2.4 Extensive case law on the distinction between the construction of a new building and reconstruction or conversion of an existing building has been largely superseded by the legislation, which provides that a building only ceases to be an existing building when demolished completely to ground level, or when the part remaining above ground level consists of no more than a single façade (or, in the case of a corner site, a double façade) required for planning consent or similar permission.[5]

Works included in construction

3.2.5 Construction commences when a start is made on the foundations of the building which will continue to the construction of the actual building. HMRC has stated that construction also includes demolition work carried out as part of a single construction project.[6] HMRC does not, however, regard merely digging a hole or preparing foundations and then leaving the site as sufficient.

---

2 Sch 8, Group 5 note (16)(b).

3 Sch 8, Group 5 note (17).

4 Sch 8, Group 5 note (15).

5 Sch 8, Group 5 note (18).

6 HMRC Notice 708/02, para 3.3.

3.2.6 HMRC regards as 'services supplied in the course of construction' any services which are supplied as part of the construction of a building, or which are directly relevant to the beginning or ending of its construction (provided they are performed before the building is occupied). Examples given by HMRC[7] extend from site preparation to first decoration and site restoration (but not landscaping, planting of trees, plants and shrubs or ornamental work, which are always standard-rated).

3.3 TREATMENT OF BUILDING SERVICES AND BUILDING MATERIALS – GENERAL

The general rule is that all supplies of goods and services in relation to construction, conversion, renovation, maintenance or upkeep of buildings or civil engineering works, including residential buildings, are chargeable to VAT at the standard rate. As an exception to this rule, however, some building services and materials in relation to non-commercial buildings are zero-rated (see **3.5.1-3.5.5** below).

3.4 CONSTRUCTION AND ALTERATION OF COMMERCIAL BUILDINGS

Standard-rating is automatically applied to all supplies of goods and services in the course of:

(a) the construction of, or any building work in connection with, commercial buildings or civil engineering works; and

(b) alteration and refurbishment of commercial buildings or civil engineering works.

3.5 CONSTRUCTION, CONVERSION AND ALTERATION OF NON-COMMERCIAL BUILDINGS

3.5.1 VAT is chargeable at the zero rate on supplies of certain goods and services (see **3.5.5** below) supplied in the course of:

(a) construction of non-commercial buildings and civil engineering works, namely:

    (i) buildings designed as dwellings;

---

7 HMRC Notice 708/02, para 3.3.

    (ii) buildings intended for use solely for a relevant residential purpose;

    (iii) buildings intended for use solely for a relevant charitable purpose; and

    (iv) civil engineering works for permanent residential caravan parks;[8]

(b) approved alterations to listed buildings within categories (a)(i)-(iii) above;[9] and

(c) conversion of an existing non-residential building (or part of one) into a dwelling or number of dwellings or a building intended for use solely for a relevant residential purpose if the supplies are made to a housing association.[10]

Non-commercial buildings other than dwellings

3.5.2 In the case of construction or conversion of non-commercial buildings other than dwellings (see **3.5.1(a)(ii)** and **(iii)**), to qualify for zero-rating the supplies must be made to a person who intends to use the building for a relevant residential or charitable purpose (see **Chapter 2**).[11] This means that supplies by sub-contractors in the course of constructing such buildings are standard-rated (as being to a main contractor and not to a person who intends to use the building for a non-commercial purpose), but supplies by the main contractor are zero-rated (subject to **3.5.3** below). The main contractor can recover the VAT charged to him by the sub-contractor, although he may suffer a cashflow cost.

Certificate of use

3.5.3 In order to obtain zero-rating for supplies in the course of construction (or conversion) of non-commercial buildings other than dwellings, HMRC requires certain formalities to be observed. Zero-rating only applies if the person who intends to use the building, and to whom the supplies are made, has (before the supplies are made) provided the supplier with a certificate of use in a form published by HMRC in Notice 708/02.[12] If a certificate of use is not obtained, the modification to the general rule does not apply and the

---

8 Sch 8, Group 5 item 2. See **Chapter 2** for the meanings of 'dwelling', 'relevant residential purpose' and 'relevant charitable purpose'.

9 Sch 8, Group 6 item 2.

10 Sch 8, Group 5 item 3.

11 Sch 8, Group 5 note (12)(a).

12 Sch 8, Group 5 note (12)(b).

supplies are standard-rated. It is therefore important to obtain a certificate of use prior to supplying any goods or services.

Dwellings

3.5.4 Supplies relating to the construction of buildings designed as dwellings are zero-rated, no matter to whom they are made (see **3.5.1(a)(i)**). Moreover, no certificate of use is required to be obtained.

Supplies to which zero-rating applies

3.5.5 To qualify for zero-rating, the supplies in question must be either:

(a) supplies of services relating to construction (or, as the case may be, conversion or alteration) other than services of an architect, surveyor or any person acting as a consultant or in a supervisory capacity; or

(b) supplies of 'building materials' to a person who is also receiving zero-rated construction, etc services which include the incorporation of the materials into the building or site from the same supplier[13] – 'building materials' are specifically defined (see **3.6** below).

3.6 BUILDING MATERIALS

3.6.1 Zero-rating only applies to building materials where the materials are supplied by a builder in the course of supplying zero-rated construction services, and are incorporated into the building or site. Building materials are defined as materials or goods of a kind ordinarily incorporated by builders into a non-commercial building.[14] In most cases, whether or not goods are 'of a kind ordinarily incorporated by builders' into a non-commercial building is largely a matter of common sense. Therefore, timber used for shelving would be zero-rated, but a snooker table or trees and shrubs on a new housing estate would not qualify as they are not articles of a kind ordinarily installed by builders. HMRC Notice 708/02, para 13.8, contains a list of items currently recognised by HMRC as being 'of a kind ordinarily incorporated by builders' into a non-commercial building.

3.6.2 Certain items are expressly excluded from zero-rating and are always standard-rated, namely:[15]

---

13 Sch 8, Group 5 item 4.
14 Sch 8, Group 5 note (22).
15 *Ibid.*

(a) fitted furniture (except fitted kitchen furniture) and materials for its construction;

(b) gas and electrical appliances (except space and water heaters; ventilation systems; door entry and waste disposal systems in multiple-occupancy buildings; burglar and fire alarms and other safety equipment; and lifts); and

(c) carpets and carpeting material.

3.6.3 All supplies of goods in relation to commercial buildings are always standard-rated.

3.7 SERVICES OF ARCHITECTS, SURVEYORS, ETC

The services of architects, surveyors and others acting as consultants or in a supervisory capacity are excluded from zero-rating and are always standard-rated,[16] subject to one exception. The exception is that where these services are subsumed in a 'design and build' contract for non-commercial buildings (whose construction is zero-rated, as set out at **3.5.1(a)** above), the whole is zero-rated as a single composite supply of construction.

3.8 APPORTIONMENT

In the case of buildings intended for mixed use, the supplies in relation to construction or conversion are apportioned on a fair and reasonable basis between zero-rated and standard-rated elements.[17]

3.9 DEMOLITION

Goods and services supplied in the course of demolition are always standard-rated, except where the demolition work is carried out as part of a contract for the construction of a non-commercial building.

3.10 CONSTRUCTION OF CIVIL ENGINEERING WORKS

Goods and services supplied in the course of construction or repair to a civil engineering work are always standard-rated. There is one exception to this, relating to goods and services supplied in the course of construction of civil engineering works for the development of a

---

16 Sch 8, Group 5 item 2.

17 Sch 8, Group 5 note (11).

permanent park for residential caravans, which are zero-rated. Holiday caravans, although permanent, are excluded from zero-rating.[18]

3.11 Undertakings under section 106 Town and Country Planning Act 1990 and similar agreements

HMRC's view is that no supply is made and no VAT is chargeable where a developer dedicates (other than for monetary consideration) new roads or new sewers to local authorities or statutory undertakers, or provides goods or services free (or for a nominal charge) under section 106 Town and Country Planning Act 1990 planning undertakings or similar agreements. The developer's ability to recover input tax in full (providing the development is not exempt) is unaffected.[19]

3.12 DIY housebuilders and self-build projects by voluntary bodies

Specific legislation permits recovery of input tax on building materials by persons carrying out certain works other than in the course or furtherance of a business.[20] This scheme puts such persons in a similar position to a developer building houses or flats for sale, who can obtain input recovery by virtue of the zero-rating of the first sale (see **Chapter 4**). The person building need not be registered for VAT to recover under the scheme. Recovery of VAT is permitted on building materials used for the purpose of:

(a) construction of buildings designed as dwellings;

(b) construction of a building for use solely for a relevant residential purpose or relevant charitable purpose; and

(c) conversion of a non-residential building (or a non-residential part of a building) into dwellings or into a building intended for use solely for a relevant residential purpose (but not a relevant charitable purpose).

On a conversion within category (c), VAT on services provided by a contractor (other than an architect, surveyor, etc) is also recoverable. Services within categories (a) and (b) are normally zero-rated (see **3.5.1(a)** above), so recovery is not necessary.

---

18 Sch 8, Group 5 note (19).
19 HMRC Notice 742/02, para 8.1 and see further **Chapter 12**.
20 Section 35.

3.13 BUILDING REGULATION FEES

All building regulation fees are standard-rated.[21] Prior to 13 January 1997, non-domestic building regulation fees were outside the scope of VAT.

---

21 See HMRC Business Brief 5/97 (**Appendix 12**).

4. DISPOSALS OF NON-COMMERCIAL PROPERTY

Summary

- Favourable treatment applies to developers of non-commercial buildings.
- The first sale of a freehold or grant of a long lease (over 21 years) by a person constructing a non-commercial building is zero-rated, enabling him to recover input VAT relating to the building without charging VAT on the sale or lease.
- The same applies to a person converting a non-residential building into dwellings or into a 'relevant residential purpose' building, and to a person substantially reconstructing a non-commercial listed building.
- In each case, however, zero-rating applies only to the first grant (ie the first sale or long lease) of the building (or of each part sold or leased separately) by the person constructing, converting or reconstructing.
- In the case of a building intended for use solely for a relevant residential purpose or relevant charitable purpose, zero-rating applies only if the developer has obtained a certificate of use from the purchaser or lessee.

4.1 DISPOSALS BY THE PERSON CONSTRUCTING

4.1.1 A 'major interest' is a freehold or a lease for a term of more than 21 years.[1] VAT is chargeable at the zero rate on the first grant of a major interest in (or in any part of) a building or its site in the following circumstances:

(a) the grant is by a person constructing a building which is:

    (i) designed as a dwelling or dwellings;

    (ii) intended for use solely for a relevant residential purpose; or

    (iii) intended for use solely for a relevant charitable purpose;[2]

(b) the grant is by a person converting a non-residential building (or a non-residential part of a building) into a building designed as a

---

1 Section 96(1).

2 Sch 8, Group 5 item 1(a). For the meaning of 'dwelling', 'relevant residential purpose' and 'relevant charitable purpose' see **Chapter 2**.

dwelling or dwellings, or intended for use solely for a relevant residential purpose;[3] or

(c) the grant is by a person substantially reconstructing a listed building which is designed to remain or become a dwelling or dwellings, or is intended for use solely for a relevant residential or charitable purpose.[4]

4.1.2 Zero-rating is advantageous, since it allows the person making the relevant supply (ie the grant of the major interest) to recover input VAT relating to the property – in particular, input VAT incurred on construction costs (see **1.10** above). The zero-rating of the first grant by a 'person constructing' thus provides favourable treatment for developers of residential property or property for charitable use.

First grant

4.1.3 Only the *first* grant (which includes an assignment or surrender) of a major interest in the building (or in any part of it or its site) is zero-rated.[5] If, however, separate parts of the building are sold or leased separately (as in the case of a block of flats), the first grant of a major interest in each part will be zero-rated.

Person constructing

4.1.4 The 'person constructing' may, in principle, be either the person building on his own land and disposing of the building, or the person who commissions and controls construction on a site. The Court of Session has held that it also includes 'a person who has constructed' the building, regardless of the timespan between the construction and disposal in question.[6] However, intermediate use for an exempt purpose (for example, if a lease is granted for less than 21 years) will result in part or all of the input VAT on the costs of construction being disallowed.

4.1.5 For the meaning of 'construction', see **Chapter 3** above.

---

3 Sch 8, Group 5 item 1(b). Note that conversion to a 'relevant charitable purpose' building is not included.

4 Sch 8, Group 5 item 1.

5 Sch 8, Group 5 item 1 and Group 6 item 1.

6 *Customs & Excise Commissioners v Link Housing Association Ltd* [1992] STC 718.

Substantial reconstruction of a listed building

4.1.6 A listed building is not regarded as 'substantially reconstructed' unless one or both of the following conditions is fulfilled when the reconstruction is completed:

(a) of the works carried out to effect the reconstruction, at least 60% (measured by reference to cost) comprise 'approved alterations' (see below); and/or

(b) the reconstructed building incorporates no more of the original building than the external walls, together with other external features of architectural or historic interest.[7]

Approved alterations

4.1.7 In relation to most listed buildings, 'approved alterations' mean alterations for which listed buildings consent has been given (separate rules apply to ecclesiastical buildings and scheduled monuments). 'Approved alterations' do not include repairs, maintenance or incidental alterations resulting from repair or maintenance work.[8]

Certificate of use

4.1.8 In the case of a building intended for use solely for a relevant residential purpose or a relevant charitable purpose, zero-rating of the first grant applies only where, before the grant is made, the person to whom the grant is made has provided the grantor with a certificate in the form set out in HMRC Notice 708/02 that he intends to use it for such purpose.[9] It is therefore imperative for the developer to obtain a certificate in such cases from the purchaser/grantee. The requirement to obtain a certificate does not, however, apply in the case of dwellings.

Dwellings

4.1.9 If the building is designed as a dwelling, or the land in question is the site of such a building, the grant or assignment of a major interest by the person constructing, converting or reconstructing the building is only zero-rated provided that the grantee is not prevented from residing in it throughout the year or using it as his principal private residence by the

---

7 Sch 8, Group 6 note (4).
8 Sch 8, Group 6 note (6).
9 Sch 8, Group 5 note (12)(b).

terms of a covenant or planning permission.[10] For example, zero-rating will not apply if (for example) the planning permission permits use only as an office.

Long leases

4.1.10 Under the above provisions, a lease or tenancy is zero-rated only to the extent of the premium or, if there is none, the first payment of rent due under the lease or tenancy.[11] Any further rental payments are consideration for exempt supplies. This means that any VAT incurred by the landlord which is attributable to the property after the premium or first rent has been paid will be irrecoverable. To avoid the cost of irrecoverable VAT falling on landlords, leases may provide that the tenant will indemnify the landlord for any VAT which he incurs in respect of the building and which is irrecoverable. Landlords should still be able to recover VAT on costs incurred in providing services under a lease in respect of which there is a separate service charge which itself carries VAT.

Short leases

4.1.11 The grant of a lease in a non-commercial building for less than 21 years by any person is exempt. The election to waive exemption (see **Chapter 6**) does not apply to non-commercial buildings, except for a building or part of a building intended for use as an office for a relevant charitable purpose.[12]

4.2 VAT IMPLICATIONS GENERALLY FOR DEVELOPERS OF NON-COMMERCIAL BUILDINGS

Dwellings

4.2.1 In relation to the construction of dwellings, developers are unlikely to incur substantial amounts of VAT. This is because services, materials and articles ordinarily installed as fixtures supplied in the course of construction of dwellings are always zero-rated (see **3.5.1** above), except for the services of architects, solicitors, surveyors, estate agents and similar persons (see **3.7**).

---

10 Sch 8, Group 5 note (13).

11 Sch 8, Group 5 note (14).

12 Sch 10, para 2(2).

Relevant residential or charitable purpose buildings

4.2.2 In the case of a building intended for use solely for a relevant residential or charitable purpose, on the other hand, goods and services supplied in the course of construction are only zero-rated if they are supplied to the person who intends to use the building for such purpose (and that person has given a certificate of his intention to so use the building). This means that supplies by the developer to such a person are zero-rated, but supplies by a sub-contractor to the developer must be standard-rated (see **3.5.2**). The developer will therefore incur input VAT. Any input VAT incurred by the developer in the construction of non-commercial buildings should normally be recoverable in full by the developer, provided he sells the freeholds or grants leases for more than 21 years, as these are zero-rated supplies (see **4.1.1** above). The grant of a lease for 21 years or less is an exempt supply, however, which may cause all or some of the input tax attributable to that property to be irrecoverable. HMRC has indicated that in such cases builders and developers should agree the basis of apportionment with their local VAT office.

4.2.3 A developer selling or letting a building intended for use for a relevant residential purpose or relevant charitable purpose need not be concerned about whether it is actually used for that purpose, provided the purchaser has given the developer a certificate in the form specified by HMRC in Notice 708/02, stating that the building is intended for such use. If the use of the building subsequently changes, the purchaser will be liable to a VAT self-supply charge (see **Chapter 8**) but the developer will not. Of course, a developer must not accept a certificate if he knows it is being given fraudulently.

Short leases – planning point

4.2.4 A developer of non-commercial property will generally be unable to recover input VAT if he grants leases for less than 21 years (see **4.1.11** above). If the intention is to grant short leases, the developer should be able to circumvent this problem by selling the property (or granting a long lease) to an associated company, which can then grant the short leases. The sale or long lease will be zero-rated, thereby enabling the developer to recover input VAT incurred in relation to the construction. The stamp duty land tax and capital gains tax implications of the sale must be considered, but generally reliefs for these taxes are available on disposals to an associated company. Also, note that, following the introduction of disclosure rules in 2004, arrangements like this are likely to require disclosure to HMRC (see **Chapter 12**).

Refurbishment

4.2.5 Owners of residential property who carry out refurbishment work will incur irrecoverable VAT (except in the case of substantial reconstruction of listed buildings). This is because any subsequent sale or lease of such properties will be exempt.

4.3 DISPOSALS BY PERSONS OTHER THAN THE PERSON CONSTRUCTING

The grant of a major interest (as explained in **4.1.1** above) in a non-commercial building by a person *other than* the person constructing it, is always exempt. The election to waive exemption (see **Chapter 6**) is not available, except in relation to an office in a building intended for use solely for a relevant charitable purpose.[13]

4.4 SURRENDERS OF LEASES OF NON-COMMERCIAL BUILDINGS

A surrender is only chargeable to VAT if the tenant has elected to waive exemption.[14] The same approach now applies to reverse surrenders, which are treated as exempt supplies by a landlord unless the landlord has elected to waive exemption. (A reverse surrender is where the landlord is paid to accept the surrender by the tenant, who wishes to surrender an onerous lease.)[15] Since an election to waive exemption cannot normally have effect in relation to non-commercial property (except as mentioned at **4.3** above), a surrender or reverse surrender will normally be exempt.

---

13 Sch 10, para 2(2).

14 Sch 9, Group 1 note (1).

15 Sch 9, Group 1 note (1A).

5. Disposals of commercial property

Summary

- Supplies of commercial property are exempt, subject to some important exceptions which are standard-rated.

- The sale of the freehold of a 'new' building (less than three years old) or an uncompleted commercial building is always standard-rated.

- An election to waive exemption by the supplier turns any exempt supply of commercial property into a standard-rated supply.

- Sales or assignments of rental properties may be transfers of going concerns and outside the scope of VAT.

- Inducements to take a lease from the landlord are not consideration for any taxable supply by the tenant, provided the tenant does no more than undertake to become a tenant and pay rent.

5.1 Introduction

The normal rule is that the grant of any interest in land (including an assignment or surrender) is exempt from VAT. However, there are a number of exceptions which are standard-rated. The most important of these is the sale of the freehold in a 'new' (ie less than three years old) or uncompleted commercial building (see **5.2** below). The legislation also contains a list of miscellaneous other transactions which are compulsorily standard-rated (see **5.9** below). Moreover, any grant of an interest in a commercial property will be standard-rated if the grantor has elected to waive exemption in relation to the property (see **Chapter 6**). Finally, bear in mind that a transfer of a rental property as a going concern will be outside the scope of VAT altogether (see **Chapter 11**).

5.2 Sales of freeholds of commercial property

5.2.1 All sales of freeholds of commercial property are exempt, except for sales of the freehold of:

(a) an uncompleted commercial building;

(b) a 'new' commercial building;

(c) an uncompleted civil engineering work;

(d) a 'new' civil engineering work;[1] and

(e) property in relation to which an election to waive exemption has been made[2] (see **Chapter 6**).

All of the transactions listed above are subject to VAT at the standard rate. The grant of an equitable right, a right under an option or a right of pre-emption to call for or be granted an interest of the types described above is also always chargeable to VAT at the standard rate.

5.2.2 Standard-rating only applies to sales of freeholds of the properties described in **5.2.1(a)-(d)**, not to the grant or assignment of leases of any length. Normally, however, grantors will be able to elect to waive exemption and charge tax in respect of such leases if desired.

5.2.3 There are also a number of other property transactions which are always standard-rated (see **5.9** below).

5.2.4 The sale of a commonhold unit (a new form of property ownership introduced in 2002) is treated in the same way as the sale of a freehold property, and so follows the normal VAT accounting rules.[3]

Meaning of 'new' – the three-year time period

5.2.5 A building or civil engineering work is 'new' for three years after it is completed.[4] Any sale of the freehold within this period is standard-rated, whoever sells it and even if it is sold more than once during this period.

Meaning of 'completed'

5.2.6 A building is completed when either an architect (and only an architect) issues a certificate of practical completion or the building is first fully occupied, whichever happens first.[5] A civil engineering work is 'completed' when either an engineer (and only an engineer) issues a certificate of completion or the work is first fully used, whichever happens first.[6]

---

1 Sch 9, Group 1 item 1(a).
2 Sch 10, para 2(1).
3 HMRC Notice 742/02 (**Appendix 8**), para 13.5.2.
4 Sch 9, Group 1 note (4).
5 Sch 9, Group 1 note (2),
6 *Ibid.*

5.3 THE GRANT OR ASSIGNMENT OF LEASES OF COMMERCIAL PROPERTY

5.3.1 The grant or assignment of a lease of commercial property is always exempt, subject to two exceptions which are always standard-rated, namely:

(a) a grant or assignment by a person who has elected to waive exemption from VAT in relation to the property (see **Chapter 6**);[7] and

(b) a grant or assignment of one of the miscellaneous standard-rated types set out at **5.9** below.[8]

This applies equally to licences and any other rights over, or interests in, commercial property, other than sales of freehold 'new' buildings or works as described at **5.2.1**.

5.4 SURRENDERS AND ASSIGNMENTS OF LEASES OF COMMERCIAL PROPERTY

Surrenders

5.4.1 The surrender of a lease of a commercial property is exempt, except where the tenant has elected to waive exemption.[9]

Reverse surrenders

5.4.2 The term 'reverse surrender' refers to a lease surrender where the landlord is paid to accept the surrender by the tenant.[10] A reverse surrender is treated as the grant of an interest in land by the landlord.[11] The transaction is therefore *prima facie* exempt from VAT. However, VAT is chargeable on reverse surrenders where the landlord has elected to waive exemption in respect of that property.

5.4.3 Table 5.1 (overleaf) sets out the VAT treatment of straight and reverse surrenders in various situations.

Assignments

5.4.4 The VAT treatment of assignments should be the same (ie substitute 'seller' for 'landlord' and 'purchaser' for 'tenant'), subject to the comments at **5.5.5** on 'reverse assignments'.

---

7 Sch 10, para 2(1).
8 Sch 9, Group 1 item 1(c)-(n).
9 Sch 9, Group 1 note (1).
10 Sch 9, Group 1 note (1A).
11 Sch 9, Group 1 note (1).

Table 5.1

VAT status of land and direction of payment	Person making supply	VAT payable?
1. Landlord (not elected) pays tenant (not elected)	Tenant	No
2. Landlord (not elected) pays tenant (elected)	Tenant	Yes
3. Landlord (elected) pays tenant (not elected)	Tenant	No
4. Landlord (elected) pays tenant (elected)	Tenant	Yes
5. Tenant (not elected) pays landlord (not elected)	Landlord	No
6. Tenant (not elected) pays landlord (elected)	Landlord	Yes
7. Tenant (elected) pays landlord (not elected)	Landlord	No
8. Tenant (elected) pays landlord (elected)	Landlord	Yes

'Virtual' assignments

5.4.5 A 'virtual' assignment is a transaction which involves the transfer of all economic benefits and burdens of a lease to a third party. Usually, an actual assignment is not possible because the tenant requires the consent of its landlord to effect an assignment, and this may not be forthcoming or take time to obtain. The VAT treatment of 'virtual' assignments was considered in the recent High Court decision of *Abbey National Plc v Customs & Excise Commissioners.*[12] The case involved a 'virtual' assignment by Abbey under which it transferred all the economic benefits and burdens of various short leasehold properties to a third party, Mapeley. Abbey

12 [2005] EWHC 831 (Ch).

remained in occupation of some of the properties it had previously occupied, and paid a principal fee (similar to the rent under the leases) to Mapeley. Mapeley paid all rents due to third-party landlords, and collected and retained all rents due from the third-party under-tenants. In these circumstances, HMRC ruled that:

(a) where Abbey remained in occupation, the supply by Mapeley to Abbey was not an exempt property supply, but a standard-rated supply of agency and property management services; and

(b) the rents paid by the under-tenants remained the property of Abbey, and when retained by Mapeley were consideration for standard-rated supplies of agency and property management services by Mapeley to Abbey.

5.4.6 Abbey contested the rulings and appealed to the VAT Tribunal and then to the High Court. The High Court upheld Abbey's arguments that the right supplied by Mapeley to Abbey was an exempt supply of property. On the second point, the High Court upheld the Tribunal's decision in finding that the correct interpretation of Schedule 10, para 8 is that rents paid by under-tenants were consideration for supplies made by Mapeley to the under-tenants, and not consideration for supplies of standard-rated agency services to Abbey. Although the High Court found in favour of the taxpayer, HMRC is appealing the first point (although not the second) to the Court of Appeal.[13] The final outcome of the case is likely to have a significant bearing on the VAT treatment of 'virtual' assignments, so care should be taken in all appropriate cases to make sure that the impact of the decision is fully considered.

Surrender and re-grant

5.4.7 Where an old lease is surrendered in exchange for a new one and the tenant has elected to waive exemption, VAT is only chargeable on the surrender if it is made for a consideration. The consideration may not only include any payment for the surrender, but also a rent-free period (see **5.6** below), or a reduced premium or rent in relation to the new lease.

Lease variations

5.4.8 Where an existing lease is varied to change the term of the lease or the property leased, English property law deems there to be a surrender of the existing lease and a grant of a new one. If either party receives any monetary

---

13 See HMRC Business Brief 16/05 (**Appendix 22**).

consideration, the surrender or re-grant is an exempt supply, subject to the option to tax. Where there is no monetary consideration, no supply is seen as taking place, and HMRC does not seem to regard the surrender as being consideration for the re-grant (or vice versa) in these circumstances.[14] However, HMRC is unlikely to take this view if the new lease is granted (or re-granted) on condition that the lessee develops the property or takes on other onerous obligations, and careful thought needs to be given to the VAT liability of the transaction in such circumstances.

5.5 REVERSE PREMIUMS

5.5.1 A reverse premium is a payment by a landlord to a prospective tenant to induce the tenant to enter into a lease. The decision of the European Court of Justice (ECJ) in *Mirror Group Plc v Customs & Excise Commissioners*[15] should be noted in this context.

5.5.2 In that case, the ECJ held that:

> 'A tenant who undertakes, even in return for payment from the landlord, solely to become a tenant and to pay the rent does not, so far as that action is concerned, make a supply of services to the landlord.'

This would not always be the position, however, and the ECJ went on to hold that:

> 'The future tenant would make a supply of services for consideration if the landlord, taking the view that the presence of an anchor tenant in the building containing the leased premises will attract other tenants, were to make a payment by way of consideration for the future tenant's undertaking to transfer its business to the building concerned.'

This means that, where a tenant has done no more than agree to enter into a lease and pay rent, the payment of a reverse premium does not create a taxable supply. No VAT should be chargeable by the tenant. Only where the tenant does something further in return for the payment is a standard-rated supply created.

5.5.3 Interestingly, the ECJ suggested that an undertaking by an anchor tenant to move its business into a particular property could be qualified as a supply of advertising services. Such a classification would produce the strange result that a supply by a UK tenant to a landlord in the UK would be chargeable to VAT at the standard rate, whereas a supply of such services to a landlord outside the UK would not be subject to UK VAT. This

---

14 Statement of practice in *Customs & Excise Manual*, vol 1, s8, para 27.1.
15 [2001] STC 1453, ECJ case no C-409/98.

is because supplies of advertising services to overseas persons are outside the scope of UK VAT.

5.5.4 Until recently, HMRC appeared to ignore the conclusions of the ECJ in the *Mirror Group* case, and regarded the payment to a prospective tenant at a reverse premium as consideration, in all cases, for a standard-rated supply of services of entering into the lease. Only recently did HMRC concede this position.[16] HMRC will now generally accept that inducements do not themselves create a supply (and are therefore outside the scope of VAT), unless the payment is for something that goes beyond merely entering into the terms of the lease. The following are examples of where HMRC is still likely to see a supply:

(a) where the payment is for the tenant to carry out works or refurbishments that are the responsibility of the landlord – HMRC will accept that normal contributions to the tenant's own works are not subject to VAT;

(b) where payment is to carry out improvements which are generally for the long-term benefit of the landlord;[17]

(c) in other cases, where the payment is linked to other extra obligations that would not normally appear in a lease; or

(d) where the tenant agrees to be an anchor tenant and move its business into the premises being leased.

5.5.5 In the case of a 'reverse assignment' (ie an assignment where the assignor pays the assignee a reverse premium to induce the assignee to take the assignment), there is slightly different analysis. The ECJ held in *Customs & Excise Commissioners v Cantor Fitzgerald International*[18] that the reverse premium was consideration for a standard-rated supply consisting of acceptance of the assignment by the assignee. The supply by the assignee does not contain the elements necessary for it to be regarded as a leasing or letting of property. The ECJ held that a letting of property essentially involves the landlord assigning the right to occupy property to the tenant (and exclude others from it) for an agreed period in return for rent.

5.6 RENT-FREE PERIODS

5.6.1 Where a landlord grants a rent-free period to a tenant entering into a lease (and the tenant does nothing, apart from entering into the lease, in

---

16 See HMRC Business Brief 12/05 (**Appendix 21**).

17 See *Ridgeons Bulk Ltd v Customs & Excise Commissioners* [1994] STC 427 and **5.6.2** below

18 [2001] STC 1453, ECJ case no C-108/99.

consideration of the rent-free period), HMRC does not regard the rent-free period as giving rise to any charge to VAT. On 18 December 1991, Gillian Shepherd, the minister then responsible for Customs and Excise, stated in the House of Commons:

> 'It is long-standing Customs policy that rent-free periods are outside the scope of VAT unless services are performed in return by the tenant for the landlord. As this is uncommon in practice, only a few cases will lead to VAT being charged.'

Care must always be taken to ensure that a rent-free period is not linked with any supplies made by the tenant to the landlord (eg surrender or construction services) which would be chargeable to VAT at the standard rate. Where a tenant surrenders one lease and accepts another with a rent-free period from the same landlord, HMRC regards the rent-free period as consideration for the surrender of the lease by the tenant, who must account for VAT on the value of the consideration if he has elected to waive exemption in respect of the property.

5.6.2 The case of *Ridgeons Bulk Ltd v Customs & Excise Commissioners*[19] illustrates the dangers of rent-free periods. The landlord agreed to grant the tenant a substantial rent-free period 'in view of' the fact that the tenant agreed to carry out certain works. The lease made no reference to the reason for the rent-free period, but HMRC obtained (it is not known how) and relied on a letter from the landlord to its solicitors setting out the terms of the agreement. The VAT Tribunal and the High Court held that the rent-free period was consideration for the taxable supply by the tenant of the construction works.

5.7 PARTNERSHIP INTERESTS

5.7.1 The VAT aspects of transactions involving transfers of partnership interests, or the contribution of property to a newly formed partnership, have never been entirely clear. It was common, prior to the introduction of anti-avoidance rules in stamp duty land tax legislation, for property to be transferred to third parties by transferring interests first into a partnership and then by transferring the partnership interests to the third party. Historically, stamp duty and stamp duty land tax at 4% could be avoided in these circumstances. Until recently, it was always assumed that contributions of properties to a partnership did not create a supply, or that the contribution itself was a transfer of a going concern (assuming the relevant conditions were met – see **Chapter 11**). Similarly, it was assumed

19 [1994] STC 427.

that the sale of an interest in a partnership did not create a supply on the basis that s45 states that:

> '... no account shall be taken, in determining [whether] goods or services are supplied to or by [partners in a partnership], of any change in the partnership.'

In 2004, HMRC appeared to change its position on the VAT treatment of partnerships, but shortly after the ECJ's decision in *KapHag Renditefonds v Finanzamt Charlottenburg*[20] HMRC published Business Briefs 21/04 and 30/04.[21] In summary, HMRC considers that:

(a) in certain circumstances, a transfer of a partnership share can create a supply (for example, dealing) and in others it will not (pure investment);

(b) subject to (c) below, a partnership contribution does not create a supply;

(c) however, if the partner held the asset to be contributed as a business asset, there was the potential for a supply; and

(d) transfer as a going concern treatment (see **Chapter 11**) could apply in appropriate cases to the contribution of business assets to a partnership.

5.8 LICENCES TO OCCUPY

5.8.1 The exemption in Schedule 9, Group 1 extends to the grant of any interest in or right over land or of any licence to occupy land. HMRC formerly maintained that a licence to occupy required an exclusive right of occupation. However, in *Abbotsley Golf & Squash Club Ltd*,[22] the VAT Tribunal held that a non-exclusive licence also qualified for exemption. In *Belgian State v Temco Europe SA*,[23] the taxpayer tried to engineer a taxable supply in order to recover input tax. In this case, the ECJ held that the exclusive occupation of a property did not mean its sole occupation, and that it was sufficient if occupation was exclusive in regard to persons not permitted by law or by the contract from exercising a right over the property.

5.8.2 In *Sinclair Collis Ltd v Customs & Excise Commissioners*,[24] on a reference from the House of Lords, the ECJ held that there was not an exempt 'letting of immoveable property' for the purposes of Article 13B(b) of the

---

20 ECJ case no C-442/01.
21 See **Appendices 18** and **19**.
22 Unreported, 1997, VAT Tribunal decision no 15042.
23 ECJ case no C-284/03.
24 ECJ case no C-275/01.

Sixth Directive[25] where an agreement between the owner of premises and the owner of vending machines did not specify any particular area for the location of the machines, and where the owner of the machines did not have the right to control or restrict access to the area in which the machines were placed.

5.8.3 Other, perhaps surprising, cases where a licence to occupy land has been held to exist have included: the exclusive use of specified rooms in a building for a few hours on a specified day;[26] hiring a specified chair in a hairdresser's salon on a regular basis;[27] the hire of a specified market stall for ten hours on a specific day;[28] and the right to install payphones, where physically attached to premises.[29]

5.8.4 HMRC has issued guidance[30] as to the meaning of 'licence to occupy'. In its view:

(a) the licence must be granted for consideration paid by the licensee;

(b) the licence must be of a specified piece of land, even if the licensor is able to change the exact area occupied;

(c) the licence must be for the occupation of the land by the licensee;

(d) another person's right to enter the specified land must not impinge on the licensee's right to occupy; and either:

    (i) the licence must allow the licensee to enjoy the land physically; or

    (ii) the licence must allow the licensee to exploit the land economically for the purpose of its business.

5.9 Miscellaneous standard-rated property transactions

5.9.1 In addition to sales of freeholds of new or uncompleted commercial buildings and civil engineering works, the VAT legislation describes 11

---

25 Council Directive 77/388/EEC of 17 May 1977 on the harmonization of the laws of the Member States relating to turnover taxes.

26 *Swindon Masonic Association Ltd v Customs & Excise Commissioners* [1978] VATTR 200.

27 *Daniels v Customs & Excise Commissioners*, unreported, 1993, VAT Tribunal decision no 12014.

28 *Tameside Metropolitan Borough Council v Customs & Excise Commissioners* [1979] VATTR 93.

29 *British Telecommunications Plc v Customs & Excise Commissioners*, unreported, 1999, VAT Tribunal decision no 16244.

30 'Licence to occupy land', HMRC Report, 12 July 1999, subsequently reproduced in HMRC Business Brief 21/99.

further categories of supplies of property which are always standard-rated,[31] namely:

(a) the grant or assignment of any interest, right or licence consisting of a right to take game or fish, except as part of the transfer of the freehold of the land;

(b) the provision in a hotel or similar establishment of sleeping accommodation, or of accommodation in rooms provided in conjunction with sleeping accommodation, or for the purpose of a supply of catering;

(c) the grant of any interest in, right over or licence to occupy holiday accommodation in a building, hut, caravan, houseboat or tent, except for a grant in respect of a building (which is not 'new') of:

(i) a freehold; or

(ii) a tenancy, lease or licence, to the extent that it is granted for a premium;

(d) the provision of pitches and other facilities for caravans other than permanent residential caravans;

(e) the provision of pitches for tents or camping facilities;

(f) the separate grant of facilities for parking a vehicle, except where provided in conjunction with domestic accommodation or where provided as part of a lease of a commercial building;[32]

(g) the grant of any right to fell and remove standing timber;

(h) the grant of facilities for housing, mooring or storage of an aircraft, ship, boat or other vessel;

(i) the grant of any right to occupy a box, seat or other accommodation at a sports ground, theatre, concert hall or other place of entertainment;

(j) the grant of facilities for sports or physical recreation, other than certain specified long-term lettings;[33] and

(k) the grant of any right (eg an equitable right, option or right of pre-emption) to call for or be granted a freehold new or uncompleted building or civil engineering work or any interest in (a)-(j) above.

---

31 Sch 9, group 1 item 1(c)-(n).

32 See further *Skatteministeriet v Henriksen* [1990] STC 768.

33 Long-term lettings include *inter alia* any letting for a continuous period of over 24 hours.

5.10 PROPERTY EXCHANGES

If A sells a property to B in exchange for another property transferred by B to A (with or without a cash equalisation sum), there is a supply by each party to the other. The normal rules apply, so that each transfer will be subject to VAT if, for example, the property transferred is the freehold of a new commercial building or the transferor has elected to waive exemption in respect of the property. The value of the supply, on which VAT is charged, is the monetary equivalent of the consideration.[34] It is important for the transferor to include provisions in the contract entitling it to charge the VAT to the transferee.

5.11 LEASE BREAK CLAUSES

HMRC accepts that where a contract (including a lease) contains a break clause providing for termination on payment of a sum of money, the payment made on exercise of the break clause is outside the scope of VAT as a payment of liquidated damages.[35] It should be noted, however, that this treatment will not be accepted where a break clause is inserted in a lease (by way of variation) and exercised, all as part of the same transaction. In *Lloyds Bank Plc v Customs & Excise Commissioners*,[36] the VAT Tribunal held that such an arrangement was, in substance, a 'reverse surrender' (see **5.4.2** above) and so was liable to VAT, since the landlord had elected to waive exemption in respect of the property.

5.12 STATUTORY COMPENSATION

Statutory compensation paid by a landlord to a tenant under the Landlord and Tenant Act 1954 or the Agricultural Tenancies Act 1995 is outside the scope of VAT.[37] Where, however, the landlord and tenant agree that the tenant will leave in return for additional payments to do so, these payments will be consideration for the tenant surrendering the lease (which will be exempt unless the tenant has elected to waive exemption).

5.13 DILAPIDATIONS

The terms of a lease may impose an obligation on the tenant to pay the landlord, at the end of the lease, an amount to cover the cost of repairing

---

34 Section 19(3).
35 *Customs & Excise Manual*, vol 1, s3, para 7.8.2.
36 Unreported, 1996, VAT Tribunal decision no 14181.
37 HMRC Notice 742/02, para 10.7.

the property (known as a dilapidations payment). HMRC accepts that such a payment is outside the scope of VAT as a payment of liquidated damages.[38] Nor does the adjustment affect the value of the supply of the property – VAT (if applicable) is charged on the price before adjustment.

5.14 RENT APPORTIONMENTS

When a rental property is sold part-way through a rent period, an adjustment is normally made to the consideration to reflect rent apportionments. For example, if the rent is payable in advance, an adjustment will be made in favour of the purchaser to compensate it for the fact that the vendor has received the whole of the rent for the current rent period. HMRC accepts that such adjustments are not consideration for any supply, and so are outside the scope of VAT.[39]

---

38 HMRC Notice 742/02, para 10.10.
39 HMRC Notice 742/02, para 10.9.

6. THE ELECTION TO WAIVE EXEMPTION

Summary

- The reason for electing is to recover input tax.

- The election only applies to commercial properties.

- An election may be revoked within three months of being made (subject to conditions) but, after that, will last for at least 20 years.

- The election applies to the person making it and members of that person's VAT group.

- The election applies to the property, not only to the particular interest held by the person making it.

- The election must be notified to HMRC in writing within 30 days of being made.

- If exempt supplies have already been made, HMRC's written permission must be obtained before electing.

6.1 WHAT IS THE ELECTION TO WAIVE EXEMPTION?

6.1.1 Where a person has made an election to waive exemption from VAT (also known as exercising the option to tax) in relation to a property, all supplies by that person of that property which would otherwise be exempt are standard-rated,[1] subject to certain exceptions set out at **6.5** below.

6.1.2 HMRC has issued Business Brief 32/04,[2] which gives details of a consultation process on the 'future of the option to tax'. The consultation primarily seeks views on the conditions under which businesses will be able to revoke their option to tax, but it also addresses other areas. The outcome of the consultation is likely to result in significant changes to this area in the near future. The timescale for implementing changes is August 2009 at the latest.

6.2 WHY ELECT?

By electing to waive exemption, input VAT incurred by developers, landlords or vendors (for example on acquisition costs, surrenders of leases, construction costs, alterations and professional fees) may be

---

1 Sch 10, para 2(1).
2 See **Appendix 20**.

recovered, in so far as it is attributable to a taxable supply of the land. It must be remembered that simply making the election does not entitle a person to recover input tax. Provided certain conditions are met (see **6.17** below), input tax incurred before the date from which an election has effect may be recovered, even where exempt supplies of the property have previously been made. There may, however, be disadvantages to making the election as well – principally, unless the sale contract or lease allows VAT to be added, the price or rent may include VAT, which means that the net amount of the price or rent and thus, indirectly, the value of the property will be reduced. These disadvantages are explained more fully in **6.22** below.

6.3. EXTENT OF THE ELECTION

6.3.1 The election is:

(a) made on a property-by-property basis;[3] and

(b) personal to the person making it (and members of the same VAT group).

The election may be made in respect of any land or building (including land not yet owned or a planned building). For the purposes of the election only, buildings linked internally or by a covered walkway, and complexes consisting of a number of units grouped around a fully enclosed concourse, are single buildings.[4] Parades, precincts and complexes divided into separate units (not being grouped around a fully enclosed concourse) are no longer regarded as single buildings and, since 1 March 1995, separate elections may be made for individual premises. For example, a number of shops on a single parade built at the same time are separate buildings, unless it is possible to go from one to the other without going outside.

6.3.2 There are no longer any special rules to determine the extent of an election in relation to agricultural land. The election can be made (or not) in relation to any separately defined area of land (for example a field).

6.3.3 Where a person makes an election in relation to a particular property, the election covers all interests in that property then owned or thereafter acquired by that person or a member of the same VAT group and, subject to special exclusions (see **6.4** below), VAT will be chargeable on all disposals by that person of the property. The election does not affect the VAT liability of

---

3 Sch 10, para 3(2).

4 Sch 10, para 3(3).

supplies by other owners of interests in the same property (for example, tenants or landlords) unless they are or become part of the same VAT group.

6.4. WHEN THE ELECTION DOES NOT APPLY

6.4.1 The election has no effect in relation to a grant or supply of:

(a) a building (or part of one) intended for use as a dwelling,[5] except in the case of a non-residential building which the purchaser or lessee intends to convert into a dwelling and grant a major interest, provided both parties agree in writing that the election shall apply;[6]

(b) a building (or part of one) intended for use solely for a relevant residential purpose[7] subject to the same exemptions as (a);

(c) a building (or part of one) intended for use solely for a relevant charitable purpose other than as an office;[8]

(d) a pitch for a residential caravan;[9]

(e) facilities for the mooring of a residential houseboat;[10]

(f) land to a registered housing association which has provided the grantor with a certificate that the land will be used (after any necessary demolition) for the construction of dwellings or a building to be used solely for a relevant residential purpose;[11]

(g) land to an individual for the construction of a dwelling for his own use and other than in the course of any business;[12]

(h) land which is a capital item and the input tax adjustment period[13] is still running if the grantor or a person who financed the property intends or expects the property to be occupied by him or any person connected with him during that adjustment period when that person is not registered for VAT (nor liable to be registered for VAT),[14] for example a small business or a non-business; or

---

5 Sch 10, para 2(2)(a).

6 Sch 10, para 2(2A)-(2B).

7 Sch 10, para 2(2)(a).

8 Sch 10, para 2(2)(b).

9 Sch 10, para 2(2)(c).

10 Sch 10, para 2(2)(d).

11 Sch 10, para 2(3)(a).

12 Sch 10, para 2(3)(b).

13 See **Chapter 9** for explanations of these terms and details of the capital goods scheme.

14 Sch 10, paras 2(3AA) and 3A with effect from 19 March 1997.

(i) land which is a capital item and the input tax adjustment period is still running if the grantor or a person who financed the property intends or expects the property to be occupied by him or any person connected with him during that adjustment period other than wholly or mainly (there is an administrative 80% threshold) for the purpose of making supplies in the course or furtherance of business and in respect of which that person is entitled to recover all the input VAT attributable to those supplies.[15]

6.4.2 The above supplies remain exempt even where an election has been made in respect of the property (although any supplies of the same property which are standard-rated under any other provisions will continue to be standard-rated).

6.5 THE ANTI-AVOIDANCE PROVISIONS

6.5.1 The measures in **6.4.1(h)** and **(i)** above are anti-avoidance provisions introduced in the Finance Act 1997. These measures do not affect grants made before 26 November 1996 or after that date but before 30 November 1999 pursuant to a written agreement made before 26 November 1996.[16]

6.5.2 These provisions only apply where:

(a) the property is or becomes a capital item in the hands of the grantor or any person to whom the property is transferred;

(b) the capital goods scheme adjustment period is still running;

(c) the property is occupied by the grantor, a person providing finance or a person connected with either of them;

(d) the property is occupied by persons not liable to register for VAT or by registered persons for the purposes of making supplies otherwise than in the course of business or in respect of which more than 20% of input tax is not recoverable; and

(e) at the time of the grant, the grantor or a person providing the finance intends or expects the above to happen.

6.5.3 'Providing finance' is very widely defined, and includes directly or indirectly providing funds or the means of raising funds or discharging liabilities. It is important to note that the person providing finance must intend or expect that the land will be used as indicated at **6.5.2(a)-(d)**

---

15 Sch 10, paras 2(3AA) and 3A with effect from 19 March 1997.
16 Finance Act 1997, s37(5)-(6).

above. Furthermore, the intention or expectation must exist at the time that the finance is provided. The finance must relate to the grantor's capital item – if it does not, then it is ignored for these purposes. For example, where a tenant pays a developer to carry out fit-out works, the payment will not be financing the developer's capital item if there is a separate contractual provision (even if contained within the agreement for lease) for the work.

6.6 WHO MAY ELECT?

A person may elect to waive exemption in relation to any property, whether or not he has any interest in it. For example, a person may elect to waive exemption in relation to Buckingham Palace, although HMRC will refuse to accept facetious elections. Therefore, a person about to acquire an interest in a property, as well as an existing owner, may elect. Special rules apply to members of VAT groups (see **6.20** below) and where land is held by nominees, etc (see **10.1.1** below).

6.7 AGREEMENTS (NOT) TO ELECT

The election to waive exemption may be made by the supplier (the lessor, vendor or assignor) at any time without consulting the recipient of the supply (the lessee or purchaser), although he can agree with the recipient as a matter of contract whether or not to elect to waive exemption. In making any such agreement, care must, however, be taken not to create a separate taxable supply on which the supplier must charge and account for VAT. An agreement not to elect in return for consideration (for example, a premium) is a supply of services by the landlord which is chargeable to VAT at the standard rate. The agreement will not be a separate taxable supply if it is merely an ancillary part of the exempt supply.

6.8 WHAT DOES THE ELECTION COVER?

Where an election is made in respect of a particular building, then it will cover all interests then owned or thereafter acquired in that building by the person making the election. If a landlord has granted several leases in a building, then the election must be made either in respect of all those leases or no election should be made over any of the leases if they are all to be exempt. The election will also cover all disposals by that person of the property, including granting new leases, assigning existing leases and disposing of the freehold (if these disposals are not compulsorily taxable anyway) and all rights to ground rent.

6.9 Effect of the Election

6.9.1 Where an election has been made, VAT is chargeable on all supplies of the property by the person making the election, except for supplies described in **6.5** above. In the case of leases, VAT will be added to the rent paid by the tenant unless the lease expressly provides otherwise. The election should allow the person making it to recover input tax incurred in relation to the property both before and after the election has effect, to the extent that the input tax is attributable to taxable supplies of the property. This means that a person refurbishing a property can wait until the work has been completed and, perhaps, a tenant or buyer is found before deciding whether or not to elect (subject to a general limitation of three years from incurring the input tax beyond which it cannot be recovered).

6.9.2 However, care may be required in certain circumstances. The issue of when a landlord incurs VAT in advance of making an option to tax was considered recently by the House of Lords in *Royal and Sun Alliance Insurance Group Plc v Customs & Excise Commissioners.*[17] Royal and Sun Alliance had held some surplus vacant properties with a view to letting or disposal, and had incurred VAT on the rent and service charges. It had not opted to tax, but when it did so at a later date it sought to recover the VAT attributable to the earlier taxable supplies. HMRC disallowed this. The House of Lords accepted HMRC's position, and denied Royal and Sun Alliance its VAT recovery. The overall outcome is that, pending a decision to opt to tax, input VAT incurred on surplus properties is likely to be treated as an 'overhead' and recoverable at the taxpayer's residual rate. HMRC has accepted this position in Business Brief 14/04.[18]

6.9.3 Another case on a similar issue was *Beaverbank Properties Ltd v Customs & Excise Commissioners.*[19] The case concerned Beaverbank, a property developer, which incurred speculative costs on a project which was abandoned owing to the fact that planning permission was unavailable. Beaverbank reclaimed input tax in relation to these costs, although it had not exercised its option to tax at the time of incurring them. HMRC therefore argued that the supplies Beaverbank would have made from the development would have been exempt, and claimed that the input tax was not recoverable. The Tribunal held that the fact that Beaverbank had not opted to tax in the course of incurring speculative costs did not necessarily negate its intention to opt to tax in the future. Beaverbank could demonstrate an intention to opt to tax, so it was entitled to reclaim input tax.

---

17 [2003] STC 832.

18 See **Appendix 17**.

19 Unreported, 2003, VAT Tribunal decision no 18099.

6.9.4 When an election to waive exemption has effect, the normal tax point rules apply (ie the date of receipt of payment or the issue of a VAT invoice, whichever is the earlier). This means that, when a landlord elects in relation to a building, all payments received after the date the election takes effect will be chargeable to VAT, even if the payment relates to a period before the election. This can be a trap, as a rent demand issued before the election has effect may not have included VAT, and no invoice will have been sent out.

6.10 WHO DOES THE ELECTION BIND?

The election only binds the person who makes it (and members of the same VAT group – see **6.20** below). Accordingly, the election does not affect other owners of interests in the same building. Thus, unless they are part of the same VAT group, if two landlords own separate interests in the same building, one may elect to charge VAT while the other landlord grants leases on an exempt basis. Nor does the election cover an unconnected subsequent purchaser of the interest from a person who has made the election, although the purchaser will normally have paid VAT on the acquisition, which he may only be able to recover by making the election himself.

6.11 REVOKING THE ELECTION

Once made, an election to waive exemption used to be irrevocable,[20] but now, with some care, it can be revoked where either:

(a) less than three months; or

(b) more than 20 years

has passed since the day on which the election was made. In the case of the three-month period, it is a condition that no tax has become chargeable and no credit for input tax has been claimed by virtue of the election, and then the election is revoked from the date on which it was made. In the case of the 20-year period, the election is revoked from the date of HMRC's written consent or such later date as may be specified.[21]

6.12 CESSATION OF THE ELECTION

Although an election in relation to a building includes the land on which the building stands, the election ceases to apply to that land when the building is

---

20 Sch 10, para 3(4).
21 Sch 10, para 3(5).

demolished or destroyed[22] (which, presumably, includes demolition down to a single façade wall or to ground level leaving foundations). Also, an election in relation to bare land does not affect any building subsequently built on the land. In effect, this means that a new election must always be made after a building is constructed or demolished.

6.13 EXAMPLE OF THE OPERATION OF THE ELECTION

To take an example, A owns a freehold which is subject to a lease to B who, in turn, has granted a sub-lease to A, out of which a further sub-lease has been granted to C.

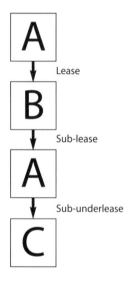

An election by A in relation to the property would cause VAT to be chargeable in respect of both the lease to B and the sub-lease to C, but it would not cause VAT to be chargeable on B's sub-lease to A (although B may well elect himself, to recover the VAT which he pays to A as the freeholder). Furthermore, if B, having elected to waive exemption in relation to the sub-lease granted by him, later assigns his lease so that he has no interest in the property but subsequently acquires the freehold from A, his earlier election would apply to any sale of or leases out of the freehold which he may make.

---

22 HMRC Notice 742A/02, para 2.4 (see **Appendix 9**).

6.14 Does the election add VAT to the rent?

6.14.1 The landlord has an absolute right to elect to charge VAT which will be added to the rent paid by the tenant unless the lease expressly provides otherwise.[23] However, although VAT is added to the rent, most tenants and purchasers should be able to recover the VAT as input tax. Where this is the case, the effect should be limited to a cashflow cost. This is discussed further in **6.18** below.

6.14.2 The making of an election may have stamp duty land tax consequences, which are discussed in **Chapter 14** below.

6.15 The timing of the election

6.15.1 The election may be made at any time, and has effect from the day on which it is made or any later day specified. If, however, the person electing has made, or makes, exempt supplies of the property before the election has effect, he must obtain HMRC's prior written permission before electing (see **6.17** below). If the election is to be made, it will normally be advantageous to make it as soon as the decision is taken, so that the input tax may be recovered at the earliest stage possible.

6.15.2 An election may be made between contract and completion, or between an agreement for lease and the grant of the lease, so that the consideration stipulated in the contract may be automatically increased by the amount of the VAT unless the contract or agreement specifically provides otherwise. An election made after contract will not make VAT chargeable on a deposit paid on exchange which has itself been treated as the time of supply, for example one paid direct to the vendors or to the vendors' agent (see **7.3.1** below). In appropriate cases, purchasers or lessees should ensure that a contract or agreement for the acquisition of exempt property contains an express clause providing that the vendor/lessor has not elected and will not elect to waive exemption, but that if an election does have effect the consideration includes any VAT which is or may become payable.

6.15.3 The election is also important where treatment of the disposal of a property as a transfer of a going concern is relevant. This is discussed in **Chapter 11**.

6.15.4 Also refer to **6.9.2-6.9.4** above concerning the timing of making an election.

---

[23] Section 89.

6.16 HOW IS THE ELECTION MADE?

6.16.1 Where a person has not made (and does not intend to make) any exempt supplies of the property before the election takes effect, there are no conditions which must be satisfied before the election is effective, although written notification of an election must be given to HMRC within 30 days of its being made.

6.16.2 Written notification of the election is required in all cases, otherwise it is ineffective. No form is prescribed for notifying HMRC that an election has been made, although HMRC suggests the use of Notification Form VAT 1614 (obtainable from HMRC's National Advice Service).[24] The written notification should give the person's name, address, VAT registration number, the date from which the election takes effect and, most importantly, identify the property in respect of which the election is made, which may be done by specifying particular properties by address with a description or plan. Alternatively, all properties that a person has an interest in could be elected by making a general election. Care must be taken when making a general election, as this could include any property acquired in the future. An example of a notification of an election is contained in **Appendix 2**.

6.16.3 There is no prescribed procedure for making the election, but large companies, partnerships and, especially, groups of companies should establish a procedure for which ensures that the decision has been taken after a full consideration of its effect. Groups of companies, in particular, should bear in mind that an election is binding on the whole VAT group. The procedure should also ensure that elections are made and notified correctly and not made by mistake, although the VAT Tribunal has held that an erroneous notification of properties as elected when no election had been made in respect of them has no effect.[25] It is important to keep a record of which properties are elected.

6.16.4 An election cannot be made retrospectively,[26] but HMRC will accept a belated notification of the election in certain circumstances. Business Brief 13A/05, issued on 5 July 2005 states that the HMRC will usually accept a belated notification if a trader provides evidence, such as the minutes of a board or management meeting or correspondence referring to the decision

---

24 The National Advice Service can be contacted between 8am and 8pm Monday to Friday on 0845 010 9000.

25 *Blythe Limited Partnership v Customs & Excise Commissioners*, unreported, 1999, VAT Tribunal decision no 16011.

26 *Fforestfach Medical Centre v Customs & Excise Commissioners* unreported, 2000, VAT Tribunal decision no 16587.

making the election. In instances where such evidence is not available, HMRC will normally accept a statement from the responsible person if it is supported by evidence that all the relevant facts have been given, output tax has been properly charged from the date of the supposed election, and the input tax recovery in respect of the land or building is consistent with the trader having made taxable supplies of it. The Business Brief also states that the decision to opt may not be accepted, even if these conditions have been met – for example, there had been correspondence concerning, or investigation into, the liability of supplies of the property in question since the supposed date of option, and no mention of the option to tax was made, or the trader or his representative has previously put forward an alternative explanation for the charging of output tax. The guidance also states that HMRC reserves the right to refuse to accept belated notification if to do so would produce an unfair result, or if the exercise of the discretion is sought in connection with a tax avoidance scheme.

6.17 ELECTING WHERE EXEMPT SUPPLIES HAVE BEEN MADE

6.17.1 Where a person has made, makes or intends to make an exempt supply of the property before the day the election takes effect, that person must obtain prior written permission from HMRC before making the election,[27] or the conditions for automatic permission specified in a notice published by HMRC must be met.[28] If a person has made exempt supplies of a property before making an election in relation to it, HMRC will only give permission for the election if it is satisfied that the amount of input tax which will be recovered as a result of the election (if permission is given) will be fair and reasonable. There is no definition of what is fair and reasonable, and this is left to HMRC's discretion. An example of a draft letter to HMRC where an exempt supply has been or will be made in relation to the relevant land prior to the day on which the election takes effect is contained in **Appendix 3**.

6.17.2 The conditions for automatic permission are set out in para 5.2 of HMRC Notice 742A/02.[29] Prior written permission to elect where exempt supplies are made before the election takes effect is not required where:

(a) it is a mixed-use development and the only exempt supplies (sales, leasing or lettings) have been in relation to dwellings;

---

27 Sch 10, para 3(6)(b)(ii).

28 Sch 10, para 3(9).

29 See **Appendix 9**.

(b) the person electing does not wish to recover any input tax on goods, services or acquisitions received before the option to tax has effect and:

(i) the consideration for the exempt supplies has, up to the date when the option to tax is to take effect, been solely by way of rent or service charge; and

(ii) the only input tax the person electing wishes to recover after the option to tax takes effect is on day-to-day overheads; or

(c) the person electing wishes to recover input tax incurred before the option to tax takes effect but:

(i) this input tax relates solely to tax charged by a tenant or tenants upon surrender of a lease;

(ii) the building or relevant part of the building has since been unoccupied; and

(iii) there will be no further exempt supplies of the property; or

(d) the exempt supplies have been incidental to the main use of the property, for example, the siting of an advertising hoarding within the curtilage of a building.

6.18 THE RECOVERY OF INPUT TAX

6.18.1 In property transactions, attribution of input tax is normally determined on a property-by-property basis. The landlord or developer should recover all the input tax directly attributable to a building in relation to which taxable supplies are made or to be made because taxable supplies of the building are made by selling or leasing it, having elected. In cases where a taxable supply would only be made by virtue of an election, input tax cannot be recovered until the election has actually been made. An owner or tenant could also recover input tax if he occupies the building to carry on a business which makes only taxable supplies.

6.18.2 A person will not recover any input tax directly attributable to a building in relation to which only exempt supplies are made or to be made. Where a property is used to make both taxable and exempt supplies, only the proportion of the input tax attributable to taxable supplies is recoverable.

6.18.3 Recovery by a vendor or landlord will often (but not always) depend on whether or not he has elected to waive exemption.

6.18.4 Where supplies are:

(a) zero-rated;

(b) exempt; or

(c) take place outside the UK,

no VAT is charged by the supplier to his customer.

Example 6.1

LANDLORD 1	**LANDLORD 2**	**TENANT (PART ONLY)**
Elected	Elected	(Manufacturer)
Charges rent of £200 + VAT of £35	Charges rent of £100 + VAT of £17.50	

Landlord 2 recovers the £35 input tax paid to Landlord 1 because it can attribute this to a taxable supply (ie it charges £17.50 output tax). It does not have to wait until it has charged £35 in output tax to make recovery of the input tax.

Example 6.2

LANDLORD 1	**LANDLORD 2**	**TENANT (BANK)**
Elected	Non-elected	
Charges rent of £200 + VAT of £35	Charges rent of £300	

Landlord 2 decides not to elect to waive exemption because the tenant (a bank) cannot recover very much of its input tax. Landlord 2 cannot recover its £35 input tax paid to Landlord 1 as this is attributable to an exempt supply (ie Landlord 2 does not charge output tax).

Example 6.3

BUILDING SUPPLIES COMPANY	**DEVELOPER**	**OLD PEOPLE'S HOME**
Charges rent of £100 + VAT of £17.50	Charges £200 + £0 VAT	

Developer buys building supplies and constructs an old people's home. It can recover the input tax involved since this is attributable to a zero-rated supply (ie it charges VAT at 0%), but this is a taxable supply.

A person making supplies which are zero-rated or treated as taking place outside the UK (provided they would be taxable if made in the UK) can recover any input tax paid by him which is directly attributable to such supplies. Supplies relating to land situated in the UK are always treated as taking place in the UK (regardless of where the person making the supplies is actually located). A person cannot recover any input tax paid by him which is directly attributable to any exempt supplies or supplies which are made otherwise than in the course of business.

6.18.5 Thus, zero rating is the most favourable VAT treatment, as it does not require the supplier to charge any amount of VAT to his customers (VAT is charged at 0%) and does not restrict recovery of input tax. The making of exempt supplies, on the other hand, has a real cost because the input tax attributable to such supplies is not recoverable and therefore is normally to be avoided. Even where an election has been made, the supply may not be taxable, for example if made in the circumstances set out in **5.5** above or for charitable use (otherwise than as an office) or residential use.

6.18.6 If a person incurs input tax attributable to taxable supplies and to exempt supplies or a non-business activity, it will be 'partially exempt', and although all output tax must still be accounted for to HMRC, special rules[30] apply to determine how much input tax may be credited against this output tax, namely:

(a) input tax incurred on supplies used exclusively for making taxable supplies is recoverable in full;

(b) input tax incurred on supplies used exclusively for making exempt supplies or for an activity other than making taxable supplies is irrecoverable; and

(c) input tax incurred on supplies used for making both taxable supplies and exempt supplies is recoverable in the same proportion as the value of the taxable supplies bears to the value of all supplies.

6.19 RECOVERY OF INPUT TAX INCURRED BEFORE AN ELECTION

6.19.1 Input tax which is incurred before the election to waive exemption has effect (but after 1 August 1989, the date when the option to tax was introduced in the UK) and which is fairly and reasonably

---

30 Value Added Tax Regulations 1995, SI 1995/2518, regs 99-111.

attributable to a taxable supply of the property is recoverable, even where the person who made the election had made exempt supplies in relation to the property before the election has effect, provided HMRC permits the recovery of such input tax when authorising the election (see above).[31]

6.19.2 See **6.9.2** and **6.9.3** concerning the outcome of the cases *Royal and Sun Alliance Insurance Group Plc v Customs & Excise Commissioners*[32] and *Beaverbank Properties Ltd v Customs & Excise Commissioners.*[33]

6.20 ELECTIONS BY MEMBERS OF VAT GROUPS

To prevent exploitation of the election, special rules apply to VAT group registration. Any election by one member of a VAT group registration is binding on the other members, and continues to be binding even if they subsequently leave the VAT group registration or cease to be a member of the corporate group. In addition, the anti-avoidance provisions in Schedule 9A may also apply to restrict the ability of companies to transfer properties in and out of VAT groups to achieve a tax advantage.

6.21 AGRICULTURAL LAND

An election in respect of agricultural land no longer has effect in respect of all such land owned by the person electing and which is not separated by other land. From 1 March 1995, it has been possible to elect in relation to discrete parcels of agricultural land without this having any effect on the adjoining agricultural land. HMRC asks persons to submit a map or plan detailing the land which is subject to the election with the notification.[34]

6.22 DISADVANTAGES OF THE ELECTION FOR PURCHASERS AND TENANTS

6.22.1 An investor who buys a property and has paid VAT has a choice – he can either bear the VAT (but hope to obtain a higher rent from the property) or elect to waive exemption and recover the VAT. A taxpayer who buys for his own occupation will normally be able to recover all the input tax charged if he is fully taxable, but not otherwise (subject to the

---

31 Sch 10, paras 2(8)-(9).

32 [2003] STC 832.

33 Unreported, 2003, VAT Tribunal decision no 18099.

34 HMRC Notice 742A/02, para 4.2 (see **Appendix 9**).

effect on him of the partial exemption rules and the capital items adjustment rules – see **Chapter 9**).

6.22.2 The result of the landlord or vendor electing to waive exemption is that tax is charged to the purchaser, assignee or tenant in addition to the premium or rent. In many cases, the purchaser, etc will be able to recover any VAT he pays as input tax – in which case the imposition of VAT will be mainly a cashflow cost – but if he cannot do so (for example, if he is a tenant carrying on a financial business), the tax paid will be a real cost and may result in either a reduction in the price or rent which such a purchaser, etc is willing to pay to the supplier who has made the election, or an increase in costs passed on to the final consumer (ie the tenants or customers of the purchaser, etc). Many industrial and commercial groups (including many high street outlets) are partially exempt – including many who are not engaged in financial businesses – and are therefore unable to recover input tax in full on their overheads. Accordingly, the supplier will need to weigh up the advantages of recovering input tax against making the election and possibly suffering a reduction in what he receives.

6.22.3 Where a purchaser/tenant believes he is taking over a property on which the vendor/landlord will not elect to waive exemption, he should ensure that this is a contractual term, and/or that the contractual price is inclusive of any VAT which may become chargeable as, if the contract is silent on the point and the election is made before completion, VAT will be added to the purchase price. It was thought that the inability of some tenants to recover VAT would lead to a two-tier market, particularly in the City of London, of properties where VAT is payable and exempt properties. The basic rent for exempt properties would be higher, although possibly still lower than the VAT-inclusive rent. This would have a consequential impact on the properties' capital values. This, however, does not yet appear to have happened to any material extent.

6.22.4 Tenants should also bear in mind that, even if they are fully taxable and can recover VAT charged by their landlord, such a tax liability may reduce the market for, and value of the lease to, potential purchasers who are exempt or partially exempt (for example, financial institutions). In some circumstances, it may be preferable for a tenant to give the landlord an indemnity against the cost of additional VAT which the landlord may have to pay (for example to his own superior landlord).

6.23 LANDLORDS OF COMMERCIAL BUILDINGS AND LAND

6.23.1 Property owners or investors who let premises must decide whether or not to elect to waive exemption and charge VAT on the rent of each building in light of the building's individual circumstances. Where there is little or no input tax to be recovered by a landlord, the increased accounting and compliance costs if the election is made may outweigh any VAT recovered. If the election is made, the landlord should be able to recover all VAT incurred in respect of the property after the election has effect, including VAT on managing and maintaining the property, together with VAT on any future refurbishment work, as well as a proportion relating to the landlord's own general overheads. VAT incurred before the date on which the election has effect is recoverable subject to certain conditions (see **6.19** above). Not opting to tax in these circumstances may mean the landlord is able to command a higher rent. The election may have an adverse effect on the value of the property, depending on the existing or potential tenants, because not all businesses can recover VAT in full (for example, financial institutions – see **6.22** above).

6.23.2 For a new landlord, the decision whether or not to elect will probably be determined by whether or not he has incurred VAT on the acquisition cost of the property. If the parties wish the sale of a tenanted property which is subject to VAT, either compulsorily or by virtue of an election, to be treated as a transfer of a going concern (and thus to avoid it being subject to VAT – see **11.1.1** below), the purchaser must elect to waive exemption.

6.23.3 A landlord who pays a tenant to surrender his lease may be charged VAT (see **Chapter 5**) but will only be able to recover that VAT if he elects (or has elected) to waive exemption in relation to the property in respect of which the surrender was made, or he goes into occupation of it himself for the purpose of making taxable supplies. Where a landlord agrees not to elect to waive exemption, the VAT paid by him in respect of a payment to obtain a subsequent surrender of the property will be irrecoverable. Therefore, the cost of agreeing not to make the election should reflect the potential loss of VAT on a surrender.

6.23.4 Also, if a landlord agrees not to elect to waive exemption in return for consideration given by the tenant or any other person, the agreement may itself be a taxable supply chargeable to VAT at the standard rate. Care is needed to avoid this situation.

6.23.5 Landlords should bear in mind that, if they do not elect to waive exemption (thereby possibly preserving the market value of their interest) they will be unable to recover input tax, for example on professional fees in connection with the purchase or on any refurbishment, until they do so. Also, for the landlord, the charging of VAT may create a cashflow advantage, provided the tenants pay on time and the landlord's VAT accounting periods are suitably timed.

6.24 VENDORS OF COMMERCIAL BUILDINGS AND LAND

6.24.1 Like landlords, vendors who have not already elected to waive exemption in respect of a property must decide whether or not to elect. The vendor may obtain two advantages from making the election, namely:

(a) the recovery of input tax attributable to the sale (subject to the usual requirements – see **6.18** above); and

(b) the cashflow advantage of holding the VAT on the purchase price from the date of payment (usually completion) to the date on which he must account to HMRC for the VAT (up to four months later).

To maximise the cashflow benefit, a vendor of a taxable property should ensure that completion takes place as early as possible in his VAT accounting period.

6.24.2 An agreement by a vendor not to elect to waive exemption is a taxable supply if entered into for a consideration. However, if such agreement is merely a term of the contract for the exempt sale, then no separate taxable supply occurs. In either case, the price of a vendor agreeing not to elect to waive exemption should be the value of the input tax lost, the cashflow benefit foregone and the amount by which the market value of the property in the hands of the purchaser is increased by virtue of it being exempt rather than taxable.

6.24.3 If a vendor decides to make the election, it is advisable to make it before the exchange of contracts. The election can be made after exchange and before completion, but if, as may be the case where an election has not already been made, the contract provides that the price is inclusive of VAT or otherwise excludes the effect of s89, the vendor should not elect, as the consideration received would effectively be reduced by 14.9% (ie the VAT element included in the price).

6.24.4 If the vendor is also a landlord, the effect of the election will be that the tenants must pay VAT on the rents from the date the election has effect until completion, when the purchaser will have a new right of election. If this is to be avoided, it may be necessary for the election to have effect on the same day as exchange and completion. In practice, it may be unlikely that a purchaser who had been charged VAT on the acquisition of a property would not elect to waive exemption in order to recover that VAT and, in such a case, the sale would be a transfer of a going concern, so no VAT would be chargeable by the vendor.

6.25 RESIDENTIAL DEVELOPERS WHO ARE VENDORS

The election to waive exemption is irrelevant to developers of residential properties, as it does not apply to sales or leases of buildings intended for use as dwellings or solely for a 'relevant residential purpose' (as defined in **2.4** above).

6.26 COMMERCIAL PROPERTY LENDERS

Lenders who take security over commercial property will want to ensure that the VAT consequences of a transaction are adequately understood and provided for, as they can materially affect the solvency of the borrower and the adequacy of the security. In particular, they may wish to check that VAT is properly payable on acquisition and that, where appropriate, an election to waive exemption is correctly made and notified to HMRC by the borrower. Covenants are often included in lending agreements to reflect these points.

7. WHEN IS VAT PAYABLE IN PROPERTY TRANSACTIONS?

Summary

- A tax point occurs when:
  - payment is received;
  - an invoice is issued; or
  - the transaction is completed.
- Special rules apply where consideration is not determinable on a sale of a freehold.

7.1 INTRODUCTION

7.1.1 The time of supply of property determines when the supplier must account for output VAT to HMRC. This chapter describes when a supply of property occurs for VAT purposes. Recovery of input VAT is discussed in **6.18** above.

7.1.2 VAT is accounted for by reference to the VAT accounting periods in which the supply occurs (the 'tax point'). As noted in **Chapter 1**, the output VAT charged on tax points occurring in a period, less the input VAT paid on supplies made to the taxpayer in that period, is the amount payable to HMRC. Except where monthly payments on account of VAT must be made, the net amount of VAT is paid to HMRC with the VAT return, which must be submitted by the last day of the month following the end of the accounting period (monthly or quarterly) in which the tax point occurs. Set out below is an explanation of when the tax points arise in certain property transactions, which in turn determines when VAT becomes payable.

7.2 CONSTRUCTION WORK

7.2.1 Where a contract for services (including goods provided with such services) of construction, alteration, demolition, repair or maintenance provides for periodic payments, the supply takes place when and to the extent that either:

(a) a payment is received by the contractor, including payments by way of reimbursement of expenses, but not normally a loan (this rule does not apply if there is a non-monetary consideration as well as cash);

(b) a tax invoice is issued by the contractor; or

(c) the work is completed if the person constructing or a person who financed the construction knows or expects that the property will be occupied by him or someone connected with him who will recover less than 80% of the VAT on the building work,[1]

whichever is the earlier. These rules also apply to retention payments.

7.2.2 A contractor should, if possible, avoid issuing a tax invoice before an interim or retention payment is received. Where a contract for construction work does not provide for periodic payments, the supply will be treated as taking place when the events at **7.2.1(a)** or **(b)** above occur, or when the work is finished, whichever of the three occurs first. Where the contract provides for consideration to be determined periodically or from time to time, but does not provide for payment (for example because the consideration is non-monetary) reg 93 VATR 1995 does not apply. The tax point only occurs when and if an invoice is issued or the services are performed, ie completion or an event at **7.2.1(b)** and **(c)** above occurs. There is no longstop in those circumstances.

7.3 SALES OF FREEHOLDS

7.3.1 Exchange of contracts:

(a) Payment of a deposit to the vendor's solicitor as stakeholder does not create a tax point because payment is not 'received' by the vendor.

(b) Payment of a deposit to the vendor's solicitor as agent of the vendor creates a tax point for the supply of the property, to the extent of the payment, provided completion subsequently occurs. The tax point is the date of the payment. If completion does not take place, and the deposit is forfeited in whole or in part, no VAT is payable in respect of it because no supply has been made. In this situation the vendor should issue a VAT credit note to the purchaser (if a tax invoice had been issued originally) and the vendor can reclaim the VAT previously accounted for on his next return.

(c) Payment of a deposit to the vendor is as for (b) above.

---

1 Value Added Tax Regulations 1995, SI 1995/2518 (VATR 1995), reg 93; VAT Information Sheet 7/99.

The VAT Tribunal decision in the case of *Higher Education Statistics Agency Ltd v Customs & Excise Commissioners*[2] appeared to suggest that a supply could take place on the date on which an equitable interest in the property is transferred to the purchaser (ie on the date of exchange of contracts, even where no deposit is paid to the vendor or his agent). HMRC has confirmed that it does not believe that the Tribunal's decision has changed the time at which a supply occurs.[3] The High Court[4] upheld the Tribunal's decision, but on slightly different grounds which appear to confirm HMRC's analysis.

7.3.2 Possession before completion – where the vendor grants the purchaser possession of the property (other than as a tenant or licensee under a separate agreement which is a supply) a supply may be treated as having taken place, because the property is 'made available' to the person to whom it is supplied.

7.3.3 Completion – a supply of the property is treated as taking place on completion (except to the extent that the supply had been treated as taking place previously) to the extent that the consideration is determinable (see **7.3.4** below) because:

(a) payment is made;

(b) possession is given; or

(c) the property is made available to the purchaser on the transfer of title to the purchaser.

7.3.4 Post-completion – where the consideration for a freehold property is not determinable at the time of completion, a supply of goods is treated as taking place each time:

(a) a tax point arises under **7.1.2** above; or

(b) any part of the consideration, which was not determinable at the time of the tax point in (a) is received by the vendor, or the vendor issues a tax invoice for such part of the consideration,[5]

whichever is earlier.

Also, where a vendor under a compulsory purchase order does not know the amount of the payment to be received at the time of

---

2 Unreported, 1999, VAT Tribunal decision no 15917.

3 HMRC Business Brief 16/99 (see **Appendix 14**).

4 [2000] STC 332.

5 VATR 1995, reg 84(2).

completion, a supply is treated as taking place each time the vendor receives a payment.[6]

7.4 GRANTS OR ASSIGNMENTS OF LEASES, ETC FOR PREMIUMS

The position is the same as for sales of freeholds, except that the rules for supplies where consideration cannot be determined do not apply to leasehold interests (unless they are the subject of a compulsory purchase order).

7.5 GRANTS OF LEASES AND LICENCES FOR RENT

The supply takes place on the earlier of:

(a) receipt of rent by the landlord; or

(b) the issue of a tax invoice by the landlord.

The landlord may issue a single invoice for a period of up to 12 months ahead, stating the dates on which payments are due, the amount payable (excluding VAT), the rate of VAT in force at the time of issue and the amount of VAT chargeable. When such an invoice has been issued, the supply is treated as occurring when each payment is due or is received, whichever is earlier. Where there is a change in the rate of VAT after the issue of an invoice for a period, the invoice ceases to be a VAT invoice in respect of any supplies occurring after the change in rate, and the landlord must issue a new invoice.

7.6 SURRENDERS OF LEASES, ETC

The supply takes place on the earliest of:

(a) execution of the deed of surrender (or, if the surrender is effected by operation of law, when that occurs);

(b) receipt of payment by the tenant (or, in the case of a reverse surrender, the landlord) to the extent of the payment; or

(c) issue of a tax invoice by the tenant (or, in the case of a reverse surrender, the landlord).

---

6 VATR 1995, reg 84(1).

7.7 VARIATIONS OF LEASES

Where there is a change in the length of the term or the extent of the property subject to the lease, English property law treats variations of leases as involving the surrender of one lease and the grant of another in its place. Where this occurs, the time of supply in such a case is therefore as in **7.4** above. Where a 'variation' is truly a variation – if it is of a very minor nature – and if a taxable supply occurs, the time of supply of a simple variation takes place on the earliest of:

(a) execution of the deed of variation;

(b) receipt of payment by the landlord or tenant (whichever is applicable) to the extent of the payment received; or

(c) issue of a tax invoice.

8. SELF-SUPPLIES

Summary

- A self-supply is a deemed taxable supply by a person to himself.

- If the person cannot recover all his input VAT, the self-supply causes a charge to VAT to arise.

- There are three property and construction self-supplies:

  - self-supply of in-house construction services;

  - self-supply of non-commercial buildings on change from non-commercial to commercial use; and

  - self-supply of assets transferred as a going concern to an exempt or partially exempt VAT group (see **11.4** below).

- The former self-supply of constructions, reconstructions, enlargements or extensions of commercial buildings or civil engineering works was abolished with effect from 1 March 1997.

8.1 WHAT IS A SELF-SUPPLY?

A self-supply is a purely notional taxable supply of goods or services by a person to himself which, if the person cannot recover all his input VAT, causes a charge to VAT to arise. The person caught by the provisions must account for output VAT on the deemed supply by him. He may recover input VAT on the deemed supply to himself only to the extent that the building will be used to make taxable supplies (for example, if he occupies the building himself, the extent of its use for taxable business activities). If the person caught by the provisions makes exempt supplies, the input VAT credit will be restricted and he must account to HMRC for the excess of the output VAT over the input VAT credit allowed.

8.2 WHO IS AFFECTED BY A SELF-SUPPLY?

The persons principally affected by a self-supply are therefore those who use a property to make exempt supplies, either when occupying the property for their own exempt business (for example financial institutions, schools, hospitals and some charities) or by making exempt supplies of the property (for example, leases when the election to waive exemption has not been made).

8.3 Self-supply of in-house construction services

8.3.1 The Value Added Tax (Self-supply of Construction Services) Order 1989[1] imposes a VAT charge on in-house construction work to prevent distortion of competition where businesses use their own labour for construction.

8.3.2 A self-supply of services occurs where, in the course or furtherance of business and for the purposes of that business but otherwise than for a consideration (ie where a business carries out construction works itself rather than using outside contractors), a person:

(a) constructs a building;

(b) extends, alters or builds an annex to a building so as to increase the floor area by not less than 10%;

(c) constructs any civil engineering work; or

(d) carries out any demolition work contemporaneously with (a)-(c) above.

8.4 The value of the self-supply of in-house construction services

The value of the self-supply is the open-market value of the services. The value of any services which would be zero-rated if supplied in connection with the construction is ignored for these purposes. No self-supply arises where the value of the services supplied would be less than £100,000. It should be noted that the value of any goods supplied in connection with the construction is ignored for the purposes of this self-supply. For these purposes, companies which are all members of the same VAT group are treated as a single person acting through the representative member, so any supply of construction services by one member of that VAT group to another will be affected by these self-supply provisions.

8.5 The impact of the self-supply of construction services

The self-supply of construction services will not have any effect on a fully taxable person, who will be able to recover all of the input tax on the deemed supply to him with the result that he will not have to account to HMRC for any VAT (although it will still be necessary to make an accounting entry). Exempt and partially exempt persons, however, will be liable to account for VAT to HMRC.

---

1 SI 1989/472.

8.6 SELF-SUPPLY ON CHANGE OF USE OF NON-COMMERCIAL BUILDING

Where a building ceases to be used for a non-commercial purpose (except where it ceases to be used as a dwelling) within ten years of its completion, VAT becomes chargeable at the standard rate.[2] Where the change of use is other than by way of a disposal (or after a disposal, but not to the vendor's knowledge), there is a self-supply by the person with the interest at the time of the change so that he must account, broadly at the time the use changes, for VAT on the value of the building as determined at completion.[3] Again, the self-supply charge only applies to that part of the building caught by the change of use provisions and the value of the self-supply is apportioned accordingly. If the change of use arises from a disposal of the building, no self-supply arises, but VAT is chargeable on the proceeds of that disposal.[4]

---

2 Sch 10, para 1(5).
3 Sch 10, para 1(6)(b).
4 Sch 10, para 1(3).

9. THE CAPITAL GOODS SCHEME

Summary

- Input tax adjustments on land and buildings over £250,000.

- Adjustments made annually for ten-year period or life of shorter interests.

- Only relevant if 'taxable use' changes during adjustment period.

9.1 INTRODUCTION

9.1.1 The capital goods scheme is a special scheme for adjusting the initial input tax deduction over (usually) a ten-year period where there is a change in the taxable person's ability to recover VAT on certain land and buildings (or parts of buildings) acquired for use in the course or furtherance of a business (other than solely for future sale) which cost £250,000 or more. The scheme also applies to computer equipment, but this is outside the scope of this book.

9.1.2 As an error in making the adjustment may give rise to a charge for default interest and also to a misdeclaration penalty, it is important to understand how these rules work. Although fully taxable traders are not expected to keep additional records on the off-chance that they might have to use the scheme, it might be prudent, at least, to identify those assets which are potentially affected where input tax is incurred on capital items. The taxable person should maintain records showing the amount of input tax that was incurred, the amount deducted initially and any adjustments made in subsequent intervals under the capital goods scheme.

9.2 WHAT LAND AND BUILDINGS ARE AFFECTED?

The categories of land and buildings which are capital items are:

(a) an interest in any land, building (or part of a building) or civil engineering work (or part of a civil engineering work) acquired on or after 1 April 1990 by way of standard-rated supply with a value of £250,000 or more excluding VAT and so much of that value as may consist of rent (other than rent payable, paid or invoiced for more than 12 months);[1]

---

1 Value Added Tax Regulations 1995, SI 1995/2518 (VATR 1995), reg 113(b).

(b) an interest in, right over or licence to occupy a building (or part of a building) acquired for a relevant residential or relevant charitable purpose which becomes treated as a taxable self-supply on or after 1 April 1990 by reason of a change of use (as in **8.6** above) and where the value of the initial zero-rated supply is £250,000 or more;[2]

(c) where, on or after 1 April 1990 but before 1 March 1997, a developer is treated as receiving a self-supply of £250,000 or more by virtue of his granting an exempt right over or licence to occupy a building or work or himself occupying or using it when not fully taxable;[3]

(d) a building, other than one subject to a self-supply charge under (b) or (c) above, constructed by the owner, which is first used by him on or after 1 April 1990 and where the value of all standard-rated supplies of the land and goods and services in the course of construction of the building incurred on or after 1 April 1990 is £250,000 or more;[4]

(e) a building altered, extended or to which an annex is added, thereby increasing the floor area by 10% or more, where the value of the standard-rated supplies made on or after 1 April 1990 in connection with the alteration, extension or annex is £250,000 or more;[5]

(f) a civil engineering work constructed by the owner and first brought into use by him on or after 3 July 1997 where the value of all standard-rated supplies of the land and goods and services in the course of construction of the civil engineering work made to the owner on or after 3 July 1997 is £250,000 or more;[6] and

(g) a building refurbished or fitted out by the owner where the value of all standard-rated supplies of services and goods affixed to the building made to the owner on or after 3 July 1997 in connection with the refurbishment or fitting out is £250,000 or more.[7]

9.3 HOW IS THE TAX ADJUSTED?

The extent to which the land or building is used for making taxable supplies must be reviewed over an adjustment period of ten intervals (or five intervals in the case of an interest in land for less than ten years). An

---

2 VATR 1995, reg 113(c).

3 VATR 1995, reg 113(d). This refers to properties subject to the developer's self-supply, which has been abolished and will become obsolete on 30 April 2010 at the latest.

4 VATR 1995, reg 113(e).

5 VATR 1995, reg 113(f).

6 VATR 1995, reg 113(g).

7 VATR 1995, reg 113(h).

interval is usually one year, but may be less. If there is any change in the extent to which the land or building is used for making taxable supplies during the adjustment period, the person must make an input tax adjustment. The scheme is, therefore, of no concern to a person who makes only taxable supplies throughout the adjustment period. If taxable use increases, the person may recover more input tax than was originally deducted. If the taxable use decreases, he must repay a proportion of the input tax originally deducted.

9.4 HOW THE ADJUSTMENT WORKS

9.4.1 Initially, input tax on the capital item acquired is recoverable in accordance with the normal rules. Where, however, there is a change in use or a change in the level of the owner's partial exemption recovery over any of the following ten years (or five years if the interest in land and buildings has less than ten years to run on acquisition) an adjustment has to be made. If appropriate, this is done annually in the second VAT accounting period after the end of each adjustment interval.

9.4.2 The first adjustment interval commences on the day on which the asset is acquired (or used by the owner if the acquisition itself does not fall within the rules) and runs until the end of the owner's longer period or, if none is applicable, his tax year. The longer period and tax year are defined in and determined by reference to the VATR 1995. There are subsequently nine (or four) adjustment intervals. The adjustment is calculated as follows:

$$\frac{\text{Total input tax on land or building}}{\substack{\text{Number of intervals in adjustment period} \\ \text{(either ten or five)}}} \quad x \quad \text{adjustment percentage}$$

9.4.3 The adjustment percentage is the difference, if any, between the extent to which the item is used in making taxable supplies in the first interval and the extent to which it is so used in the subsequent interval in question. If taxable usage has increased, a further sum is deductible. If taxable usage has decreased, a further amount of VAT is payable to HMRC.

9.4.4 If, during an interval, the asset in question ceases to be used wholly in making either taxable or exempt supplies and starts to be used on a partially (or wholly) taxable or exempt basis, the degree of taxable use for the interval is computed on a daily basis by reference to actual usage.

9.4.5 If the land or building is disposed of (or deemed to be disposed of, for example on deregistration) before the end of the adjustment period, the adjustment for that period is generally calculated as follows:

(a) the use to which the asset has been put in that interval until disposal is treated as being for the whole of that interval;

(b) if the disposal is itself a taxable supply the trader is treated as using the asset for each of the remaining complete intervals wholly for taxable purposes; and

(c) if the disposal is an exempt supply, the land or building is treated as being used for each of the remaining complete intervals wholly for non-taxable purposes.

However, the amount recoverable in respect of the remaining complete periods cannot exceed the output tax chargeable by the owner on the relevant disposal.[8] Furthermore, if all the input tax deducted in respect of the past periods together with the input tax deductible in respect of the remaining complete periods exceeds the output tax chargeable by the owner on the relevant disposal, the owner must pay the excess to HMRC.[9]

9.4.6 Because of the above method of calculation, the timing of any disposal may be important. Generally, if the sale is taxable it should take place at or before the end of the tax year, whereas if it is to be exempt, it should be deferred until the next tax year.

9.5 SHORT LEASES

Where a lease expires before the end of the adjustment period, no further adjustment is made in respect of any remaining complete intervals.

9.6 TRANSFER OF A BUSINESS AS A GOING CONCERN

Where a business is transferred as a going concern (see **Chapter 11**), the then current interval is brought to an end and the vendor must make any adjustment in the normal way. The purchaser then becomes responsible for the next interval, which runs from the date of the transfer to the end of the purchaser's longer period or tax year, as the case may be. Where, however, the purchaser takes over the vendor's VAT registration number, the interval during which the transfer takes place continues without a

---

8 VATR 1995, reg 115(3).
9 VATR 1995, reg 115(3A)-(3B).

break, and the purchaser is responsible for making any adjustment for that interval. The purchaser must ensure that he obtains all the information required to make adjustments (or has access to such information).

9.7 VAT GROUPS

If a company owning land or buildings subject to the adjustment rules joins or leaves a VAT group during the adjustment period, the interval is brought to an end and an adjustment is made in the normal way. Responsibility for making future adjustments passes in the former case to the representative member of the group and in the latter to the company itself. If a company leaves a VAT group but does not register for VAT, the representative member's adjustment for the interval in which the company leaves the group is the final adjustment.

10. Legal and beneficial owners

Summary

- Beneficial owner treated as making supplies of property.
- Only beneficial owner can make a valid election to waive exemption.
- Special rules apply to pension funds and certain trustees.
- A special procedure applies to transfers of a going concern of property to a nominee.

10.1 Elections by beneficial owners

10.1.1 Where the legal title in land is vested in a person other than the beneficial owner (eg property held by a nominee or trustee), the legal owner is generally disregarded for VAT purposes, and the beneficial owner is deemed to make all the supplies of the property. Where such land is sold or let, the beneficial owner is therefore treated for VAT purposes as having made the sale or letting.[1] In terms of the election to waive exemption, this means that only the beneficial owner's election is effective. Also, it is the beneficial owner who should account for VAT and issue a tax invoice.

10.1.2 As an exception to this general rule, HMRC has confirmed that, where pension funds are concerned, the trustees and not the beneficial owner are the persons by and to whom supplies of property held on behalf of the pension fund are made. Thus, only an election by the trustees has effect in respect of a grant and only the trustees (or the representative member of any applicable group registration) can recover input tax attributable to such a grant. The VAT registration should be in the name of the trustees.

10.1.3 A further exception to the general rule applies in cases where the legal title is held by a trustee who is not a bare trustee. An example would be a property held by a discretionary trust, where the trustees would normally be treated as the taxable person and should register and make any election in relation to the property.

---

1 Sch 10, para 8.

10.1.4 An election made by a beneficial owner will be binding on a sale or other supply by a receiver, administrator, liquidator or mortgagee in possession, who should charge VAT accordingly.

10.1.5 Special considerations arise where the purchaser of a property as a transfer as a going concern is a nominee for the beneficial owner (see below).

10.2 TRANSFER OF A BUSINESS AS A GOING CONCERN AND NOMINEES

Strictly, the transfer of a rental property is not regarded as a transfer of a business as a going concern where the transferee is a nominee, because the beneficial owner will be the person carrying on the business, not the nominee. However, HMRC has issued a statement of practice[2] stating that, from 1 June 1996, it will consider the named beneficial owner of the land (and not the nominee who actually acquires legal title) to be the transferee for the purpose of determining whether or not the transfer of a property letting business is a transfer of a business as a going concern. The practice is optional and requires the agreement of the transferee, the nominee and the beneficial owner and should be evidenced in writing. HMRC has published a standard form of agreement.[3] The optional practice cannot apply if the nominee is acting for an undisclosed beneficial owner. The optional practice is not necessary where the nominee is the transferor of legal title as, in such cases, the beneficial owner is deemed to be the transferor.[4]

10.3 RECENT DEVELOPMENTS

In a number of recent cases, HMRC appears to have taken a narrow view of the application of Schedule 10 para 8:

(a) In *Abbey National Plc v Customs & Excise Commissioners*,[5] HMRC took the view that it was still Abbey which made supplies to tenants where it had 'virtually' assigned the economic benefit and burden of short leases to a third party. Both the VAT Tribunal and the High Court saw the supplies as by the third party under Schedule 10 para 8 (note that this part of the case is not under appeal).

---

2 HMRC Business Brief 10/96 (see **Appendix 11**).

3 See **Appendix 4**.

4 Sch 10, para 8.

5 [2005] EWHC 831 (Ch). See further **5.4.5-5.4.6** above.

(b) In *Customs & Excise Commissioners v Latchmere Properties Ltd,*[6] the taxpayer was a property developer which entered into an agreement with a freehold owner to sell units at a determined price, the proceeds of which would be divided. HMRC took the view that Latchmere's receipts were consideration for a supply of building works to the freehold owner. The VAT Tribunal and the High Court disagreed, and held that Latchmere had an interest in the property and that receipts were a disposal of that interest.

---

6 [2005] STC 731.

11. Transfers of property as a going concern

Summary

- A transfer of a business as a going concern (TOGC) is outside the scope of VAT.

- Where the transfer includes property which is standard-rated, either because the seller has opted to tax it or because it is a 'new' or uncompleted commercial building or civil engineering work, a condition of TOGC treatment is that the purchaser must opt to tax the property and notify the option to HMRC no later than the date of the supply. This may be the date of completion or, if earlier, the date of receipt of payment or part payment (eg of a deposit).

- The transferee must notify the transferor by the same date that the transferee's election will not be disapplied under certain anti-avoidance provisions.

- Where the vendor is a 'taxable person', a condition of TOGC treatment is that the purchaser must already be, or become as a result of the transfer, a 'taxable person' (ie registered or liable to be registered for VAT). In determining whether the purchaser is liable to be registered, supplies made in the course of the business by the vendor are deemed to have been made by the purchaser.

- The transfer of a leased property subject to and with the benefit of the lease is generally treated as a TOGC of a property rental business.

- HMRC considers that a wide range of property transfers qualify as TOGCs under this principle. For example, TOGC treatment applies:
  - even if the tenant is enjoying a rent-free period;
  - even if the tenant is not yet in occupation;
  - where property is sold subject to an agreement for lease; and
  - on a sale of a development containing a mixture of let and unlet, finished and unfinished properties.

- Transactions other than transfers do not qualify as TOGCs (for example the grant or surrender of a lease).

- TOGC treatment does not apply on a sub-sale (or a series of immediately consecutive transfers).

- On a TOGC to a partly exempt group, a self-supply charge arises on the purchaser's group of the open-market value of certain assets transferred.

11.1 Introduction

11.1.1 The sale or transfer of a business as a going concern to a person who will carry on the business as the transferor has done is treated as not involving any supply for VAT purposes, and is therefore outside the scope of VAT, provided certain conditions are met.[1] The same applies to the sale or transfer of part of a business which is capable of separate operation.

11.1.2 Where the business assets being transferred include property in relation to which the vendor has elected to waive exemption from VAT, or which would (but for the TOGC rules) be standard-rated as the sale of a 'new' or uncompleted commercial building or civil engineering work, the transfer of the property will only be outside the scope of VAT if the transferee elects to waive exemption in relation to the property, and gives written notification of the election to HMRC no later than the date on which a supply of the property would (but for the TOGC rules) be treated as having been made.[2] The requirement for the transferee to elect to waive exemption in relation to taxable properties applies not only to the sale of tenanted properties (see below) but also to the sale of properties as part of the assets of a non-property business (eg the sale of a retail business) which the transferee will occupy for the purpose of carrying on the business. For TOGCs to nominees, see **10.2** above.

Appendix 5 contains standard VAT and TOGC wording for a property sale contract where the vendor has elected to tax the land being sold, and **Appendix 6** contains additional clauses to be inserted into such a contract where the purchaser is acting as a nominee.

11.2 TOGCs OF RENTAL PROPERTIES

11.2.1 The sale or transfer of a fully or partially tenanted property by a landlord to another person is generally treated as a TOGC and is not chargeable to VAT, even where the election to waive exemption has been made or the sale is of a freehold of a 'new' building, provided the following conditions are met:[3]

(a) The purchaser must intend to carry on the business of letting the building as the vendor has done.

(b) The purchaser must take over as landlord with immediate effect from the date of completion.

(c) There must be no break in the business (ie the tenancy).

(d) Where the vendor is a 'taxable person', the purchaser must already be,

---

1 Value Added Tax (Special Provisions) Order 1995, SI 1995/1268 (VSPO 1995), Art 5.
2 *Ibid.*
3 *Ibid*; HMRC Notice 700/9/02, paras 2.3-2.5 (see **Appendix 10**).

or become as a result of the transfer, a 'taxable person' (ie registered or liable to be registered for VAT – see further **11.2.4** below).

(e) Where the vendor has elected to waive exemption in relation to the property, or the transfer would (but for the TOGC rules) be standard-rated as the sale of a 'new' or uncompleted commercial building or civil engineering work, the purchaser must elect to waive exemption in relation to the property and give written notification of the election to HMRC by no later than the date on which the grant of the property would (apart from the TOGC rules) be treated as having been made. If there is more than one such date, the election must be made and notification given to HMRC by the earliest of them. HMRC interprets the reference to the date of the grant as equivalent to the 'time of supply' (see **11.2.2** below).

(f) The transferee must also notify the transferor by the same date as in (e) above that the transferee's election will not be disapplied under certain anti-avoidance provisions.

(g) Where part of a property is transferred, that part must be capable of separate operation as a property rental business.

(h) There must not be a series of immediately consecutive transfers of the property (transfers within a VAT group are allowed).

(i) A separate point is that, where the purchaser has made exempt supplies of the property, written permission must be obtained from HMRC before the election takes effect (see **Chapter 6** above).

If any of the conditions are not met, the transfer of the property will be a supply, and VAT must be charged and accounted for by the transferor if it has elected to waive exemption in relation to the property or if the transfer falls within one of the standard-rated categories (eg sale of the freehold of a 'new' commercial building).

Notification by the transferee

11.2.2 HMRC interprets the reference to the date of the grant as equivalent to the 'time of supply'. The time of supply would usually be completion, but may be earlier (for example, exchange) if payment is received by the vendor or its agent (as opposed to an independent stakeholder) before completion. Thus, if a deposit is paid to the vendor or its agent on exchange, notification must be given no later than the date of exchange.[4] Some confusion was caused by the VAT Tribunal's decision in *Higher*

---

4 HMRC Notice 700/9/02, para 2.4.1.

Education Statistics Agency Ltd v Customs & Excise Commissioners,[5] but the High Court confirmed that the notification must always be made before the first time of supply (for example, payment to an agent). HMRC has announced that it is reviewing this area of the law generally. In *Chalegrove Properties Ltd v Customs & Excise Commissioners,*[6] the tribunal held that written notification of the election is given by the transferee when it puts it in the post. In response, HMRC has issued guidance as follows:

> 'Where the written notification of the buyer's option is made by letter, it is sufficient for the purpose of notification under Article 5 of Statutory Instrument 1995/1268, that the buyer has, on the relevant date, properly addressed, pre-paid and posted the letter. You may wish to retain evidence of posting. This guidance will apply to future transactions and can also apply to transactions having occurred within three years of the date of any claim (subject to the usual capping rules).'[7]

Surrenders, new leases and 'sales and leasebacks'

11.2.3 Surrenders, grants of new leases and 'sales and leasebacks' are not regarded as transfers of a business as a going concern. Nor will a transfer qualify if it is by the landlord to the lessee itself.[8]

Taxable persons

11.2.4 In deciding whether a transferee is liable to be registered for VAT, the rule is that, where a business carried on by a taxable person is transferred to another person as a TOGC, the transferee is treated as having carried on the business before as well as after the transfer, and supplies by the transferor are treated as supplies made by the transferee. Accordingly, if the supplies made by the transferor in the preceding 12 months in the business transferred exceed the registration threshold (currently £60,000), the transferee must be registered on or before the day of transfer. If not already registered, the transferee must notify HMRC of its liability to register within 30 days after the transfer, and HMRC must register the transferee with effect from the date of transfer.

Incorrect analysis of a transaction

11.2.5 The consequences of an incorrect analysis of whether the business has been transferred as a going concern can be severe. If there is no TOGC,

---

5 Unreported, 2001, VAT Tribunal decision no 15917.

6 Unreported, 2001, VAT Tribunal decision no 17151.

7 HMRC Business Brief 11/01 (see **Appendix 16**).

8 HMRC Notice 700/9/02, para 7.3.

VAT is chargeable at the appropriate rate, and if the contract does not impose an obligation on the transferee to pay VAT in addition to the consideration, the transferor is still liable to account to HMRC for the VAT element included in the consideration. Conversely, if VAT is charged when there is a TOGC, the transferee is, strictly, unable to recover the amount incorrectly charged because there is no taxable supply. HMRC may, in practice, allow an input tax claim by the transferee if the output tax is declared and paid by the transferor.[9] There are also serious misdeclaration penalties and default interest charges which may be payable.

TOGC rulings

11.2.6 Although rulings can be sought from HMRC if there is any doubt as to whether a particular transaction is a TOGC, HMRC is not generally obliged to provide them. Furthermore, HMRC has stated that it will no longer be prepared to give rulings in relation to property TOGCs where the circumstances are clearly covered by its guidance.

11.3 MISCELLANEOUS EXAMPLES OF PROPERTY TOGCS

11.3.1 The TOGC provisions apply equally to domestic (for example, a flat above a shop) as well as commercial property rental businesses.[10]

11.3.2 The sale of a portfolio of properties, including some dormant properties, may qualify as a TOGC. This depends, however, on the general requirement that the assets should be capable of operation as a going concern. If it is reasonable that, in continuing the business, some premises would be closed, HMRC has indicated that TOGC treatment should apply.

11.3.3 The transfer of a single property, which is the single asset of a business or part of a larger business, may be treated as a TOGC.

Transfer during a rent-free period

11.3.4 HMRC has confirmed that, if the property is leased but there is an initial rent-free period, a sale subject to the lease will qualify as a TOGC of a property rental business, even though no rent payments have yet been received.[11]

---

9 *Customs & Excise Manual*, vol 1, s10, Ch 2, para 3.2.

10 *Customs & Excise Manual*, vol 1, s10, Ch 2, para 5.4(j).

11 HMRC Notice 700/9/02, para 7.2.

Tenants not yet in occupation

11.3.5 HMRC has also confirmed that, where a lease has been granted but the tenants are not yet in occupation, the lessor is regarded as carrying on a property rental business capable of transfer as a going concern.[12]

Sale with the benefit of prospective tenancy

11.3.6 HMRC has stated further that if the vendor has 'found a tenant but not actually entered into a lease agreement', and transfers the property 'with the benefit of the prospective tenancy but before a lease has been signed', this is capable of qualifying as a transfer of a property rental business.[13] The meaning of this statement is somewhat unclear. However, it is clear that if, for example, the property is pre-let (under an agreement for lease) but the lease has not yet been granted, the sale of the property subject to the agreement for lease will qualify as a TOGC, even though no rent payments have been received and the property is not yet occupied.

Sale of a mixed development

11.3.7 HMRC has also stated that if a property developer sells a site as a package (to a single buyer) which is a mixture of let and unlet, finished or unfinished properties, and the sale of the site would have otherwise been standard-rated then, subject to the purchaser electing to waive exemption for the whole site, the whole site can be regarded as a business transferred as a going concern.[14] Moreover, the mere fact that the vendor held the property as a developer (with a view to a sale), whereas the purchaser acquires it as an investment, does not prevent TOGC treatment from applying.

Sale to or by an owner-occupier

11.3.8 A sale of investment premises to an owner-occupier (or a sale by an owner-occupier to an investor) will not, however, constitute a TOGC.

Tenant in a VAT group of the vendor or purchaser

11.3.9 A sale will also not qualify if either the vendor or the purchaser is in the same VAT group as the tenant – since the VAT-grouped companies are

---

12 HMRC Notice 700/9/02, para 7.2.

13 *Ibid.*

14 *Ibid.*

treated for VAT purposes as one person, a lease to a VAT group member is treated in effect as occupation by the lessor, and so is not regarded as a property rental business. However, this rule is disapplied (ie TOGC treatment will apply to the sale) where the tenant who is a member of the landlord's VAT group is only one of a number of tenants.[15]

Sub-sales

11.3.10 Where there is a sub-sale (eg A agrees to sell to B who agrees to sell to C and, on completion, A conveys direct to C), HMRC's view is that there will not be a TOGC by either A or B (see **Figure 11.1**), although the position may be different in Scotland. Accordingly, VAT may be payable on both sales (although the VAT on at least the first sale should be fully recoverable). The same view is taken where assets are transferred to a purchaser who immediately transfers them to another purchaser.[16]

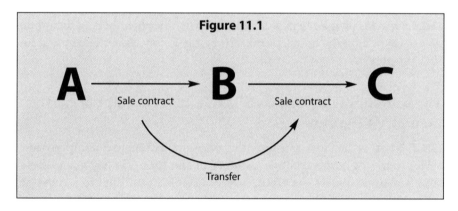

Figure 11.1

11.3.11 However, if A and B, or B and C, belong to the same VAT group at all material times, HMRC accepts that the sale by or to the party outside the group is capable of qualifying as a TOGC (see **Figure 11.2**). The effect is that no VAT is payable on either sale (since the sale within the group is disregarded for VAT purposes).

11.3.12 Where the parties are not in the same VAT group, it may be possible to avoid the problem by structuring the transaction not by way of sub-sale but by way of an assignment or novation of the sale and purchase contract by B to C. The transfer by A to C pursuant to the contract would qualify as a TOGC, and so the consideration paid by C to A under the contract would not be liable to VAT, although any additional consideration paid by C to B

---

15 HMRC Business Brief 26/98 (see **Appendix 13**).
16 HMRC Notice 700/9/02, para 2.3.3.

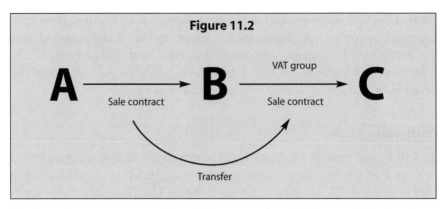

Figure 11.2

for the assignment or novation of the contract would be consideration for a taxable supply.

11.4 TOGCs AND VAT GROUPS

11.4.1 Supplies by members of a VAT group to other members of the group do not fall within the above provisions being, in any case, disregarded for VAT purposes.

The self-supply charge on a TOGC to an exempt or partly exempt VAT group

11.4.2 Where assets are transferred as part of a TOGC to a company in a VAT group, the representative member of the group is liable to a 'self-supply charge', unless the group is fully taxable (ie entitled to recover all input VAT incurred) during the period in which the assets are transferred to it.[17] The self-supply charge arises because, under the legislation, the representative member is treated as supplying to itself the assets transferred (except those assets set out at **11.4.3** below), for an amount equal to their open-market value. The effect of the deemed self-supply is that the representative member must account for output tax on the open-market value of the assets transferred to it, and will only be entitled to recover part of the tax as input tax in accordance with its agreed partial exemption method (see **Chapter 8**).

11.4.3 No self-supply charge arises on:

(a) assets which HMRC is satisfied were acquired by the vendor more than three years before the date of transfer;

---

17 Section 44.

(b) assets which are subject to the capital goods scheme (see **Chapter 9**);

(c) assets which are zero-rated or exempt; or

(d) goodwill.

11.4.4 The tax chargeable may be reduced if HMRC is satisfied that the vendor did not receive credit for the full amount of input tax incurred by it on the assets (otherwise, there would, in effect, be a double charge to tax, since both the vendor and the purchaser's group would suffer irrecoverable VAT). HMRC has issued guidance setting out a suggested approach for calculating the reduction.[18] Where the vendor recovered a smaller proportion of the input tax than the purchaser is entitled to recover, HMRC suggests that the self-supply charge should be cancelled in full.

> **Example 11.1**
>
> As part of a TOGC, the vendor (V) sells to the purchaser (P) assets worth £100,000 which are subject to the self-supply rules. P is a member of a partly exempt group which (in the relevant period) is entitled to recover 70% of its input VAT incurred on overheads. V itself had bought the assets for £100,000 exclusive of VAT (not as part of a TOGC) and was entitled to recover only 50% of the VAT of £17,500.
>
> The self-supply charge will be cancelled, since V had a lower recovery rate than P's group and has therefore incurred a higher proportion of irrecoverable VAT than would result from the self-supply charge.
>
> Where the vendor recovered a larger proportion of the input VAT than the purchaser's group would be entitled to recover, HMRC suggests that the net tax due as a result of the self-supply charge should be reduced to the difference between the vendor and the purchaser's respective recovery rates.
>
> **Example 11.2**
>
> Suppose that in the same circumstances, P's group is entitled to 50% recovery and V was entitled to recover 70% of the £17,500 VAT incurred on purchase.
>
> Since irrecoverable VAT of 30% of the tax incurred on acquisition by V has already arisen, the net tax due as a result of the self-supply charge will be reduced to the difference between V and P's recovery rate, namely 20% of £17,500 = £3,500.

11.4.5 Arguably, a TOGC within a partly exempt VAT group can trigger a self-supply charge under the above provisions. However, HMRC has confirmed that it does not take this point in practice.

11.5 INPUT TAX ON TRANSACTION COSTS

11.5.1 The purchaser's right to recover VAT on costs of the purchase depends on the purpose to which the assets acquired are put. If the assets are used exclusively to make taxable supplies, the VAT on purchase costs can be

---

18 *Customs & Excise Manual*, vol 1, s10, Ch 2, para 4.8.

recovered in full. Thus, full recovery will be available where the TOGC is of a leased commercial building in relation to which the purchaser has elected to waive exemption. If the assets are to be used exclusively to make exempt supplies, none of the VAT on purchase costs can be recovered. If the assets are to be used in making both taxable and exempt supplies, the input VAT is treated as incurred on an overhead cost, and is recoverable in accordance with the purchaser's agreed partial exemption method.[19]

11.5.2 In *Abbey National Plc v Customs & Excise Commissioners*[20] the European Court of Justice (ECJ) held that the cost of the services required by the transferor in order to carry out the transfer formed part of the transferor's overheads, and must be regarded as part of the economic activity of the business before the transfer. The ECJ ruled that:

> 'If the various services acquired by the transferor in order to effect the transfer have a direct and immediate link with a clearly defined part of his economic activities, so that the costs of those services form part of the overheads of that part of the business, and all the transactions relating to that part of the business are subject to VAT, he may deduct all the VAT charged on his costs of acquiring those services.'

What the ECJ did not decide was whether or not the 'clearly defined part' of the business was the properties transferred, or all of the properties held immediately before the transfer.

11.5.3 Following the ECJ's decision in *Abbey National*, HMRC adopted a new policy, which was set out in Business Brief 8/01.[21] HMRC's policy on the deduction of input tax incurred on expenses relating to a sale by way of TOGC is as follows:

> '... VAT incurred on services that wholly relate to the transfer of part of a business, should be treated as an overhead of that part of the business.
>
> Where that part of the business makes only taxable supplies, then the VAT incurred is deductible. Conversely, where only exempt supplies are made then the VAT incurred is not deductible. In instances where both taxable and exempt supplies are made then the VAT incurred is partly deductible, determined by reference to the partial exemption method in place. If the partial exemption method in place fails to achieve a fair and reasonable result Customs may be prepared to approve an alternative method.'

HMRC has applied this policy to transfers on or after 1 August 2001, but businesses may apply it from an earlier date, provided they do so consistently and subject to the normal three-year limit on refunds. The policy does not say what constitutes a part of the business, but the clear

---

19 HMRC Notice 700/9/02, para 2.7.

20 [2001] STC 297.

21 See **Appendix 15**.

implication is that any disposal of part of a business that qualifies as a TOGC (ie part of a business capable of separate operation) will be regarded as a 'clearly defined part'.

12. Abuse of law and VAT disclosure rules

Summary

- The doctrine of 'abuse of law' is being developed by HMRC and the courts in an increasing number of cases.
- Businesses that exceed prescribed turnover limits are under an obligation to disclose the use or marketing of certain VAT avoidance schemes.
- Schemes that must be disclosed are divided into 'designated' and 'hallmarked' schemes.
- Financial penalties apply in the event of non-compliance.

12.1 Introduction

12.1.1 HMRC is using the developing doctrine of 'abuse of law' to counteract VAT advantages obtained by taxpayers where avoidance is a primary motive.

12.1.2 From 1 August 2004, businesses which use or market certain VAT avoidance schemes ('notifiable schemes') are required to disclose details to HMRC.[1]

12.1.3 This chapter is intended to provide a basic summary of recent cases involving 'abuse of law' and how the disclosure rules operate.

12.2 Abuse of law principles

12.2.1 During 2002-2003, the VAT Tribunal referred three cases for reference to the European Court of Justice (ECJ), two of which involved complex property transactions:

(a) The first case was *Halifax Plc v Customs & Excise Commissioners*.[2] Halifax is a banking company. As such, its supplies are generally exempt for VAT purposes, and at the relevant time its VAT recovery rate was under 5%. For the purpose of its business, Halifax decided to

---

1 Finance Act 2004, s19 and Sch 2.

2 ECJ case no C-255/02.

construct call centres at four different sites on which it held leases. In order to save part of the VAT cost, Halifax implemented a VAT saving scheme. This consisted of a sale and leaseback structure involving three other companies, each of which separately registered for VAT but within the Halifax group for the purposes of the Companies Act 1985 (CA 1985).

(b) The second case was *University of Huddersfield Higher Education Corporation v Customs & Excise Commissioners.*[3] The supplies provided by the University relate to education and are therefore mainly VAT-exempt. However, a small number of the supplies are taxable. In 1995, the University decided to refurbish two mills in which it had previously acquired the leasehold estates. Since the input VAT on the refurbishment costs would be largely irrecoverable if the mills were refurbished directly by the University, the University sought a way in which to save tax or defer its liability to it. The University opted to tax the lease of the mills, and granted a taxable full repairing lease to a trust. In turn, the trust granted an internal repairing underlease back to the University. A wholly owned subsidiary company of the University, which was not part of the same VAT group, then invoiced the University for future construction services on and refurbishment of the mill, which were completed by an independent third party.

(c) The third case was *BUPA Hospitals Ltd v Customs & Excise Commissioners.*[4] From 1 January 1998, UK law was amended so that supplies of drugs and prostheses were no longer zero-rated, but instead became exempt supplies. There were no anti-forestalling provisions applicable to this new legislation. Due to previous litigation on this subject, BUPA had known that the UK government was considering implementation of this change in law. To ensure recovery of input VAT, BUPA entered into an agreement in 1997 for the prepayment of more than £100m VAT-worth of drugs and prostheses from a company which was part of the same VAT group.

12.2.2 The general issues the ECJ was asked to consider were:

(a) whether transactions carried out with the sole purpose of enabling input tax to be recovered could constitute an 'economic activity'; and

---

3 ECJ case no C-223/03.
4 ECJ case no C-419/02.

(b) could the doctrine of 'abuse of rights' apply, given the circumstances of the cases.

12.2.3 The Advocate General delivered his opinion on 7 April 2005, and in answer to the first question, he said that transactions carried out for the sole purpose of enabling input tax to be recovered are able to constitute an 'economic activity'. In response to the second question, he stated that abuse could apply when:

(a) there was objectively no economic justification for the scheme; and

(b) the purpose of the Community provisions giving rise to the right would be frustrated if the right were conferred.

In particular, the Advocate General emphasised that the doctrine could only apply when there was no other explanation for the scheme. Transactions with mixed tax planning and commercial motives are therefore, arguably, not caught.

12.2.4 The Advocate General's opinion is only a preliminary ruling, and the full decision of the ECJ is not expected until late 2005 at the earliest. The cases, however, highlight the increasing lengths to which taxpayers will go to develop schemes to avoid the incidence of VAT or to enable recovery. It is expected that HMRC will develop the 'abuse of law' doctrine much more rigorously in the future.

12.3 WHICH SCHEMES MUST BE DISCLOSED?

12.3.1 As noted above, from 1 August 2004 businesses are required to disclose certain arrangements involving a tax advantage to HMRC. Businesses are under an obligation to disclose if:

(a) the notifiable scheme leads to an alteration in the amount of VAT paid or payable by the business on a VAT return; or

(b) the notifiable scheme leads to a VAT claim by the business in respect of a past VAT return, and the amount claimed is greater than it would have been but for the notifiable scheme.[5]

12.3.2 Notifiable schemes are divided into two categories:

(a) those specified in a statutory list ('designated schemes'); and

---

5 Sch 11A, para 6.

(b) schemes that contain one or more specified 'hallmarks of avoidance' and have as a main purpose the obtaining of a tax advantage by any person ('hallmarked schemes').[6]

12.4 DO ALL BUSINESSES HAVE TO DISCLOSE?

12.4.1 VAT-registered businesses generally do have to disclose. However, disclosure is not required where the business (or any other undertaking in the same group as the business)[7] meets both the following conditions:

(a) the total value of its taxable and exempt supplies in the 12 months ending immediately before the VAT return period in which the notifiable scheme has effect is less than the relevant turnover limit;[8] and

(b) the total value of its taxable and exempt supplies in the VAT return period ending immediately before the VAT return period in which the notifiable scheme has effect is less than the appropriate proportion of the relevant turnover limit.[9]

12.4.2 There are rules to prevent businesses from separating their activities in order to fall below the relevant turnover limits.[10]

12.4.3 Notification is also not required when the prescribed accounting period for the affected VAT return, or the period to which the affected claim for VAT relates, begins before 1 August 2004.[11]

12.4.4 In the case of hallmarked schemes, it is possible for advisers to a business to make voluntary disclosure to HMRC, thereby absolving the business from the responsibility of disclosure.[12] This has the advantage, if done correctly, of preserving anonymity for the business.

---

6 Sch 11A, para 5. See **12.5** below.

7 For companies, the definition of 'connection' in the VAT disclosure rules is by reference to CA 1985, s259. In the case of a trust, persons are connected if they are connected to the same trust (eg if they are the settlor, trustee or beneficiary, or if they hold shares in a company in accordance with the terms of the trust).

8 The relevant turnover limit is currently £600,000 per annum for designated schemes and £10m per annum for hallmarked schemes.

9 Sch 11A, para 7 – for businesses that submit quarterly/monthly VAT returns the appropriate proportion will be a quarter/a twelfth of the limit respectively.

10 Sch 11A, para 8.

11 Value Added Tax (Disclosure of Avoidance Schemes) Regulations 2004, SI 2004/1929 (DASR 2004).

12 Sch 11A, para 9.

12.5 DESIGNATED AND HALLMARKED SCHEMES

Designated schemes

12.5.1 Of the eight specified schemes,[13] two are particularly relevant to property transactions.

Scheme 1 – the first grant of a major interest in a building

12.5.2 This covers:

> 'Any scheme comprising or including the first grant of a major interest in any building of a description falling within item 1(a) of Group 5 of Schedule 8 (construction of buildings etc) where:
>
> (a)   the grant is made to a person connected with the grantor; and
>
> (b)   the grantor, or any body corporate treated as a member of a VAT group under section 43 of the Act of which the grantor is a member, attributes to that grant input tax incurred by him –
>
>   (i)   in respect of a service charge relating to the building; or
>
>   (ii) in connection with any extension, enlargement, repair, maintenance or refurbishment of the building, other than for remedying defects in the original construction.'[14]

12.5.3 Developers of certain buildings are able to zero-rate the sale of those buildings or the grant of a long lease in them. The VAT on costs associated with, for example, making alterations to the building so that it can be sold is therefore recoverable. Scheme 1 is intended to target abuse of this practice when the grant of a major interest is to a connected person.

Scheme 4 – leaseback arrangements

12.5.4 This covers:

> 'Any scheme comprising or including the supply of goods,[15] or the leasing or letting on hire of goods, ("the relevant supply") by a taxable person to a connected relevant person[16] where:
>
> (a)   the taxable person or another taxable person connected with him, including the relevant person, is entitled to credit for all the input tax arising on the purchase of the goods;

---

13 The full list of designated schemes is set out in the Value Added Tax (Disclosure of Avoidance Schemes) (Designations) Order 2004, SI 2004/1933 (DASO 2004).

14 DASO 2004, Sch 1.

15 The 'supply of goods' does not include property transactions.

16 'Relevant person' is defined as 'any person who, in respect of the relevant supply, is not entitled to credit for all the input tax wholly attributable to the supplies he makes'. See notes to DASO 2004, Sch 1.

(b)   the relevant person uses the goods in the course or furtherance of a business carried on by him, and for the purpose of that business, otherwise than for the purpose of selling, or leasing or letting on hire, the goods; and

(c)   the relevant person or a person connected with him has directly or indirectly provided funds[17] for meeting more than 90% of the cost of the goods.'[18]

12.5.5 Although Scheme 4 does not include property transactions or supplies of services, it does cover a separate supply of fittings or the materials element in building work. It is intended to cover various arrangements. For example, a bank (which is unlikely to be able to recover all its input tax) establishes a subsidiary that can fully recover. The subsidiary buys equipment and leases it to the bank, giving rise to the benefit that the bank's irrecoverable VAT is spread over the term of the lease.

12.5.6 In addition, it is expected that a third relevant scheme will be specified in late 2005.[19] Details of this scheme have not yet been finalised, but it is anticipated that it will cover attempts to remove the effect of a prior election to waive exemption on supplies of land and property.

Hallmarked schemes

12.5.7 A main purpose of a hallmarked scheme must be the obtaining of a 'tax advantage'. The meaning of tax advantage is drafted widely, and an advantage will be obtained by a person when:

(a) the net payment due to HMRC on a VAT return is less than it otherwise would be;

(b) a VAT credit is obtained, or a larger or earlier VAT credit is obtained by the person than would otherwise be the case;

(c) if the person is the recipient of a supply, the period between the supplier accounting for output tax and the person recovering input tax is greater than would otherwise be the case;

(d) the amount of the person's non-deductible VAT is less than it otherwise would be.[20]

12.5.8 The specified hallmarks of avoidance[21] are broadly:

---

17 The provision of funds includes loan or equity funding. See notes to DASO 2004, Sch 1.

18 Schedule 1 VAT (Disclosure of Avoidance Schemes) (Designations) Order 2004.

19 HMRC Budget Note 6 (2005).

20 Sch 11A, para 2.

21 The full list of specified hallmarks of avoidance is set out in Parts 1 and 2 of Schedule 2 DASO 2004.

(a) a confidentiality condition preventing or limiting disclosure of the scheme;

(b) agreement that the tax advantage is shared between the beneficiary of the scheme and the person promoting it;

(c) agreement that the promoter's fees are contingent on tax savings arising from the scheme;

(d) payment for goods or services made between connected persons before those goods or services are supplied;[22]

(e) supply between connected persons funded by the subscription for shares in, or securities issued by, a connected person;[23]

(f) use of an 'offshore loop' (for example, services are supplied VAT-free to a non-EU party and then used in making a supply to a UK party where that supply is not subject to UK VAT); and

(g) any standard-rated or exempt property transaction between connected persons, unless both persons are fully taxable.[24]

12.6 HOW AND WHEN SHOULD DISCLOSURE BE MADE?

12.6.1 Disclosure must be made within 30 days of either the last date on which the affected VAT return was required to be filed, or the date on which the affected claim for VAT was made.[25]

12.6.2 Disclosure can be made either by post or by e-mail. The correct method of disclosure depends upon whether the notifiable scheme is a designated scheme or a hallmarked scheme, and exact details of how disclosure should be made are contained in HMRC Notice 700/8/04.[26]

12.7 PENALTIES FOR FAILING TO COMPLY WITH DISCLOSURE REQUIREMENTS

12.7.1 The penalties for failure to disclose at the correct time are:

(a) 15% of the VAT involved in the case of failure related to a designated scheme; and

---

22 This hallmark does not apply when the parties form part of the same VAT group.
23 This hallmark does not apply when the parties form part of the same VAT group.
24 The wording of the legislation suggests that transactions within a VAT group are covered by this hallmark.
25 DASR 2004, para 2.
26 Available on the HMRC website: www.hmrc.gov.uk.

(b) £5,000 in the case of failure related to a hallmarked scheme (although cumulative and/or multiple penalties may be imposed).[27]

---

27 Sch 11A, para 11.

13. Transactions under planning agreements

Summary

•   Dedication of road sewers to a local authority is not treated as a supply.

•   Goods and services supplied under a section 106 agreement do not constitute a supply.

13.1 Introduction

Agreements drawn up between developers, local authorities and water and sewerage undertakers make provision for a wide variety of land, buildings and works to be provided, at the developer's expense, in connection with the granting of planning permission for the development. HMRC's views of the VAT consequences of some of these transactions are set out below.

13.2 Dedication of roads and sewers

Where a developer, for no monetary consideration, dedicates new roads and sewers to local authorities and sewerage undertakers, there is no supply and no VAT is, therefore, chargeable to the local authority or sewerage undertaker. Input tax on the construction of such works is, however, attributable to the developer's supplies of the development (ie the land or buildings – houses, shops, factory units etc), and if these are taxable supplies, then the input tax incurred on constructing the roads and sewers is recoverable subject to the normal rules. Where, however, exempt supplies of buildings or areas of land on the development are made, the developer will not be able to recover all the input tax.[1]

13.3 Section 106 and similar agreements

Where a developer provides other types of goods and services free (or for a purely nominal charge) to the local or other authority under s106 of the

---

1 HMRC Notice 742/02, para 8.1 (see **Appendix 8**).

Town and Country Planning Act 1990, or other similar agreements, or agrees to construct something on land already owned by the authority or a third party (for example, community centres, schools, amenity land, civil engineering works), such transactions do not constitute a supply for consideration to the local or other authority. Consequently, no VAT is chargeable on the handing over of the land, building or completion of the works. The input tax is attributable to the developer's supplies of land and buildings on the development as in **13.2** above.[2]

13.4 Cash contributions made by developers

Sums of money paid or payable by a developer, in addition to buildings or works, to a local authority under section 106 and similar agreements (for example, for the future maintenance of a building or land, or as a contribution towards improvement of the infrastructure) are not consideration for taxable supplies to the developer.[3] This does not apply, however, to payments made to water companies in connection with the supply of mains water and sewerage services.

13.5 Transfers of roads, etc to management companies

If the developer of a private housing or industrial estate transfers the basic amenities of estate roads and footpaths, communal parking and open space to a management company which maintains them, no supply is regarded as taking place.[4] The transfer is usually for a nominal monetary consideration, but this is not a condition of HMRC's view that there is no supply. The input tax incurred is attributable to supplies of land and buildings, as in **13.2** above. This does not apply to transfers of buildings, land and amenities apart from the basic amenities specified above.

---

2 HMRC Notice 742/02, para 8.3.

3 HMRC Notice 742/02, para 8.5.

4 HMRC Notice 742/02, para 8.2.

14. Some other implications of VAT in property transactions

Summary

- Stamp duty land tax is payable on any VAT payable by a purchaser or lessee of property.

- Non-recoverable VAT incurred on acquiring capital items may qualify for capital allowances or be added to the cost of an asset for capital gains tax purposes.

- VAT on service charges and insurance service charges will normally follow the VAT liability of the rent.

- There is no separate supply of fixtures when a property is sold.

14.1 Stamp duty land tax

Stamp duty land tax (SDLT) was introduced on 1 December 2003, and replaces stamp duty in relation to land transactions in UK property. The main points to note about the interaction of SDLT and VAT are as follows:

(a) Where VAT is payable compulsorily (eg on the sale of the freehold of a new commercial building or civil engineering work) SDLT is chargeable on the gross purchase price including VAT.[1]

(b) Where VAT is payable because the vendor has elected to waive exemption, SDLT is similarly chargeable on the gross purchase price, premium or rent including VAT.[2]

(c) Where the transaction is not compulsorily standard-rated and no election has yet been made at the effective date of the transaction, SDLT is not charged on VAT that may have been payable if the option to tax had been exercised, or which may at some future date be exercised. In the past, stamp duty would be charged on the gross amount (including VAT) if an election could still have applied to the payment in question. In the case of a transaction involving further supplies after the date of execution (such as a lease of commercial property under which payments of rent will continue to be due in the future), SDLT will be charged on the gross

---

1 Finance Act 2003 (FA 2003), Sch 4 para 2.

2 FA 2003, Sch 2 para 2.

(ie VAT-inclusive) amount of payments (such as rent) to which an election applies at the 'effective date' of the lease.

(d) SDLT is not chargeable on a formal notice of election to waive exemption made to HMRC, or on any notification to the purchaser or lessee that such an election has been made.

14.2 STAMP DUTY LAND TAX AND VAT ON LEASES

Paragraph 2 of Schedule 4 to the FA 2003 provides that, where VAT is chargeable on the rent under the lease as at the effective date of the lease (ie where the landlord has opted to tax the property before granting the lease), VAT is included in the rent for the purposes of calculating the SDLT payable.

14.3 STAMP DUTY LAND TAX AND TRANSFERS OF A GOING CONCERN (TOGC)

14.3.1 According to the Law Society,[3] the Stamp Office's approach in relation to stamp duty was as follows. If the document allows for VAT to be charged subsequently, for instance, if HMRC refused transfer of a going concern (TOGC) clearance, then the Stamp Office stamps the document on the initial consideration stated (ie without the addition of VAT), subject to confirmation being provided that:

(a) the transaction was believed to involve a TOGC and consequently no VAT was added to the consideration stated in the document;

(b) the client had been advised that he was obliged to tell the Stamp Office if that position changed, in line with his obligations under s5 Stamp Act 1891; and

(c) the client undertook to arrange for the document to be returned to the Stamp Office and to pay the extra duty if VAT was charged.

A written undertaking from the client or the firm of solicitors acting to that effect had to be enclosed with the letter to the Stamp Office.

14.3.2 It is not certain how this practice applies in the context of SDLT. The better view is that where there is uncertainty over whether TOGC treatment applies, a land transaction return should be submitted on the VAT-exclusive amount of chargeable consideration, and the taxpayer should seek a post-transaction ruling from HMRC on the applicability of TOGC treatment. If TOGC treatment does not apply, the taxpayer should submit

3 *Law Society Gazette*, 13 January 1999.

an amended land transaction return in accordance with para 6 of Schedule 10 to the FA 2003 and pay any additional SDLT.[4]

14.4 LAND REGISTRY FEES

Land Registry scale fees on first registration and for registration of transfers and leases are assessed on the value of the monetary consideration paid. Where standard-rated VAT is payable on the transaction, HM Land Registry takes the view that the fee for registration is based on the VAT-inclusive amount.

14.5 CAPITAL ALLOWANCES

Generally, any input tax which is not recoverable can be added to the capital costs of the asset for the purpose of computing capital allowances, if applicable. Where the amount of non-deductible input tax changes over the capital items adjustment period (see **Chapter 9**), capital allowances will be given as if extra qualifying expenditure has been incurred, or (as the case may be) as if a refund has been received, generally on the last day of the VAT accounting period for which the relevant VAT return is submitted.[5] Earlier computations are not in any way affected.

14.6 CAPITAL GAINS TAX

14.6.1 The general position on the interaction of VAT and capital gains tax (CGT) computations is that, where input tax on the purchase of an asset can be recovered, the cost of the asset for CGT purposes is the cost exclusive of VAT. Where no recovery is available, the cost will be inclusive of the VAT borne. Where an asset is disposed of, any VAT chargeable is disregarded in computing the capital gain.

14.6.2 Where VAT adjustments are made, for example under the capital items adjustment rules, corresponding adjustments may be made to expenditure in computing capital gains and losses. Although in certain circumstances a VAT adjustment may reduce the amount of expenditure on an asset qualifying for rollover relief on the replacement of business assets, HMRC has said that where a VAT adjustment is made after a claim to rollover relief has been determined, it will not normally seek to reopen the claims.

---

4 SDLT Manual, para 3800.
5 Capital Allowances Act 2001, ss235, 238.

14.7 SERVICE CHARGES

Maintenance charges, additional rent or service charges (however phrased) paid by the tenants to the landlord, in addition to the basic rent, towards the general upkeep of the structure and common areas of the premises and grounds, are treated for VAT purposes as part of the rent and follow its VAT liability (ie exempt or standard-rated depending on the particular building). However, service charges for services supplied for a tenant's particular office or flat, such as heating, lighting (where the landlord operates a secondary credit meter) or cleaning, are treated separately from the rent and other general service charges, and are chargeable to VAT at their own rate regardless of the VAT liability of the rent.[6] If the tenants pay into a maintenance fund and the moneys are paid out of the fund on behalf of the tenants to the service providers, there is no supply other than the supply of the services to the tenants by the service providers. If, on the other hand, the payments are made to a person (such as a trustee) who has a legal entitlement to the moneys and who uses the moneys himself to employ the service providers, there is a taxable supply by that person, who must therefore charge and account for VAT on the payments received.[7]

14.8 INSURANCE PREMIUMS PAID BY TENANTS TO LANDLORD

Where a landlord has insured a building and the lease provides that a tenant will contribute to the insurance premium by means of a charge additional to the basic rent, the VAT liability of the charge will follow the VAT liability of the rent. Where the tenant is the insured person, or where the landlord and tenant are jointly insured under the policy, the insurance premium or share of the premium paid by the tenant will be a disbursement rather than a consideration for a supply of the property by the landlord.

14.9 PAYMENTS OF LANDLORDS' COSTS BY TENANTS

14.9.1 Normally, a landlord's costs may be paid by a tenant in three situations, namely:

(a) on obtaining the grant of a lease;

(b) on obtaining an additional right under a lease (for example, a right to sublet where the lease prohibited it); or

---

6 For further details see HMRC Notice 742/02, s11 (see **Appendix 8**).

7 *Nell Gwynn House Maintenance Fund Trustees v Customs & Excise Commissioners* [1999] STC 79.

(c) on exercising an existing right under a lease (for example, a right to assign, subject to the landlord's consent which may not be unreasonably withheld or registration of a notice of assignment).

14.9.2 HMRC's view is that all payments in the situations at (a)-(c) above are consideration for a supply by the landlord which will be either taxable or exempt. The payments in situations (a) and (c) above are regarded as part of the consideration for the supply of the property under the lease and, like rent or a premium, chargeable to VAT (or not) according to the VAT status of the property.8 The payment in situation (b) above is regarded as consideration for a separate supply (not necessarily of property), which will be chargeable to VAT at the standard rate unless the grant of the additional right is an exempt supply. In either case, it is important that the reimbursement obligation should be properly drafted, to enable the landlord to charge VAT in addition to the costs in the situation where the landlord is making a taxable supply, and to enable the landlord to claim reimbursement of the costs inclusive of irrecoverable VAT in the situation where the landlord is making an exempt supply. Where VAT is charged and invoiced by the landlord (ie in the case where the landlord is making a taxable supply), the tenant may be able to recover the VAT, thus reducing the real cost to the tenant of the reimbursement obligation.

Invoicing

14.9.3 Where the tenant agrees to pay the landlord's costs, special care must be taken with invoicing. If a landlord is making a taxable supply to the tenant, the landlord must issue the tenant with a VAT invoice as normal. The value of the supply will be the net amount (ie excluding VAT incurred by the landlord) of the costs, to which the landlord will add VAT. The landlord will not be charging 'VAT on VAT' since, by virtue of making the taxable supply, the landlord should be able to recover the VAT incurred on the costs. Where the landlord is making an exempt supply, he cannot recover the VAT he incurs, nor can he charge VAT. The tenant is therefore not entitled to receive a VAT invoice from the landlord, but receives a non-VAT invoice, the amount of which is increased to take into account the VAT charge which the landlord suffers. In the latter case, the tenant cannot recover the VAT. Although often tenants will ask to be sent a VAT invoice direct from the suppliers, an invoice from the suppliers would not enable the tenant to recover VAT, since the supply has not been made to the tenant. The only exception would

---

8 *Law Society Gazette*, 28 October 1992.

be if the tenant enters into a direct contractual relationship with the supplier and pays the supplier.[9]

14.10 FIXTURES AND FITTINGS

Fixtures supplied on the disposal of a freehold or leasehold interest in land are treated as 'flowing' with the land, so that their VAT liability follows that of the land itself. Although supplies of fittings are, technically, not part of the land and are, in principle, subject to tax at the standard rate, HMRC has agreed in relation to commercial premises that, provided a single charge is made for the supply of the land and any associated fixtures and fittings (or where a separate consideration is assigned to 'fixtures and fittings' but the fittings as such are not charged for separately), the sale of the fixtures and fittings together may be treated as part and parcel of the disposal of the land, and may take on the same liability as the grant of the interest in the land itself. However, items valued and invoiced separately as fittings, either individually or as a group, would be regarded as a separate supply of goods and taxed accordingly.

14.11 COVENANTS CONCERNING LAND

The release of a restrictive covenant for consideration is regarded as an exempt supply, except where the person receiving the payment has elected to waive exemption.[10]

14.12 RIGHTS OF LIGHT

The grant or assignment of a right of light is an exempt supply, subject to the election to waive exemption. Following the European Court of Justice decision in *Lubbock Fine & Co v Customs & Excise Commissioners*,[11] it is considered that the same applies to a variation or release of an existing right.

14.13 CRANE OVER-SAILING LICENCES

The grant of a crane over-sailing licence is neither an interest in nor a right over land. Neither is it a licence to occupy land. Therefore, it is not an exempt supply, but is liable to VAT at the standard rate.[12]

---

9 *Customs & Excise Commissioners v Redrow Group Plc* [1999] STC 161.

10 HMRC Notice 742/02, para 10.6.

11 [1994] STC 101.

12 *Carter t/a Protheroe Carter & Eason v Customs & Excise Commissioners*, unreported, 1994, VAT Tribunal decision no 12047.

14.14 DEFAULT ON RENT BY TENANT

Landlord's VAT position

14.14.1 Where a tenant defaults in payment of rent, the landlord should not be liable to account for VAT unless he either:

(a) issues a VAT invoice (see **7.5** above);

(b) has issued a VAT invoice for a period of up to 12 months and payments become due (see **7.5** above);

(c) appropriates a rent deposit held as security in respect of which he has not already accounted for VAT; or

(d) receives a payment from a guarantor, former tenant or sub-tenant.

Planning point

14.14.2 In view of the fact that issue of a VAT invoice will trigger a tax liability, a planning point for the landlord is to avoid issuing a VAT invoice until payment has been received. An invoice issued with the rent demand will not be a VAT invoice if it omits requisite details, such as the landlord's VAT registration number. Such an invoice can also specifically state that it is not a VAT invoice.

Landlord's rights

14.14.3 In the event of default by the tenant, the landlord may in certain circumstances claim the rent (including VAT) from earlier tenants under the same lease. In the case of a lease entered into before 1 January 1996 (or pursuant to an agreement dated before 1 January 1996), the original tenant remains liable for the rent for the whole term (ie even for periods after he has assigned the lease). An assignee who has entered into a direct covenant with the landlord in relation to a pre-1 January 1996 lease will likewise remain liable for the whole of the residue of the term. In the case of a lease entered into on or after 1 January 1996 (and not pursuant to an agreement before that date), a tenant who assigns will not normally remain liable, unless he has entered into an 'authorised guarantee agreement' (AGA) under the Landlord and Tenant (Covenants) Act 1995. Moreover, even where the outgoing tenant has entered into an AGA, he will usually remain liable for the rent only for the period of tenure of his immediate assignee.

14.14.4 Where an earlier tenant is liable for the rent, the liability includes any VAT thereon, even if VAT only became payable after he parted with his interest.

14.14.5 Section 6 of the Law of Distress Amendment Act 1908 provides that, where the head lessor, whose tenant is in arrears with his rent, serves on the underlessee a notice stating the amount of the rent due and requiring him to pay the rent to the head lessor until such arrears are paid, the giving of the notice operates to transfer to the head lessor the right to recover, receive and give a discharge for the underlessee's rent. The underlessee cannot be required to pay more than the rent payable to the head lessee.

Invoices and recovery

14.14.6 In cases where the rent is paid by a person other than the current tenant, HMRC regards the landlord as continuing to make a supply to the current tenant. Accordingly, the landlord should not issue a tax invoice to the guarantor, former tenant or underlessee, and such persons are not able to recover any VAT which they pay to the landlord.

APPENDICES

Appendix 1: Summary of VAT in commercial and non-commercial property transactions

Type of transaction	VAT treatment as at August 2005
Commercial properties	
Freehold sale of 'new' building (ie less than three years old)	17.5% (compulsory)
Freehold sale of building not yet completed (whether or not preceded by a letting)	17.5% (compulsory)
Freehold sale of 'new' civil engineering work	17.5% (compulsory)
Freehold sale of civil engineering work not yet completed	17.5% (compulsory)
Separate grant of facilities for parking a vehicle, playing sports or housing aircraft	17.5% (compulsory)
Grants of certain rights in respect of theatre boxes, hotels, holiday accommodation, caravans and camping facilities and rights to take fish, game and timber	17.5% (compulsory)
Grants of any right (eg an option) to call for any of the interests or rights listed above	17.5% (compulsory)
Any sale or lease covered by election to waive exemption	17.5% (compulsory)
Payment of capital sum ('reverse' premium) to prospective tenant to induce him to take up lease	No supply for VAT purposes (see **Chapter 5**)
'Straight' or 'reverse' premium for surrender of a lease	Exempt (unless recipient has elected)
'Reverse' premium for assignment of lease	17.5% (compulsory)
Payment for release of restrictive covenant or easements	Exempt (unless recipient has elected)
Grant of lease for a premium or at a rent (whether of 'new' building, one not yet completed or otherwise)	Exempt (unless grantor has elected)
Any sale of a lease (including sale of leasehold of 'new' or uncompleted building or civil engineering work)	Exempt (unless vendor has elected)
Sale of existing (old) building whether freehold or leasehold	Exempt (unless vendor has elected)

Continued overleaf

Type of transaction	VAT treatment as at August 2005
Commercial properties (cont)	
Exercise of power of sale by mortgagee (whether or not mortgagor has exercised option over mortgaged land)	Supplies by mortgagee deemed to be made by mortgagor
Self-supply of in-house construction services	17.5% (compulsory – see **Chapter 8**)
Non-commercial properties	
Grant of a major interest (which is also the first supply) in a new non-commercial property by 'person constructing'	Zero-rated
Grant of a major interest in a non-commercial property by someone other than 'person constructing'	Exempt
Grant of any other interest in a non-commercial property	Exempt
Self-supply on change to commercial use (not dwellings)	17.5% (compulsory)
General	
Transfer of a going concern	No supply for VAT purposes

APPENDIX 2: DRAFT LETTER TO HMRC NOTIFYING IT OF AN ELECTION WHERE NO EXEMPT SUPPLIES HAVE BEEN MADE OR WILL BE MADE IN RELATION TO THE RELEVANT LAND PRIOR TO THE DAY ON WHICH THE ELECTION TAKES EFFECT

HM Revenue & Customs

[Local VAT Office]

Dear Sirs,

[Property Owner Ltd]

VAT Registration No: […]

As required by paragraph 3(6), Schedule 10, Value Added Tax Act 1994, [Property Owner Ltd] of [address] hereby notifies HM Revenue & Customs that, on [date], [Property Owner Ltd] elected to waive exemption under paragraph 2, Schedule 10, Value Added Tax Act 1994 in respect of the property described below:

[insert *full* details of properties (eg address and description, with plan if necessary) in respect of which election has been made or refer to a schedule of such properties attached to the letter]

The election has effect from the beginning of [insert date when election has effect].

[Property Owner Ltd] has not made [and will not make] any exempt supply of the property described above between 1 August 1989 and the beginning of [insert date on which election has effect].

The election in respect of which notice is hereby given is not made and has no effect in relation to any land (which, for the avoidance of doubt, includes any buildings on the land or works on or under it) which is now owned or may be subsequently acquired by [Property Owner Ltd] other than the land referred to above.

Yours faithfully,

For and on behalf of

[Property Owner Ltd]

APPENDIX 3: DRAFT LETTER TO HMRC WHERE AN EXEMPT SUPPLY HAS BEEN OR WILL BE MADE IN RELATION TO THE RELEVANT LAND PRIOR TO THE DAY ON WHICH THE ELECTION TAKES EFFECT

HM Revenue & Customs

[Local VAT Office]

Dear Sirs,

[The Property]

Paragraph 2, Schedule 10, Value Added Tax Act 1994

We are writing to seek your permission under sub-paragraph 3(9), Schedule 10, Value Added Tax Act 1994 to our making an election in respect of the above property to take effect from [...].

We should mention that:

(a) the total value of exempt supplies in relation to the relevant property which we have made and/or will make before [the day on which the election is to take effect] is £[...];

(b) the expected total value of supplies in relation to the above property that would be taxable if the election were to take effect on [the day on which the election is to take effect] is £[...]; and

(c) the total amount of input tax which we have incurred or are likely to incur on or after 1 August, 1989 in relation to the above property is £[...].

We would be grateful if you could confirm your consent to our making the election to take effect on the date set out above.

Yours faithfully,

APPENDIX 4: PRO FORMA NOTICE OF AGREEMENT FOR TRANSFER OF A GOING CONCERN TO NOMINEE PURCHASER

Notice of agreement to adopt statement of practice

Property: […]

Vendor: […]

Purchaser: […]

Future Beneficial Owner: […]

[Vendor, Purchaser and Future Beneficial Owner] confirm that they have agreed to adopt the optional practice set out in HMRC's Business Brief 10/96 in relation to the purchase of the Property pursuant to an agreement dated […] between [Vendor] and [Purchaser].

Following the transfer of the Property, [Purchaser] will hold the legal title as nominee for [Future Beneficial Owner], the beneficial owner.

Signed on behalf of [Vendor]

Signed on behalf of [Purchaser]

Signed on behalf of [Future Beneficial Owner]

Date: […]

APPENDIX 5: STANDARD VAT AND TRANSFER OF A GOING CONCERN WORDING FOR PROPERTY SALE CONTRACT WHERE VENDOR HAS ELECTED TO TAX THE LAND BEING SOLD

1. Value added tax and TOGCs

1.1 All payments made pursuant to this Agreement shall be exclusive of VAT and any VAT chargeable in respect of the matters giving rise to such payments shall be added to the amount thereof and paid in addition thereto.

1.2 [Any VAT payable in addition to amounts paid hereunder shall be paid on the later of the date of Completion and the date the Vendor provides a valid VAT invoice for the said VAT.]

1.3 The Vendor and the Purchaser warrant to each other that they are duly registered for the purposes of VAT.

1.4 The Purchaser hereby confirms that Article 5(2B) of the Value Added Tax (Special Provisions) Order 1995 does not apply to the Purchaser.

1.5 The Vendor warrants that it has exercised the election to waive exemption for VAT purposes under paragraph 2 of Schedule 10 to the Value Added Tax Act 1994 ('VATA') in respect of the Property and has notified such election to HM Revenue & Customs.

1.6 The Vendor and the Purchaser consider that the sale of the Property is for VAT purposes the transfer [of part of] the business of the Vendor as a going concern and falls within Section 49 of the VATA and Article 5 of the Value Added Tax (Special Provisions) Order 1995.

1.7 [The consideration for the Property is apportioned as to [£...] in respect of the tenanted part and [£...] which relates to the part of the Property [being occupied by the Vendor/used for residential/charitable purposes].]

1.8 The Vendor shall (unless already sent) as soon as practicable send a letter to HM Revenue & Customs seeking a direction that the Vendor be permitted to keep and preserve the records referred to in Section 49 of VATA and paragraph 6 Schedule 11 VATA relating to the Property for such periods as may be required by law PROVIDED THAT:

    (a) if HM Revenue & Customs requires such records be delivered to the Purchaser, then the Vendor will upon written demand deliver the same to the Purchaser;

    (b) if HM Revenue & Customs directs that such records may be retained by the Vendor then the Vendor will on or after the date of Completion deliver, on written demand, to the Purchaser, complete copies of such records as may be reasonably required by the Purchaser from time to time.

1.9   Whichever party retains the records referred to above shall preserve the said records for such a period as may be required by law and during that period shall at all reasonable times permit the other party or its agents to inspect such records and (at the other party's expense) to take copies of such records.

1.10   The Purchaser warrants that it has exercised the election to waive exemption for VAT purposes under paragraph 2 of Schedule 10 to the VATA in respect of the Property with effect from the relevant date (as defined in Article 5(3) of the Value Added Tax (Special Provisions) Order 1995) or the date hereof (whichever is earlier).[1]

1.11   The Purchaser warrants that for so long as it is necessary for this transaction to be treated as a transfer [of part of] a business as a going concern it will continue to use the Property in carrying on the same kind of business as that carried on by the Vendor and in particular will continue to let the Property.

1.12   In the event that HM Revenue & Customs assess the Vendor to VAT in relation to the sale of the Property pursuant to this Agreement or determine that the sale of the Property is not a transfer of a business [or part of a business] as a going concern the Purchaser shall within three days of the Vendor notifying the Purchaser of the assessment and producing to the Purchaser a copy of the determination of HM Revenue & Customs in this regard and producing a VAT invoice addressed to the Purchaser pay to the Vendor such VAT [and interest and penalties due thereon].

---

1. If deposit has been paid by Purchaser to Vendor's Solicitor as agent for Vendor, the Purchaser is required to elect and notify the election on or prior to exchange.

APPENDIX 6: ADDITIONAL VAT TRANSFER OF A GOING CONCERN CLAUSES WHERE THE PURCHASER IS BUYING LAND AS NOMINEE FOR ANOTHER PERSON

1. The Purchaser is buying the property as nominee for [named beneficial owner].

2. The Vendor and the Purchaser agree to adopt the optional practice detailed in HMRC Business Brief 10/96 and to that effect shall sign the Notice of Agreement set out in Schedule […]. The Purchaser shall procure that the [Future Beneficial Owner] shall also sign the Notice of Agreement.

Appendix 7: Draft letter notifying transfer of a going concern and asking to return records

[Date]

HM Revenue & Customs

[Local VAT office]

Dear Sirs,

[Insert Vendor's name and VAT registration number]

[Insert purchaser's name and VAT registration number]

Transfer of a going concern of [property or properties]

On […], [the Vendor] agreed to sell [describe property or properties] to [the Purchaser]. The sale was by way of a transfer of a going concern ('TOGC'). I enclose a copy of the Agreement for Sale.

The purpose of this letter is to:

1. notify HM Revenue & Customs that the sale and purchase of [the property/properties] was treated as a transfer of a going concern and, therefore, not subject to VAT; and

2. obtain a written direction from HM Revenue & Customs under section 49(1)(b) VAT Act 1994 that, in the event, that [the Vendor] shall preserve any records relating to the business which are required by law to be preserved following the transfer.

The reason for the application for the direction is [that the records relate to many properties] [the records are part of other records] [the records are kept in electronic form] and separation is not easily achievable in practice. Such records can be made available for inspection at [the Vendor] if required.

If you require any further information or have any questions concerning anything contained in this letter, please contact […] at the above address.

Yours faithfully,

Appendix 8: HMRC Notice 742/02 – Land and property

1. Introduction

1.1 What is this notice about?

This notice explains when transactions involving land and buildings are exempt from VAT. We recommend that you also read *Notice 742A Opting to tax land and buildings*. The land law in Scotland differs in many ways from that in England and Wales. *Notice 742/3 Scottish land law terms* may help you to understand these differences.

This notice has been restructured to improve readability. It contains text on parking, sporting rights and letting of facilities for sport and physical recreation, which did not appear in the previous edition.

This notice and others mentioned are available both on paper and on our Internet website at www.hmce.gov.uk.

1.2 Who should read this notice?

You should read this notice if you make, or intend to make, supplies of any interest in land, buildings or civil engineering works.

1.3 What area of law covers this notice?

Section 31 of the VAT Act 1994 holds that goods and services specified in Schedule 9 to the Act are exempt supplies. Schedule 9, Group 1 specifies those supplies of land and buildings that are exempt from VAT.

2. Supplies of land

2.1 What constitutes land?

For the purposes of VAT, the term 'land' includes any buildings, civil engineering works, walls, trees, plants and any other structure or natural object in, under or over it as long as they remain attached to it.

2.2 How do I make a supply of land?

You make a supply of land by making a **grant** of an interest in, right over or licence to occupy land in return for a payment or consideration. If you make free supplies of land you should read paragraph 7.6. A grant includes an **assignment** or **surrender**:

- a grant is the sale of a freehold or other interest, or a lease or a letting of land.

- an assignment is the transfer of a lease by the existing tenant to a new tenant.

- a surrender is giving up an interest in land to the person who granted it to you. More information on surrenders can be found in paragraphs 10.3 and 10.4.

2.3 What is an interest in land?

An interest in land can be **legal** or **beneficial**:

An interest in land can be a...	which is the...
legal interest	formal ownership of an interest in or right over land, such as a freehold or leasehold interest.
beneficial interest	right to receive the benefit of any supplies made of the land, such as sale proceeds or rental income. A beneficial interest can be held and transferred separately from the legal interest in the land.

2.4 What are rights over land?

Rights over land include...	which...
rights of entry	allow an authorised person or authority to enter land. For example you might allow someone to come onto your land to perform a specific task.
easements	grant the owner of neighbouring land a right to make their property better or more convenient, such as a right of way or right of light.
wayleaves	are a right of way to transport minerals extracted from land over another's land, or to lay pipes or cables over or under another's land.
profits a prendre	are rights to take produce from another's land, such as to extract minerals.

2.5 What is a licence to occupy land?

A licence is an authority to do something that would otherwise be a trespass. A licence to occupy land is created when the following criteria are met:

(a) the licence is granted in return for a consideration paid for by the licensee;

(b) the licence to occupy must be for a specified piece of land, even if the licence allows the licensor to change the exact area occupied, such as to move the licensee from the third to fourth floor;

(c) the licence is for the occupation of the land by the licensee;

(d) another person's right to enter the specified land does not impinge upon the occupational rights of the licensee; and **either**

(e) the licence allows the licensee to physically enjoy the land for the purposes of the grant, such as to hold a party in a hall; **or**

(f) the licence allows the licensee to economically exploit the land for the purpose of its business, such as to run a nightclub.

For examples of supplies that are licences to occupy land see paragraph 2.6. For examples of supplies that are not licences to occupy see paragraph 2.7.

2.6 Examples of supplies that are licences to occupy land

The following are examples of licences to occupy land. This list is not exhaustive:

• the provision of office accommodation, such as a specified bay, room or floor, together with the right to use shared areas such as reception, lifts, restaurant, rest rooms, leisure facilities and so on;

• the provision of a serviced office that includes use of telephones, computer system, fax machine, photocopiers and so on;

- granting a concession to operate a shop within a shop, where the concessionaire is granted an area from which to sell their goods or services;

- granting space to erect advertising hoardings;

- granting space to place a fixed kiosk on a specified site, such as a newspaper kiosk or flower stand at a railway station;

- hiring out a hall or other accommodation for meetings or parties and so on. The use of a kitchen area, lighting and furniture can be included;

- granting a catering concession, where the caterer is granted a licence to occupy a specific kitchen and restaurant area, even if the grant includes use of kitchen or catering equipment; or

- granting traders a pitch in a market or at a car boot sale.

2.7 Examples of supplies that are not licences to occupy land

The following are examples of supplies that are not licences to occupy land:

- sharing business premises where more than one business has use of the same parts of the premises without having their own specified areas;

- providing another person with access to office premises to make use of facilities, such as remote sales staff away from home having access to photocopiers and the like at another office;

- allowing the public to tip rubbish on your land;

- storing someone's goods in a warehouse without allocating any specific area for them;

- granting of an ambulatory concession, such as an ice cream van on the sea front or a hamburger van at a football match;

- allowing the public admission to premises or events, such as theatres, historic houses, swimming pools and spectator sports events. This includes admission to a series of events, such as a season ticket; or

- any grant of land clearly incidental to the use of the facilities on it, such as hiring out safes to store valuables, the right to use facilities in a hair dressing salon or granting someone the right to place a free standing or wall mounted vending or gaming machine on your premises.

3. The liability of a supply of land

3.1 How do I establish the VAT liability of a supply of land?

The grant, assignment or surrender of an interest in, right over or licence to occupy land is normally exempt from VAT. There are exclusions from this general exemption:

Description	Liability/further information
Freehold sale or long lease in 'qualifying' buildings – including new dwellings, relevant residential or relevant charitable buildings by the person constructing	Generally zero-rated. See *Notice 708 Buildings and construction.*
Freehold sale of new or partly completed 'non-qualifying' buildings	See paragraph 3.2.
Freehold sale of new or partly completed civil engineering works	See paragraph 3.3.
Parking	See section 4.

Description	Liability/further information
Letting facilities for sport and physical recreation	See section 5.
Sporting rights	See section 6.
Hotel and holiday accommodation	Standard-rated. See *Notice 709/3 Hotels and holiday accommodation*
Pitches for caravans on seasonal sites	Standard-rated. See *Notice 701/20 Caravans and houseboats.*
Pitches for tents or camping facilities	Standard-rated. See *Notice 701/20 Caravans and houseboats.*
The right to fell and remove timber	Standard-rated If you sell land that happens to contain standing timber your supply is of exempt land.
Mooring and storage facilities	Generally standard-rated. Moorings for houseboats may qualify for exemption, see *Notice 701/20 Caravans and houseboats.* If the mooring charge is for a 'qualifying ship' the supply may be zero-rated, see *Notice 744C Ships, aircraft and associated services.*
Viewing accommodation	See paragraph 3.4.

You can opt to tax your interest in land. Once you have opted to tax all the supplies you make in relation to your interest in the land will normally be standard-rated. Please read *Notice 742A Opting to tax land and buildings* for more information.

3.2 Freehold sales of new or part completed 'non-qualifying' buildings

If you sell the freehold of a new, or partly completed, non-qualifying building your supply is standard-rated. Non-qualifying buildings are commonly commercial buildings and include offices, warehouses, retail premises and factories. A building is new for three years from the date that it is completed. The date of completion is the date the certificate of practical completion is issued, or the date the building is fully occupied – whichever happens first. All freehold sales that take place within the three-year period are standard-rated.

3.3 Freehold sales of new or part completed civil engineering works

If you sell the freehold of a new or, partly completed, civil engineering work your supply is standard-rated. A civil engineering work is new for three years from the date it is completed. The date of completion is the date the certificate of completion is issued by an engineer, or the date it is first fully used – whichever happens first. All freehold sales that take place within the three-year period are standard-rated.

If you sell the freehold of some bare land, but that land is ancillary to new or part completed civil engineering works, such as an airfield or oil refinery, you are making a single standard-rated supply.

If you sell the freehold of land containing new civil engineering works but those works are a minor part of the supply, you are making a supply of exempt land (unless you have opted to tax) and standard-rated civil engineering works. An example of this is building land on which you have built a road or laid pipes for connection to mains services. You must apportion your charge fairly and reasonably between the land and the civil engineering works.

3.4 Viewing accommodation

If you grant viewing accommodation, such as boxes at a sports ground, theatre, concert hall or other place of entertainment, your supply is standard-rated. This includes any accommodation that is intended for use by individuals or groups for viewing a sporting event, show or other form of entertainment, regardless of whether the entertainment is actually in progress when the accommodation is used. If you let an entire theatre, concert hall or other place of entertainment your supply is normally exempt, unless you have opted to tax.

4. Parking

4.1 The basic VAT position

If you provide facilities for parking vehicles your supply will normally be standard-rated. There are exceptions to this general rule. This section will help you decide the liability of your supplies.

4.2 When do I make a standard-rated supply of parking facilities?

If you make a specific grant and the facilities are designed for, or provided specifically for parking vehicles your supply is standard-rated. The following are examples of standard-rated supplies of parking facilities:

> • a letting or licence of a garage or designated parking bay or space. The letting of a garage is standard-rated even if it is not used for storing a vehicle;

> • a right to park vehicles (including trailers) in, for example, a car park or commercial garage;

> • a letting or licence of land specifically for the construction of a garage, or for use solely for parking a vehicle;

> • a letting or licence of a purpose built car park. For example, a car park let to a car park operator;

> • a letting of a taxi rank;

> • the provision of storage for bicycles;

> • the provision of storage for touring caravans; or

> • a freehold sale of a 'new' or partly completed garage, car park or car parking facility other than in conjunction with the sales of new dwellings. (A garage or car park is 'new' for three years following the date on which it was completed).

4.3 When will a supply be of land rather than parking facilities?

If you grant an interest in, right over or licence to occupy land in the following circumstances, your supply will be exempt, unless you have opted to tax:

> • letting of land or buildings (but not lock-up or other garages) where the conveyance or contract makes no specific reference to use for parking vehicles;

> • letting of land or buildings where any reference to parking a vehicle is incidental to the main use;

> • letting of land or buildings to a motor dealer for storing stock-in trade;

> • letting of land or buildings to a vehicle transportation firm, to a vehicle distributor or to a vehicle auctioneer for use in the course of their business;

> • letting of land, including land used at other times as a car park, for purposes such as holding a market or a car boot sale (this also includes the charge to the car owners selling their goods at a car boot sale);

> • letting of land for the exhibition of vehicles;

> • letting of land to a travelling fair or circus (and the incidental parking of vehicles); or

- the freehold sale of garages, car parks or car parking facilities that are not new (more than three years from the date on which they were completed).

4.4 Grants of parking facilities with dwellings

The sale or long lease of a new dwelling together with a garage or parking space by the person constructing that dwelling is zero-rated. However, if the new dwelling is holiday accommodation the supply is standard-rated, see *Notice 708 Buildings and construction* for more information.

The letting of garages or parking spaces in conjunction with the letting of dwellings for permanent residential use is exempt providing:

(a) the garage or parking space is reasonably near to the dwelling; **and**

(b) the tenant takes up both the lease of a dwelling and the lease of a garage from the same landlord. In these circumstances the garage forms part of the domestic accommodation.

Where a garage is let separately from the letting of a dwelling it cannot be exempt from VAT and will be standard-rated. This is because there is no letting of domestic accommodation with which to associate the garage. This scenario commonly occurs when a local authority tenant renting a dwelling and garage then decides to purchase the dwelling. The local authority retains the garage and continues to lease it to their former tenant. As the local authority is only supplying a garage, and not domestic accommodation, the supply is standard-rated.

4.5 Grants of parking facilities with commercial premises

The supply of commercial premises together with parking facilities is treated as a single supply of the commercial premises, providing:

(a) the facilities are within or on the premises, or reasonably near to it; **or**

(b) the facilities are within a complex (for example, an industrial park made up of separate units with a 'communal' car park for the use of the tenants of the units and their visitors); **and**

(c) both lettings are to the same tenant by the same landlord.

If the rents from the commercial premises are exempt from VAT, the parking facilities will also be exempt. In any other circumstances the provision of parking facilities in conjunction with commercial property is a separate standard-rated supply.

4.6 Grants of garages and parking spaces at caravan parks

If you supply a garage or parking facility at a seasonal or holiday caravan park your supply is always standard-rated.

If you supply a garage in conjunction with the sale of a new caravan your supply is standard-rated.

If you supply a garage or parking space in conjunction with the supply of a permanent residential caravan pitch your supply is exempt providing:

(a) you retain ownership of the land on which the garage or parking space is sited; **and**

(b) the garage or parking space is reasonably close to the caravan pitch.

4.7 Moorings and parking facilities for houseboats

If you supply a mooring for a houseboat of a type described in *Notice 701/20 Caravans and houseboats* your supply is exempt. The supply of a garage or parking space to a houseboat owner is also exempt providing:

(a) the garage or parking space is supplied by the person who is supplying the mooring; and

(b) the garage or parking space is reasonably close to the mooring.

5. Sports facilities and physical recreation

5.1 The basic VAT position

If you let facilities for playing any sport or for taking part in any physical recreation your supply is normally standard-rated. But, if the let is for over 24 hours or is for a series of sessions your supply may be exempt. Please see paragraph 5.3 and 5.4 for more details. If you are a sports club or a non-profit making body you should read *Notice 701/45 Sport*.

5.2 What is a sports facility?

Premises are sports facilities if they are designed or adapted for playing any sport or taking part in any physical recreation, such as swimming pools, football pitches, dance studios and skating rinks. Each court or pitch (or lane in the case of bowling alley, curling rink or swimming pool) is a separate sports facility.

5.3 Lets for over 24 hours

If you make a single let of sports and physical recreation facilities for a continuous period of over 24 hours to the same person your supply is exempt, unless you have opted to tax. However, the person to whom you let the facilities must have exclusive control of them throughout the letting period.

5.4 Lets for a series of sessions

If you let out sports and physical recreation facilities for a series of sessions your supply is exempt (unless you have opted to tax) when you meet all the following conditions:

Step	Condition
1.	The series consists of 10 or more sessions.
2.	Each session is for the same sport or activity.
3.	Each session is in the same place, although a different pitch, court or lane, or different number of pitches, courts or lanes is acceptable.
4.	The interval between each session is at least 1 day but not more than 14 days. The duration of the sessions may be varied, however there is no exception for intervals greater than 14 days through the closure of the facility for any reason.
5.	The series is to be paid for as a whole and there is written evidence to the fact. This must include evidence that payment is to be made in full whether or not the right to use the facility for any specific session is actually exercised. Provision for a refund given by the provider in the event of the unforeseen non-availability of their facility would not affect this condition.
6.	The facilities are let out to a school, club, association or an organisation representing affiliated clubs or constituent associations, such as a local league.
7.	The person to whom the facilities are let has exclusive use of them during the sessions.

6. Sporting rights

6.1 What are 'sporting rights'?

A sporting right is the right to take game or fish from land. The supply of sporting rights is normally standard-rated.

If the sporting rights form part of the supply of some land, there are occasions when the liability of the sporting rights will follow the liability of that land. Please see paragraph 6.2 for more information.

6.2 Sporting rights forming part of a supply of land

If you sell sporting rights as part of the freehold sale of the land over which those rights may be exercised, your supply will be exempt unless you have opted to tax.

If you lease land together with sporting rights over that land, and the sporting rights represent no more than 10% of the value of the whole supply, your supply will be of exempt land unless you have opted to tax.

If the sporting rights represent more than 10% of the value of the whole supply, you are making a standard-rated supply of those rights in addition to the lease of the land. You must apportion your charge fairly and reasonably between the sporting rights and the land.

6.3 Supplies relating specifically to shooting

6.3.1 Shooting in hand

The term 'shooting in hand' is used where a landowner keeps control of a shoot, makes all the necessary arrangements to stock the land with game and decides who participates in a shoot.

If you accept contributions towards the cost of maintaining a shoot from other 'guns' you invite to a shoot, you are not making a supply in the course of any business when all the following conditions are met:

Step	Condition
1.	Only friends and relatives shoot with you.
2.	You do not publicly advertise the shooting.
3.	Your shooting accounts show an annual loss at least equal to the usual contribution made by a 'gun' over a year.
4.	The loss is not borne by any business but by you personally.

In these circumstances you must not charge VAT to the 'guns' and you cannot recover as input tax any VAT that you incur in maintaining the shoot.

6.3.2 Shooting syndicates

If you set up a syndicate for individuals to contribute towards sharing the expenses of shooting, the syndicate does not normally make a supply of sporting rights to its members.

However if the syndicate is regularly paid to provide shooting facilities to individuals who are not members, or it makes taxable supplies of other goods or services, then it is in business. The syndicate must, if registrable, account for VAT on all its supplies including those to its members.

6.3.3 Landowners as syndicate members

If you are a landowner or a tenant, and you grant shooting rights for less than their normal value to a syndicate of whom you are a member, you must account for VAT on the open market value of those rights. If you supply other goods or services, such as the services of a gamekeeper or beater, you should charge VAT in the normal way.

6.4 Supplies relating specifically to fishing

6.4.1 Still-water fisheries

If you operate a still-water fishery, the charges you make are standard-rated even if you supply both fishing rights and fish.

However, if:

(a) you allow a person to choose whether to take away fish caught or to throw them back into the water; and

(b) you make a separate charge solely for those fish taken away; and

(c) the fish taken away are of a species generally used for food in the UK (see *Notice 701/14 Food*), then the separate charge is zero-rated as a supply of those fish.

6.4.2 Lakes

If you let a lake that is empty of fish to a person who will stock it with fish, you are supplying the lake and not the right to take those fish. You are making an exempt supply of land, unless you have opted to tax.

7. Other land transactions

7.1 Beneficial owners of land or buildings

For VAT purposes, a beneficial owner who directly receives the benefit of the proceeds from selling, leasing or letting land or buildings is treated as being the person selling, leasing or letting the land or buildings. This is the case even though that person is not the legal owner. An example of this is a bare trust where a trustee is the legal owner of the land, but the beneficial ownership belongs to another person. We treat the beneficial owner as the person making the grant.

If the beneficial owner is making taxable supplies above the registration threshold they will have to register for VAT. They will then need to account for the VAT due on the supply and can claim any input tax that arises, subject to the normal rules. The beneficial owner may also request voluntary registration where the value of taxable supplies is below the registration threshold. *Notice 700/1 Should I be registered for VAT?* gives more information on registering for VAT.

Where the benefit accrues directly to trustees, it is the trustees who should register for VAT as a single person if the value of their taxable supplies is above the registration threshold.

7.2 Joint owners of land or buildings

Where more than one person owns land or buildings, or receives the benefit of the consideration for the grant of an interest in land or buildings, we treat them as a single person making a single supply for VAT purposes.

If the joint owners are making taxable supplies above the registration threshold they will have to register for VAT as a partnership, subject to the normal rules, even if no legal partnership exists. The joint owners may also request voluntary registration where the value of taxable supplies is below the registration threshold. For more information on VAT registration please read *Notice 700/1 Should I be registered for VAT?*

7.3 Compulsory purchases

If you are obliged to dispose of land or buildings under a compulsory purchase order you are making a supply for VAT purposes. Your supply will generally be exempt, unless you have opted to tax.

If at the time of supply you do not know how much you will receive, there will be a tax point each time you receive any payment for the purchase.

7.4 Options to purchase or sell an interest in land or a building

If you grant someone the right to purchase an interest in your land or building within a specified time for a stated price you are making a supply of an interest in land. The person acquiring such a right is said to have a 'call option' as he can call on you to sell your interest in the land or building as originally agreed. The liability of your supply will be whatever the liability of the land or building would be if supplied at that time.

If you are granted the right to require someone to purchase your interest in the land or building within a specified time for a stated price you will have a 'put option'. It is the prospective purchaser that is making the supply, which will generally be standard-rated.

7.5 Recovery of rent from a third party

There are two common ways in which a landlord can recover rent from a third party. If you do receive payment from a third party you should still address any related VAT invoice to the tenant to whom you have leased or let the premises. Your supply is still to the tenant, not the third party.

7.5.1 Law of Distress Amendment Act 1908

If a tenant sub-lets land or buildings to a third party and the tenant defaults on payment of rent to the landlord, the landlord can issue a notice under the Law of Distress Amendment Act and collect the rent arrears from the third party. In turn the third party can reduce his rent payable to the tenant by the amount he has paid to the landlord. If this happens the supply chain remains the same; there is a supply of the land or building from the landlord to the tenant and a supply of the land or building from the tenant to the third party. If the landlord has opted to tax, any tax invoice must be issued to the tenant.

7.5.2 Sureties and guarantors

A surety or guarantor is normally party to any agreement between the landlord and the tenant. In the event that the tenant is unable to meet his liability to make the agreed periodic rental payments to the landlord then the surety or guarantor will make the payment on the tenant's behalf. However, there is no supply by the landlord to the surety or guarantor. The surety or guarantor will not be able to recover any tax paid.

7.6 What if I make free supplies of land and buildings?

If you transfer or dispose of land or buildings that form part of the assets of your business free of charge you may still be making a supply. You may also make a supply if you use the land or building, or make it available for anyone else to use, free of charge or for a private or non-business purpose. You must account for output tax on such supplies if:

(a) you were charged tax on the purchase, construction, reconstruction or refurbishment of the land or building;

(b) you have treated all that tax as input tax and did not apportion between business and non-business use;

(c) you were eligible to treat all or part of the input tax as deductible; and

(d) your supply is standard-rated (see below).

If you transfer or dispose of such land or buildings, then the supply is taxable if it is standard-rated in its own right or you have opted to tax (and the option is not disapplied). The value is the market value at the time of its disposal. You must account for output tax on any taxable supply.

The charge for making the building available for free of charge, private or non-business use is always taxable. The amount of the charge is equal to that part of the input VAT you deducted on the building that is fairly attributable to this use. If you did not incur VAT on the building before 9 April 2003, then this charge only arises if you change your intended use of the building after incurring the VAT, as a single output tax charge at the time of the change of use. If the free of charge, private or non-business use is intended when you incur the VAT, then you must apportion the VAT you incur at that point and there will be no further charge when the free of charge, private or non-business use actually happens.

7.7 What if I transfer my business as a going concern?

If you are transferring land or buildings that are let to tenants or are in the process of being let, you should read *Notice 700/9 Transfer of a business as a going concern*.

If you are transferring land or buildings that are capital items for the purposes of the capital goods scheme, you must make the purchaser aware of any capital goods scheme adjustments you have made. You will need to provide the purchaser with sufficient information to enable them to carry out any future adjustments under the scheme that might be necessary. Please see *Notice 706/2 Capital goods scheme for details*.

7.8 What if I have land and buildings on hand when I cancel my registration?

If you cancel your VAT registration because you are closing down your business or trading below the registration limits, some or all of the assets on hand (including land and buildings) may be treated as supplied by you when you deregister. You will have to account for VAT on these assets if you previously claimed the input tax, unless the value is under £1000. Please see *Notice 700/11 Cancelling your registration* for more information.

If the land or buildings are capital items for the purposes of the capital goods scheme you may need to make a final adjustment under the scheme. Further information can be found in *Notice 706/2 Capital goods scheme*.

If you are a farmer operating under the Agricultural Flat Rate Scheme and can produce a certificate of evidence to that effect, then this paragraph does not apply to you.

7.9 What if the land or building includes fixtures?

If the fixtures are included with a building or land they are not treated as separate supplies for VAT purposes. This means that their liability is the same as that of the land or building with which they are being supplied.

7.10 Stamp duty

The Stamp Office administers stamp duty. Any enquiry you have on liability to pay stamp duty, or on calculation of the amount payable, should be made to the Stamp Office.

8. Developers' agreements

8.1 Dedicating or vesting new roads or sewers

Agreements drawn up between developers, local authorities and water sewerage undertakers make provision for a wide variety of land, buildings and works to be provided, at the developer's expense, in connection with the granting of planning permission for the development.

If you, as a developer, dedicate or vest, for no monetary consideration:

(a) a new road (under the provisions of the Highways Act 1980 or the Roads (Scotland) Act 1984); or

(b) a new sewer or ancillary works (under the provisions of the Water Industries Act 1991 or the Sewerage (Scotland) Act 1968),

it is not a supply by you. No VAT is chargeable to the local authority or sewerage undertaker.

The input tax you incur on the construction of such works is attributable to your supplies of the development that is served by the road or sewer. For example, if your supplies of the land or buildings are taxable supplies, such as new houses, then the input tax you incur on constructing the roads and sewers is recoverable according to the normal rules. Where you make exempt supplies you will not be able to recover all your input tax.

8.2 Transfers of common areas of estates to management companies

As a developer of a private housing or industrial estate you may transfer, for a nominal monetary consideration, the basic amenities of estate roads, footpaths, communal parking and open space to a management company that will maintain them. This is not a supply, but the input tax you incurred on the building costs is attributable to the supplies of the land and buildings of the development itself.

8.3 Planning gain agreements

As a developer you may provide many other types of goods and services free, or for a purely nominal charge, to the local or other authority under section 106 of the Town and Country Planning Act 1990 or other similar agreements. These agreements are sometimes described as 'planning gain agreements'.

Such goods and services may include buildings such as community centres or schools, amenity land or civil engineering works. Alternatively, they may be in the form of services such as an agreement to construct something on land already owned by the authority or a third party. Any such provision of goods or services is not a supply for a consideration to the local or other authority, or to the third party. Consequently, no VAT is chargeable by you on the handing over of the land or building or the completion of the works. However, the input tax you incur is attributable to your supplies of land and buildings on the development for which the planning permission was given.

8.4 Agreements with the Highways Agency

When a development is undertaken there may need to be road improvements. These road improvements will normally be undertaken in one of the following ways:

8.4.1 Works carried out by the Highways Agency

The Highways Agency will arrange for the works to be carried out. Under Section 278 of the Highways Act 1980, the Highways Agency may then recover from you, the developer, the costs incurred by the Highways Agency on certain road improvements. These costs will normally include irrecoverable VAT that has been charged to the Highways Agency by a contractor. As there is no supply between the Highways Agency and yourself, but merely a reimbursement by you of VAT inclusive costs, you are not entitled to recover the VAT element as your input tax.

8.4.2 Works carried out by the developer.

If you, the developer, are permitted by the Highways Agency to carry out the works at your own cost, then there is no supply by you of the works to the Highways Agency. This is because you do not receive any consideration for the works from the Highways Agency. However you may recover the input tax as attributable to your own ultimate supply of land and buildings from the development. For example, if the development is a taxable supply you can recover all the input tax.

8.5 What if I am required to make a cash contribution?

You may be required to pay sums of money, or sums of money in addition to buildings or works, to a local authority or a third party under section 106 of the Town and Country Planning Act 1990 and other similar agreements. You may, for example, pay money towards the future maintenance of a building or land, or as a contribution towards improvement of the infrastructure. Such sums are not consideration for taxable supplies to you by the local authority or by the third party.

9. Mortgages

9.1 The basic position

If you mortgage your property, as security for borrowing money, you are not making a supply of that property.

9.2 What if my land or buildings are repossessed and then sold?

Sales of repossessed property take place in two ways:

9.2.1 Under a power of sale

If a financial institution, or any other person, sells land or buildings belonging to you in satisfaction of a debt owed by you, a supply by you takes place. If tax is due on that supply, the person selling the land or buildings is responsible for accounting for that VAT (please see paragraph 9.4 for more information).

9.2.2 Foreclosures

If a person obtains a Court Order and forecloses on land or buildings belonging to you, there is a supply by you to that person of the land or building. However, it is possible that the land or building could be treated as an asset of a business that is transferred as a going concern.

Please see *Notice 700/9 Transfer of a business as a going concern* for details. The person foreclosing can opt to tax. If the land or building is subsequently sold the person foreclosing makes the supply.

9.3 What if my land or buildings are repossessed and then rented out?

A lender may repossess land or buildings, or appoint an LPA receiver without foreclosing, where the land and buildings are rented out to tenants. If the rental income received by the lender is used to reduce the debt you owe, or to make interest payments due in respect of that debt, a supply by you to the tenant takes place. If the supply is standard-rated the lender or LPA receiver should account for VAT on your behalf (please see paragraph 9.4 for more information).

9.4 How does the lender or LPA receiver account for the VAT?

There are a number of methods under which the lender or LPA receiver can account for VAT. If you require details of how to remit VAT on behalf of a borrower please see *Notice 700/56 Insolvency*.

10. Supplies between landlords and tenants

10.1 What if I pay an inducement to a prospective tenant?

If you pay an inducement to a prospective tenant for them to enter into a lease, the prospective tenant is making a standard-rated supply of services to you. The input tax you incur on the payment to the tenant is attributable to the leasing of the land or building and will generally only be recoverable if you have opted to tax.

An inducement paid by a tenant to a third party to accept the assignment of a lease, or the grant of a sublease, is not consideration for the assignment or grant but is a standard-rated supplies of services by the third party.

10.2 Rent-free periods

Rent is the periodic payment made by a tenant to a landlord and is normally the subject of a written agreement. Rent payments can be non-monetary, and can include costs incurred by the landlord under the agreement which are recharged to the tenant. This will include items such as service charges and rates where the landlord is the rateable person.

If you grant a rent-free period or a rental reduction to a tenant who agrees to do something in return, then you have both made and received a supply. Both supplies will be of equal value, but will not necessarily have the same VAT liability. If nothing is done or received in return for the rent-free period then, so far as that period is concerned, no supply has been made.

10.3 What if I pay my tenant to surrender a lease?

If you pay a tenant or licensee to surrender any interest in, right over or licence to occupy land that is a supply to you by the tenant. That supply is generally exempt, unless the tenant has opted to tax.

10.4 What if I accept the surrender of a lease from my tenant?

If you accept the surrender of a lease in return for payment from the tenant (sometimes referred to as a 'reverse surrender'), your supply is exempt unless you have opted to tax.

10.5 Variations to leases

Some variations to leases simply alter one or more of the terms, such as permitting the building to be used for a purpose that was originally prohibited. Other variations to a lease are more fundamental, such as an extension to the length of the tenancy or an alteration to the demised area. The effect of this type of variation is that the old lease is treated as surrendered and a new lease granted in its place. Any consideration you receive for either type of variation is exempt, unless you have opted to tax. However, where there is no consideration, no supply is seen as taking place.

10.6 Restrictive covenants

Restrictive covenants are placed on land to control its use. A typical restrictive covenant is one that forbids any development of the land.

If you agree to give up a restrictive covenant in return for payment your supply will be exempt, unless have opted to tax the land the restrictive covenant applied to.

10.7 Statutory payments

Any statutory compensation you pay to a tenant under the terms of the Landlord and Tenant Act 1954 or the Agricultural Tenancies Act 1995 is outside the scope of VAT. This applies even if an agricultural tenant has issued a 'notice to quit' having decided to retire from farming. Examples of items for which statutory compensation is given on the tenant quitting property are milk quotas left behind, manurial values and standing crops.

Where you and the tenant agree that the tenant will leave in return for additional payments to do so, the payment you make will be consideration for the tenant surrendering the lease and will generally be exempt, unless you have opted to tax.

10.8 Indemnity payments

Generally any payment that you, as a prospective tenant, have to make in order to obtain the grant of a lease or licence is part consideration for that grant. This is the case even if the payment is described as a reimbursement or indemnification of the landlord's costs. Whether the payment attracts VAT depends on whether the landlord has opted to tax.

Many leases provide that an existing tenant shall make good any legal or other advisory costs incurred by the landlord as a result of the tenant exercising rights already granted under the lease. For example the tenant may be entitled to assign the lease, to sublet or to make alterations to the building provided that the tenant first obtains the landlord's consent. As a result the landlord may incur legal or surveyors' fees. In these circumstances the reimbursement payments by the tenant to the landlord are consideration for the principal supply of the lease.

If you have to make a payment to your landlord to obtain some additional right, it is consideration for the variation of the lease and is exempt unless the landlord has opted to tax.

10.9 What if rent adjustments are needed when a building is sold?

When a tenanted building is sold or a lease is assigned mid-way through a rent period, an adjustment is normally made to the consideration at the point of completion. These rent adjustments are not consideration for any supply and are outside the scope of VAT.

For VAT purposes the consideration for the sale of the building or the assignment of the lease is the full value of the supply before any rent adjustment is made.

Rent adjustments may be made as follows:

Where...	the amount paid for the purchase is...
a landlord selling a building has received rent from tenants in occupation that relates to the period when the incoming landlord will be in ownership,	reduced to reflect the rent paid in advance
a building is sold and the incoming landlord will receive rent from tenants in occupation which relates to the period when the outgoing landlord was in ownership,	increased to reflect that rent.
an outgoing tenant assigning a lease has paid rent which relates to the period of occupation by the incoming tenant,	increased to reflect the rent paid in advance.

Where...	the amount paid for the purchase is...
a lease is assigned and the incoming tenant pays rent which relates to the period of occupation by the outgoing tenant,	is reduced to reflect that rent.

10.10 Dilapidation payments

The terms of a lease may provide for the landlord to recover from tenants, at or near the termination of the lease, an amount to cover the cost of restoring the property to its original condition. The amount is often agreed between the parties and may be based on a surveyor or contractor's estimate.

A dilapidation payment represents a claim for damages by the landlord against the tenant's 'want of repair'. The payment involved is not the consideration for a supply for VAT purposes and is outside the scope of VAT.

10.11 What if I refurbish a building having received a dilapidation payment?

If, as a landlord, you carry out refurbishment works following receipt of a dilapidation payment, the input tax you incur in carrying out those works should be treated as follows:

- if the refurbishment works are used exclusively in making taxable supplies, then the related input tax is wholly recoverable;

- if the refurbishment works are to be used exclusively in making exempt supplies, then the related input tax is wholly irrecoverable;

- if the refurbishment works are to be used in making both taxable and exempt supplies, then related input tax is residual and should be recovered in accordance with your normal partial exemption method. See *Notice 706 Partial exemption* for more information.

11. Service charges on commercial buildings

11.1 What are service charges?

It is common for leases between landlords and tenants to lay down that the landlord shall provide, and the tenants shall pay for, the upkeep of the building as a whole. The lease may provide for an inclusive rental, or it may require the tenants to contribute by means of a charge additional to the basic rent. These charges are generally referred to as service charges, maintenance charges or additional rent.

11.2 What is the liability of leasehold service charges?

If, as a landlord or licensor, you provide services of a general nature to your tenants the service charges normally follow the same VAT liability as the premium or rents payable under the lease or licence (normally exempt, unless you have opted to tax). For the service to be considered of a general nature it must be:

(a) connected with the external fabric or the common parts of the building or estate, as opposed to the demised areas of the property of the individual occupants; and

(b) paid for by all the occupants through a common service charge.

11.3 What if I supply services to freehold occupants?

If you provide services to someone who owns the freehold of a building your charge is always standard-rated. This is because there is no continuing supply of accommodation that the service charge can be linked to.

11.4 What if I supply services to the occupants of holiday accommodation?

If you provide services to the occupants of holiday accommodation your supply is standard-rated. Please see *Notice 709/3 Hotels and holiday accommodation* for more information.

11.5 Services provided by someone other than the landlord or licensor

If you are responsible for providing services to the occupants of a building in which you have no interest, your services will always be standard-rated as they are not part of the supply of the accommodation itself.

If your contract is to arrange for the services and to collect the service charge on the landlord's behalf as a managing agent, then your supply is to the landlord and not to the occupants. Your supply is still standard-rated.

11.6 Payments collected by a tenant for the landlord

If you collect payments from the other occupants for their share of the rent, rates and other costs, and you pass the full amount of these to the landlord, you should treat the sums collected from the other occupants as disbursements. Please see *Notice 700 The VAT Guide* for more information on disbursements.

11.7 Other charges made by landlords to tenants

As a landlord you may make charges to your tenants for items other than general services. These charges tend to fall into three categories:

- further payment for the main supply of accommodation, and follow the liability of that supply (normally exempt, unless you have opted to tax);

- for supplies other than accommodation (normally standard-rated); or

- disbursements (outside the scope of VAT). Further information on disbursements can be found in *Notice 700 The VAT Guide*.

The rest of this paragraph outlines the VAT treatment of some of the most common charges.

11.7.1 Insurance and rates

If you (the landlord) are the policyholder or rateable person, any payment for insurance or rates made by the tenants is further payment for the main supply of accommodation. If the tenant is the policyholder or rateable person, and you make payments on the tenant's behalf, you should treat those payments as disbursements.

11.7.2 Telephones

If the telephone account is in your name, any charge you make to tenants is payment for a standard-rated supply by you. This includes the cost of calls, installation and rental. If the account is in the name of the tenant, but you pay the bill, the recovery of this from the tenant is a disbursement.

11.7.3 Reception and switchboard

If you make a charge under the terms of the lease to tenants for the use of facilities that form a common part of the premises, such as reception and switchboard services, any payment you receive will be further consideration for the main supply of accommodation.

11.7.4 Office services

If you make a separate charge for office services, such as typing and photocopying, this is a separate standard-rated supply. However, if under the terms of the lease, there is one inclusive charge for office services and accommodation together, and the tenants are expected to pay for the services regardless of whether they actually use them, the liability of the services will follow that of the main supply of office accommodation.

11.7.5 Fixtures and fittings

Fixtures and fittings are regarded as part of the overall supply of the accommodation and any charges for them are normally included in the rent. However if you provide fixtures and fittings under a separate agreement your supply will normally be standard-rated.

11.7.6 Electricity, lighting and heating

If you make a separate charge for un-metered supplies of gas and electricity used by tenants, it should be treated as further payment for the main supply of accommodation. However, where you operate a secondary credit meter, the charges to the tenants for the gas and electricity they use are consideration for separate supplies of fuel and power. These supplies will be standard-rated. See *Notice 701/19 Fuel and power* for more information.

11.7.7 Management charges

The charge raised by you to the occupants for managing the development as a whole, and administering the collection of service charges and so on, is further payment for the main supply of accommodation.

11.7.8 Recreational facilities

If the charges for the use of recreational facilities are compulsory, irrespective of whether the tenant uses the facilities, then the liability will follow the main supply of accommodation.

11.8 Shared premises

If you are the owner or tenant of the premises and you do not grant other occupants an exempt licence to occupy land (see paragraphs 2.5 and 2.6), then any service charge you make is standard-rated. This applies even if you are simply passing on appropriate shares of your costs. The only exception is if you are paying and recharging a bill that is entirely the liability of another occupant, such as a telephone bill or insurance premium in the other occupant's name. You can treat such payments as disbursements. You can find more information on disbursements in *Notice 700 The VAT Guide*.

12. Service charges on dwellings

12.1 The basic position

Service charges relating to the upkeep of common areas of an estate of dwellings, or the common areas of a multi-occupied dwelling, are exempt from VAT so long as:

> • they are required to be paid by the leaseholder or tenant to the landlord under the terms of the lease or tenancy agreement.

This is because the service charge is treated as ancillary to the main supply of exempt domestic accommodation.

12.2 What if I provide services to freehold owners of dwellings?

If you provide services to freehold owners of dwellings your supply is taxable because there is no supply of domestic accommodation to link those services to. However this is unfair to freehold owners, especially those living on the same estate as leaseholders. To address this inequity an extra-statutory concession allows all mandatory service charges paid by occupants of dwellings toward the:

> (a) upkeep of the common areas of a housing estate, such as paths, driveways and communal gardens; or

> (b) upkeep of the common areas of a block of flats, such as lift maintenance, corridors, stairwells and general lounges; and

> (c) general maintenance of the exterior of the block of flats or individual dwellings, such as painting, if the residents cannot refuse this; and

> (d) provision of an estate warden, house manager or caretaker,

to be treated as exempt from VAT.

Where you apply the concession and treat the service charges as exempt your right to recover the associated input tax may be restricted. This may also have an impact on your eligibility to remain registered for VAT.

12.3 What if the landlord supplies additional services to occupants?

If the landlord makes a separate charge for un-metered supplies of gas and electricity used by occupants, it should be treated as further payment for the main supply of exempt domestic accommodation. However, if the landlord operates a secondary credit meter, the charges to the occupants for the gas and electricity they use are separate supplies of fuel and power subject to VAT at the reduced rate.

Optional services supplied personally to occupants, such as shopping, carpet cleaning or painting a private flat, are standard-rated.

The charge made by the landlord to the occupants for managing the estate and collecting the service charges is further payment for the main supply of exempt domestic accommodation.

12.4 What if a managing agent provides services to occupants on behalf of a landlord?

A managing agent acting on behalf of a landlord can treat the mandatory service charges to occupants as exempt, providing the agent invoices and collects the service charges directly from the occupants.

However, any management fee collected from the occupants is standard-rated because it relates to the managing agent's supply to the landlord.

12.5 What if a tenant-controlled management company provides the services?

Occupants of an estate may form a tenant-controlled management company. Sometimes that company will purchase the freehold of the estate and engage a service provider to maintain the common areas and provide any necessary warden or housekeepers. Providing the tenant-controlled management company is bound by the terms of the lease to maintain the common areas of the estate (or provide a warden), and the occupants are invoiced by and pay the service charges directly to the service provider the service charges may still be treated as exempt.

However, any management fee collected from the occupants is standard-rated because it relates to the service provider's supply to the tenant-controlled management company.

13 Commonhold and leasehold reform

13.1 The Commonhold and Leasehold Reform Act 2002

Until the Commonhold and Leasehold Reform Act 2002 English law recognised only two forms of property ownership. These are:

- **Freehold** – which confers upon the person designated as the freeholder an absolute title in a property and

- **Leasehold** – which confers upon the person designated leaseholder a lesser interest in a property such as holding that interest for a fixed number of years. Until the reforms brought in by the Act leasehold was the most practical means of enforcing positive legal obligations to bind successive owners of parts of buildings, occupied in common, such as a block of flats.

The new form of property ownership introduced in 2002 is:

- **Commonhold** – which confers upon owners of parts of a building, occupied in common, freehold interests in their respective parts (units) of the property. The freehold interest in the property's communal area and often its structure (the common parts) is owned by a commonhold association whose membership comprises the owners of the units.

In addition to introducing a new alternative to leasehold as a means of property ownership the Act of 2002 also reformed residential leasehold law.

13.2 Commonhold (Part 1 of the Commonhold and Leasehold Reform Act 2002)

Commonhold will be available for residential, commercial or mixed-use developments. Those who own the interests in individual units under commonhold are referred to as 'unit-holders'.

13.3 The reforms

The reforms are intended to give unit-holders the security of freehold ownership by addressing some of the drawbacks of leasehold (such as the diminishing value of leases). They also seek to overcome the difficulties in enforcing positive obligations, such as such as an obligation to keep property in good repair, in freehold land.

13.4 The commonhold arrangement

A commonhold may only be registered upon the agreement of all those with a prescribed interest in the property.

The developer of a property, or a landlord, may enter into an agreement with existing occupants or future (identified) unit-holders to set up a commonhold. This is most likely to happen where a leasehold development is being converted to a commonhold.

Alternatively, property may be registered as a commonhold in advance of the future unit-holders being identified. The developer will then sell the units in the same way as any other freehold property.

The unit-holders acquire a freehold interest in a specific unit. It is the commonhold association, a type of management company, that owns the freehold of the common parts. The members of the commonhold association will be unit-holders. However, where a unit is jointly owned, only one of the joint owners will become a member.

The commonhold association is responsible for the upkeep of the common parts and will provide an estimate of annual expenditure, the commonhold assessment.

13.5 What is the correct VAT treatment of transactions?

A commonhold unit is a freehold in a property that follows the normal VAT accounting rules. These rules are set out in Section 3.

13.5.1 The liability of supplies of qualifying buildings (eg residential property)

The developer of a qualifying building (that is a building designed as a dwelling or number of dwellings or intended for use solely for a relevant residential or a relevant charitable purpose) may **zero-rate** the first supply of a commonhold unit in the property if the normal conditions for zero-rating are met (see *Notice 708 Buildings and construction*).

If the conditions are met the zero-rating will apply in both of the following circumstances:

- The first sale of the freehold units in a commonhold to prospective unit-holders; and

- The transfer by operation of law of the freehold of the common parts in the commonhold to the commonhold association, on the registration of the commonhold.

Any subsequent supplies of the units are **exempt**.

13.5.2 The liability for supplies of non-qualifying buildings (eg commercial property)

These will be **exempt** from VAT unless the supply is either:

- Any sale of a commonhold unit or freehold of a new building (a new building is one that is less than three years old) or a partly-completed 'non-qualifying' building; or

- Any sale of a commonhold unit or freehold of a commercial property that has been opted to tax (subject to the disapplication test – see *Notice 742A Opting to tax land and buildings*),

in which case it will be **standard-rated**.

13.6 VAT treatment in specific transactions creating a commonhold

In setting up a commonhold there are three basic forms of transaction. These are set out below together with their VAT treatment.

13.6.1 A developer constructs a new building and sets up a commonhold

With regard to the first supply of each unit where this involves

> • *Commercial property*, it will be **standard-rated** – provided that the supply is made before the property is three years old or if not, the developer has opted to tax (subject to the disapplication rules)

and where it involves

> • *Residential property*, the supply will be **zero-rated**.

For both residential and commercial property, the freehold interest in the common parts is vested in the commonhold association. Normally there will be no consideration attributed to the disposal but it is a supply for VAT purposes and there will be a requirement to charge VAT if the conditions of paragraph 7.6 apply.

13.6.2 A number of freeholds are converted into a single commonhold

This may occur when the proprietors of existing freehold properties apply for commonhold status because they have communal facilities such as shared roadways, paths or services etc. This could entail some or all of the existing freeholders giving up title to areas of their land (constituting what are to become the common parts). Any payment made to a former freeholder is likely to be seen as consideration for the surrender of the freehold interest. The liability being as follows:

> • *Commercial property* – **exempt**. However, if the property is still new (less than three years old) or if an option to tax has been made (subject to the disapplication rules) the supply will then be **standard-rated**.

or,

> • *Residential property* – **exempt**. However, if a major interest has not been previously granted in this property (probably because the freeholder was also the person who constructed the building for his own occupation), then the supply will be **zero-rated**.

13.6.3 A leasehold is converted into commonhold

Leasehold conversions will generally occur in developments that already have existing leaseholders in place prior to the establishment of the commonhold. Following agreement between the interested parties and the land being registered as commonhold all pre-existing leases are extinguished.

Where the former leaseholder gains ownership of a commonhold unit in the same property that was demised under the lease, the only supply is that of the freehold. The lease ceases to have legal effect and there is no supply of it for VAT purposes.

However when the lease is extinguished and the freehold is transferred to some other person, or the freehold units have different boundaries from the previous leasehold premises, for VAT purposes there is a supply of a surrender of an interest in the property by the former leaseholder.

The surrender of a lease in:

> • *Commercial property* – **exempt**. However, if the lessee has opted to tax the supply will then be standard-rated (subject to the disapplication rules).

And in

> • *Residential property* – **exempt**.

Where the leaseholder pays a consideration for the freehold interest in the unit he acquires, the liability for

> • *Commercial property* – **exempt** unless the property is less than three years old or it has been opted to tax, or

- *Residential property* – **exempt**, unless it is the first supply of a major interest in which case it will be zero-rated.

13.7 Other commonhold transactions

13.7.1 Sale of a commonhold unit by a unit holder

The individual disposal of a unit follows the normal rules on VAT and therefore if

- *Commercial property* – **exempt**. However, if the property is still new (less than three years old) or if an option to tax has been made (subject to the disapplication rules) the supply will then be standard-rated.

And if

- *Residential property* – **exempt**.

Through the purchase of a commonhold unit the purchaser can acquire membership of the commonhold association and therefore, an interest in the common parts. Normally there will be no consideration attributed to the transfer of interest but it is a supply for VAT purposes and there will be a requirement to charge VAT if the conditions of paragraph 7.6 apply.

13.7.2 The termination of a commonhold

A commonhold may be terminated as a result of a voluntary winding-up or by court order.

- *Voluntary winding-up.* The commonhold association must specify proposals for the transfer of the commonhold land and explain how the assets of the association are to be distributed. Any payment received by either the commonhold association or by the unit-holders will be seen as a consideration for a freehold interest and the liability will be in accordance with the normal rules, as explained above.

- *Winding-up by court.* Where a commonhold association becomes insolvent, a successor commonhold association may be registered as the proprietor of the freehold estate in the common parts. Normally there will be no consideration attributed to the disposal but it is a supply for VAT purposes and there will be a requirement to charge VAT if the conditions of paragraph 7.6 apply.

13.8 How is the commonhold assessment to be treated for VAT purposes?

Charges can be levied by the commonhold association to pay for the upkeep of common parts. These charges are referred to as commonhold assessments and reserve fund levies and are treated in the same way as service charges to a long leaseholder or a non-commonhold freeholder.

- The VAT treatment of service charges raised in respect of commercial buildings is explained in Section 11 of this notice.

- For dwellings it is set out in Section 12. Where the commonhold association is providing the services as outlined in paragraph 12.2 directly to the unit holders of dwellings, the charges may be treated as **exempt** under the extra statutory concession for mandatory service charges.

Alternatively, the commonhold association may engage a service provider to maintain the common parts of an estate. In this case its position is akin to that of a tenant-controlled management company as explained in paragraph 12.5. As the commonhold association is obliged under the commonhold community statement to maintain the common parts, then providing the unit-holders are invoiced by and pay the service charges directly to the service provider, the charges raised under the commonhold assessment may still be treated as **exempt**.

However, any management fee collected from the occupants is standard-rated because it relates to the service provider's supply to the commonhold association.

13.9 Leasehold Reform – Part 2 of the Commonhold and Leasehold Reform Act 2002

This part of the legislation is generally directed at residential leaseholders in a multi-occupancy building. It amends the Leasehold Reform Housing and Urban Development Act

1993 which permitted leaseholders to acquire the freehold interest in a property through collective enfranchisement and to extend the length of their individual leases. Amendments are also made to other legislation including the Landlord and Tenant Act 1985, which introduced rights for tenants in relation to the payment of service charges.

13.10 The reforms

These include various provisions concerning the rights to collective enfranchisement. The freehold title of the property is vested in a nominee that must be a qualifying Right to Enfranchisement Company (RTE). The reforms also confer a new right upon leaseholders, who do not wish to buy the freehold of a property, that enables them to form a 'Right to Manage' (RTM) company that will take over these duties from the landlord or the service provider. There are provisions for up to 25% of a block to be occupied for non-residential purposes although these occupants will not be qualifying tenants for the purpose of collective enfranchisement or the Right to Manage.

13.11 What is the liability of service charges raised by an RTM company?

The rules for service charges for dwellings are as per Section 12 of Notice 742 and services provided by the RTM Company may be treated as exempt if, within the terms of the agreement leaseholders are invoiced by and pay the service charges directly to the RTM Company. Section 11 covers the liability of leasehold service charges raised to tenants who are in occupation for commercial purposes.

13.12 Can VAT be recovered by an RTE Company?

An RTE company may recover VAT if part of the premises to which it has freehold title has commercial tenants. It must opt to tax the property and account for VAT on all rents to commercial tenants. The VAT on costs will be recoverable to the extent that they relate to the commercial rents. More information is available in *Notice 742A Opting to tax land and buildings*.

Appendix 9: HMRC Notice 742A/02 – Opting to tax land and buildings

1. Introduction

1.1 What is this notice about?

This notice explains the effect of an option to tax and will help you to decide whether to exercise that option. It will tell you whether you need permission from us before you can opt to tax, and how to notify us of your decision. The option to tax is also referred to as the election to waive exemption.

We recommend that you also read *Notice 742 Land and property* which gives basic information relating to supplies of land.

This notice assumes that you have a working knowledge of basic Value Added Tax (VAT) principles, as outlined in *Notice 700 The VAT Guide*.

This notice replaces chapter 8 of *Notice 742 Land and property* (December 1995 edition). The text has been generally updated and revised, and includes additional guidance on the scope of an option, input tax, transfers of going concerns and anti-avoidance measures. The notice includes revised conditions for automatic permission to opt to tax in paragraph 5.2.

This notice and others mentioned are available both on paper and on our Internet website at www.hmce.gov.uk.

1.2 What effect does an option to tax have?

Supplies of land and buildings, such as freehold sales, leasing or renting, are normally exempt from VAT. This means that no VAT is payable, but the person making the supply cannot normally recover any of the VAT incurred on their own expenses.

However, you can opt to tax land. For the purposes of VAT, the term 'land' includes any buildings or structures permanently affixed to it. You do not need to own the land in order to opt to tax. Once you have opted to tax all the supplies you make of your interest in the land or buildings will normally be standard-rated. And you will normally be able to recover any VAT you incur in making those supplies.

1.3 Who should read this notice?

You should read this notice if you make, or intend to make supplies of any interest in land, buildings or civil engineering works.

1.4 What law covers this notice?

The area of VAT law which specifies the supplies of land and buildings that are exempt from VAT is Group 1 of Schedule 9 to the Value Added Tax Act 1994. The law detailing the option to tax is found in Schedule 10 to the Value Added Tax Act 1994.

The conditions for automatic permission found in paragraph 5.2 of this notice have the force of law.

2. The scope of an option to tax

2.1 What am I opting to tax?

You are opting to tax land. For the purposes of VAT, the term 'land' includes buildings. When you opt to tax you can specify an area of land or a 'building'. Commonly, you will specify a 'building' because that is the prominent feature of the land.

2.2 What constitutes a 'building'?

Usually it will be clear what constitutes a 'building', for instance an office block or a factory. However in some instances the law treats more than one building as being a single 'building' for the purpose of the option to tax. These are:

- buildings that are, or if not yet built are planned to be, linked. Please see paragraph 2.3 for more information on links and

- a complex consisting of a number of units grouped around a fully enclosed concourse, such as a shopping mall.

2.3 What is a 'link'?

A link is an internal access or a covered walkway between buildings the purpose of which is to allow movement of goods and people.

It does not include:

- a car park, either above or below ground
- a public thoroughfare or
- a statutory requirement, such as a fire escape.

2.4 What is covered by the option to tax?

We use a number of basic principles to determine how far your option to tax extends over the land and associated buildings.

Option	Principle
Land	Your option to tax covers all the land, and any buildings or civil engineering works which are part of the land.
	Your option to tax will cover the discrete area of land that you specify, and will not affect any adjoining land.
	if you later construct a building on land that you have opted, the building will not be covered by the option to tax.
Buildings	your option to tax will cover the whole of the building, and the land under and immediately around that building such as forecourts and yards. If your interest in the building is restricted to one floor, your option to tax will still cover the remaining floors of the building.
	if the building stands in a large area of land, how far the option to tax extends over the land depends on how far the services of the building can be utilised. For example, a racecourse grandstand may provide electricity and shelter for stalls, or other facilities, within its peripheral area. An option to tax on the grandstand would extend over the whole area of land that uses the benefits.
	if the building is demolished or destroyed your option to tax will not apply to the land on which the building stood. If you later construct another building on that land it will not be covered by the option to tax.

2.5 What if I make changes to a building after I have opted to tax?

If you make changes to a building after you have opted to tax you will need to consider whether your option to tax covers those changes. This table below sets out the basic principles for the most common changes made.

Change	Principle
Extensions	if you have opted to tax a building and you extend it at a later date, upwards, downwards or sideways, your option to tax will apply to the whole of the extended building.
Linked buildings	if you have opted to tax a building and at a later date you decide to link it to another building, your option to tax will not flow through with the link unless you are creating a single building, see paragraph 2.2 for more information on single buildings.
Forming a complex	if you have a group of units that have been treated as separate buildings for the option to tax and you later decide to enclose them, the option to tax will not spread to the un-opted units.

3.Supplies not affected by an option to tax

3.1 What supplies are not affected by an option to tax?

There are some supplies where, even if you have opted to tax, the option will not apply. **If you make any of the supplies described in this section your supplies will remain exempt from VAT even if you have opted to tax. This may have an impact on how much input tax you can claim.**

3.2 Buildings to be used as dwellings

Your option to tax will not apply if you supply a building, or part of a building, and the purchaser or tenant informs you that they intend to use it as a dwelling.

3.3 Buildings to be converted into dwellings

Your option to tax will not apply if you supply a building, or part of a building, and the purchaser or tenant informs you that they intend to convert it into a dwelling or dwellings. The purchaser or tenant must be intending to carry out the conversion. For example, you may sell a warehouse to a developer who is going to convert it into flats.

However, if your supply is to a developer who intends to make zero-rated supplies of the new dwellings created by the conversion you can agree that the option to tax will apply. You must have a specific written agreement with the developer. You must do this either before or on the date you supply the building.

3.4 Buildings to be used solely for a relevant residential purpose

Your option to tax will not apply if you supply a building, or part of a building, and the purchaser or tenant informs you that they will be using it solely for a relevant residential purpose. Where a building or part of a building is used for both relevant residential purposes and business purposes, your option to tax will not apply to the part used for relevant charitable purposes, provided that the different functions are carried out in clearly defined areas. In these circumstances the value of your supply should be fairly apportioned between the exempt and taxable elements. A building used for a relevant residential purpose is one in which some of the facilities, such as dining rooms and bathrooms are shared but this does not include use as a hospital, prison, hotel or similar establishment. Examples include residential homes for children, the elderly or disabled persons and student halls of residence. See *Notice 708 Buildings and construction* for full definitions and further details.

3.5 Buildings to be used solely for a relevant charitable purpose

Your option to tax will not apply if you supply a building, or part of a building, and the purchaser or tenant informs you that they will be using it solely for a relevant charitable purpose, other than as an office for general administration eg head office functions of the charity. Where a building or part of a building is used for relevant charitable purposes and business or general administration purposes, your option to tax will not apply to the part used for relevant charitable purposes, provided that the different functions are carried out in clearly defined areas. In these circumstances the value of your supply should be fairly apportioned between the exempt and taxable elements. Relevant charitable purpose means use by a charity for its non-business activities, or as a village hall or similarly to provide social or recreational facilities for a local community. Please see *Notice 701/1 Charities* for more information on non-business activities carried out by such bodies.

3.6 Land sold to a relevant housing association

Your option to tax will not apply if you supply land to a relevant housing association, which provide you with written confirmation that, after any necessary demolition work, they will be constructing dwellings or relevant residential buildings on it.

A relevant housing association is a:

• registered social landlord within the meaning of Part 1 of the Housing Act 1996

• registered housing association within the meaning of the Housing Associations Act 1985, (Scottish registered housing associations) or

• registered housing association within the meaning of Part II of the Housing (Northern Ireland) Order 1992, (Northern Irish registered associations).

3.7 Land sold to a 'DIY' housebuilder

Your option to tax will not apply if you supply land to someone who will build a dwelling on it for their own use, and not in the course or furtherance of any business carried on by them.

3.8 Pitches for residential caravans

Your option to tax will not apply if you supply a pitch for a permanent residential caravan. A residential caravan is one where residence is permitted throughout the year, and is not restricted by planning consent, covenant or similar provision.

3.9 Moorings for residential houseboats

Your option to tax will not apply if you supply facilities for the mooring or berthing of a residential houseboat. A houseboat is a floating decked structure that is designed or adapted for use solely as a place of permanent habitation. A houseboat does not have the means of, nor is capable of being readily adapted for, self-propulsion. A residential houseboat is one where residence is permitted throughout the year, and is not restricted by planning consent, covenant or similar provision.

3.10 Building to be used for both commercial and residential purposes

You may supply a building, or part of a building, which the purchaser or tenant will be using partly for commercial and partly for residential purposes, such as a flat above a shop. If that is the case you must apportion your supply between the taxable element of the shop and the exempt (or zero-rated) element of the dwelling. You may choose the method of apportionment but it must provide a fair and reasonable result. You can find out more about apportionment in *Notice 700 The VAT Guide.*

3.11 Land or building affected by the anti-avoidance measures

The option to tax has no effect in relation to supplies resulting from a grant that falls within the anti-avoidance measures described within section 13.

4. How to opt to tax

4.1 What do I need to do if I want to opt to tax?

There are two stages in opting to tax. The first stage is making the decision to opt. This may take place at a board meeting or similar, or less formally. However you reach your decision, we recommend that you keep a written record, showing clear details of the land or buildings you are opting to tax, and the date you made your decision.

If you have previously made exempt supplies of the land or building you may need our permission before you can opt to tax. You can find more information about this in section 5.

The second stage is to notify us of your decision by writing to your local VAT office. For your option to tax to be valid you must make this notification within 30 days of your decision. Please see paragraph 4.2 for more information on notification.

4.2 How do I notify my option to tax?

Your notification must state clearly what land or buildings you are opting to tax, and the date from which the option has effect (see paragraph 4.3). We suggest you use the Notification Form VAT 1614 which you can obtain from our National Advice Service. If you are opting to tax discrete areas of land we suggest that you send a map or plan clearly showing the opted land with your notification. It is important that an appropriate person signs the notification, and any accompanying list or schedule. Please see section 7 for more information.

Please send the notification to your local VAT office. We will normally acknowledge receipt of your notification, although this is not necessary for the option to tax to have legal effect. You should not delay charging VAT just because you have not received our acknowledgement.

If you are notifying an option to tax in relation to land or buildings which are being transferred as a going concern you should read paragraph 11.2.

4.3 What is the effective date of my option to tax?

Your option to tax will have effect from the date of your decision, or any later date that you have specified, providing you notify us within 30 days of making your decision. If you realise that you did not notify us within 30 days, you should contact us immediately.

In no circumstances can an option to tax have effect from a date before you made your decision to opt.

4.4 Who is bound by the option to tax?

It is for you alone to decide whether to opt to tax any land or buildings. If you do decide to opt to tax, only the supplies you make of your interest in the land or building will be affected. Your option to tax will not affect supplies made by anyone else. For example, if you are selling an opted building the purchaser has the choice of whether to opt to tax or not. Similarly, if your tenant is sub-letting, they too have this same choice. For this reason, we suggest that you inform your tenant of your decision at the earliest opportunity so that they may safeguard their right to recover input tax by opting to tax, should they wish to.

5. Permission to opt to tax

5.1 When do I need permission from Customs?

You will need our permission before you opt to tax if you have made, or you intend to make, an exempt supply of the land or building between 1 August 1989 and the date you intend the option to tax to take effect.

5.2 Automatic permission

Since 1 March 1995 you have not needed to obtain our written permission before you opt to tax provided you meet the conditions we have set out in a notice. The conditions have changed from time to time. If you meet any of the four conditions below you do not need written permission before you opt to tax:

These conditions have the force of law and come into force on 2 March 2005

*** Number	Condition
1.	It is a mixed-use development and the only exempt supplies have been in relation to the dwellings.
2.	You do not wish to recover any input tax in relation to the land or building incurred before your option to tax has effect; **and** • the consideration for your exempt supplies has, up to the date when your option to tax is to take effect, been solely by way of rents or service charges and excludes any premiums or payments in respect of occupation after the date on which the option takes effect. Regular rental and/or service charge payments can be ignored for the purposes of this condition. Payments are considered regular where the intervals between them are no more than a year and where each represents a commercial or genuine arms length value; **and** • the only input tax relating to the land or building that you expect to recover after the option to tax takes effect will be on overheads, such as regular rental payments, service charges, repairs and maintenance costs. **If you expect to claim input tax in relation to refurbishment or redevelopment of the building you will not meet this condition.** **Notes:** When deciding whether you meet this condition you should disregard: • VAT refundable to local authorities and other bodies under section 33(2)(b) of the Value Added Tax Act 1994; • any input tax you can otherwise recover by virtue of the partial exemption de minimis rules (Regulation 106, VAT Regulations 1995); **and** • any input tax you are entitled to recover on general business overheads not specifically related to the land or building, such as audit fees.
3.	The only input tax you wish to recover in relation to the land or building incurred before your option to tax takes effect relates solely to tax charged by your tenant or tenants upon surrender of a lease; **and** • the building or relevant part of the building has been unoccupied between the date of the surrender and the date the option to tax is to take effect; **and** • there will be no further exempt supplies of the land or building; **and** • you do not intend or expect that you will occupy the land or building other than for taxable purposes.
4.	The exempt supplies have been incidental to the main use of the land or building. For example, where you have occupied a building for taxable purposes the following would be seen as incidental to the main use and the condition would be met: • allowing an advertising hoarding to be displayed; • granting space for the erection of a radio mast; • receiving income from an electricity sub-station. The letting of space to an occupying tenant, however minor, is not incidental.***

5.3 What do I need to do if I meet one of the conditions?

If you meet one of the conditions and you decide that you want to opt to tax you still need to write to us to notify your option. You should state in your notification that, although you have made previous exempt supplies of the land or building, you satisfy the conditions for automatic permission. Section 4 gives more information on notifying an option and the records you need to keep.

5.4 What if I don't meet any of the conditions?

If you do not meet any of the conditions for automatic permission you must obtain our written permission before you can opt to tax. Before permission is granted we will consider the facts of each case and you will need to provide the information set out in paragraph 5.5.

5.5 What information do I need to send?

You should write to your local VAT office asking for permission to opt to tax and stating the date from which you would like your option to tax to be effective. This can only be a future date and you should allow a period of at least one month for us to consider your request for permission.

We will need the following information:

(a) a brief description of your future plans for the land or building, should we grant permission to opt to tax

(b) details of any input tax you incurred in the ten years before opting to tax that you wish to recover. We need details of the amount of input tax you wish to claim, how this has been calculated, what the input tax relates to and when it was incurred. You also need to give us details of any input tax that you expect to incur in the period between your request for permission and the date you wish the option to tax to take effect

(c) the value of input tax you expect to incur in the future if we grant permission to opt to tax, and what this input tax will relate to. For example rents, premiums, surrenders or refurbishments

(d) the total value of your exempt supplies of the land or building in the ten years before your request for permission. You will also need to give us the value of any supplies you expect to make between the date of your request for permission and the date the option is to be effective. We need details of any grants you have made for a premium or prepayment of rent, including the dates they were made, their values and the period to which they relate

(e) the expected value of the taxable supplies you intend to make in the foreseeable future after the date of your option to tax, should we grant permission. Where these taxable supplies are the result of the granting of standard-rated leases you should advise how long the leases already in place are expected to run, and if you have any reason to suspect they will not run their full course. You should indicate whether you are likely to make any exempt grants after your option to tax takes effect, for example supplies where the option to tax will not apply for any reason. Please see section 3 for examples of where an option to tax will not apply and

(f) whether you, or anyone who has helped to fund the land or building, or anyone connected to you or the financier is occupying or intending to occupy any part of the land or building. Please see section 13 for more information.

5.6 When will you grant permission?

We cannot grant you permission to opt to tax until you provide all the information detailed in paragraph 5.5, and any additional information that we may ask for. Occasionally we will refuse permission, if we are not satisfied that granting permission would result in a fair and reasonable attribution of input tax. Once we are satisfied we will advise you in writing and ask you to confirm that you wish to put the option into effect.

5.7 What if I fail to ask for permission?

We are not able to grant retrospective permission. Any VAT you may have charged in error is not output tax, and unless you refund it we will collect it as a debt due to us. Any input tax you may have claimed in error is exempt input tax and is not allowable. If we grant you permission and you opt to tax from a current date we will need to take account of any exempt supplies you incorrectly treated as taxable when agreeing an apportionment of your pre-option input tax.

If you have incorrectly relied on automatic permission conditions as set out in a previous notice we will allow you to retain your option to tax effective from the date it was originally made, as long as you would have qualified under the conditions set out in paragraph 5.2.

5.8 What do I do once I receive permission?

If you still wish to opt to tax the land or building you must formally notify us as explained in paragraph 4.2. Providing you do not make any further exempt supplies of land or building you are entitled, where appropriate, to reclaim the agreed amount of pre-option input tax on your first VAT return following the date of your option. If the land or building is a capital item for the purposes of the capital goods scheme you will need to adjust the pre-option input tax as part of the capital goods scheme adjustment calculation on future VAT returns. Please see paragraph 13.11 and *Notice 706/2 Capital goods scheme* for more details.

6. Option to tax and VAT registration

6.1 Liability to register for VAT

If you are not already registered for VAT, you should read *VAT Notice 700/1 Should I be registered for VAT?*. If you are required to, or wish to register you should complete an application form and send it to the appropriate Registration office (listed in *VAT Notice 700/1*). The Registration office will need to be satisfied that you will be making taxable supplies, so you should send a copy of your option to tax notification with your application form. If you need our permission before opting to tax, you cannot register before we have given permission so you should also enclose a copy of your written permission with your application.

If your turnover falls below the registration threshold and you deregister, the option to tax does not cease because you have deregistered. Please see section 12 for more details.

6.2 How long must I keep records?

You must keep your correspondence and any record of your decision to opt to tax for a minimum of 6 years. Once you have charged VAT or recovered input tax because of your option to tax, the option cannot be revoked until at least 20 years have passed (see section 8). We strongly recommend you keep your option to tax records for longer than 6 years.

6.3 How does the option to tax affect group registrations?

If you opted to tax land or buildings and at a later date joined a VAT group, any supply made of those land or buildings by any member of the VAT group is taxable. Similarly if you are a member of a VAT group, and any member of that group has opted to tax any land or buildings, you are bound by that option. This is the case even if the option to tax was made before you joined the VAT group. If you leave the VAT group but retain an interest in land or buildings on which the VAT group would have charged VAT, you too must charge VAT on any supplies of the land or buildings which you subsequently make. For more information about VAT groups you should read *Notice 700/2 Group treatment*.

7. Responsibility for opting to tax

7.1 Who is responsible for making the decision and notifying the option to tax?

The person responsible for making the decision and notifying the option to tax depends on the type of legal entity holding (or intending to hold) the interest in the land or building, and who within that entity has the authority to make decisions concerning VAT. In most cases it will be the sole proprietor, one or more partners (or trustees), a director or an authorised administrator. If you have appointed a third party to notify an option to tax on your behalf, we require written confirmation that the third party is authorised to do so. We would also wish to be notified if you withdraw that authority. The following paragraphs explain who is responsible in other, slightly more unusual situations.

7.2 Beneficial owners

In some cases there may be both a beneficial owner and a legal owner of land or buildings. An example of this is a bare trust, where a trustee is the legal owner but the benefit of the income from the land or building passes to the beneficial owner. For VAT purposes it is the beneficial owner who is making the supply of the land or building. It is the beneficial owner who should opt to tax, and who must account for any VAT due on the supply and claim any input tax that arises.

This is not the case, however, where the beneficiaries are numerous, such as unit trusts and pension funds. In such situations the person making the supply is the trustee who holds the legal interest and receives the immediate benefit of the consideration.

7.3 Joint owners

Joint ownership will arise if you and another person buy land or buildings together, or if you sell a part share of your land or building to someone else. If you are a joint owner it is likely that the only supply that can be made of the jointly owned land or building is by you and the other person together.

You and the other person should together notify a single option to tax if you want supplies of the jointly owned land or building to be standard-rated. The taxable supply of the land or building is then made by both of you as one taxable person. To account for output tax and to be able to recover input tax, you and the other person should register for VAT together as if a partnership, even if you are not in partnership for any other purpose.

7.4 Limited partnerships

A limited partnership is made up of one or more 'general' partners, who have unlimited liability, and one or more 'limited' partners, who are not liable for debts and obligations of the firm. A limited partner is unable to take part in the management and running of the partnership business, and where we find that a limited partner is doing so, we will treat them as a general partner.

If there is only one general partner and one or more limited partners, the general partner is treated as a sole proprietor for VAT registration purposes. Likewise if there are two or more general partners and one or more limited partners, the general partners are treated as a partnership for VAT registration purposes. It is the general partner(s) who should opt to tax and account for any VAT due on the supply and claim any input tax that arises.

Where title to the land or building is held jointly in the names of the general partner(s) **and** the limited partner(s), only the title holders can make any supplies of that land or building together. That suggests that the limited partner is involved in the management and running of the partnership, and as such we treat them as a general partner and amend the VAT registration to reflect that. If the partnership decides to opt to tax, one or more of the partners should sign the notification.

7.5 Limited liability partnerships

A limited liability partnership has a separate legal status from its members and is able to enter into contracts in its own right. This means that the individual members of the limited liability partnership are protected from debts or liabilities arising from negligence, wrongful acts or conduct of another member, employee or agent of the partnership.

A limited liability partnership is a corporate body and is liable to register for VAT, subject to the normal registration rules. If the partnership decides to opt to tax, one or more members must sign the notification.

8. Revoking an option to tax

8.1 Can I revoke my option to tax?

If you change your mind within three months of the effective date of your option to tax, you can ask us to revoke your option. We will normally allow you to revoke as long as you have not put the option into practical effect by:

- charging rent or receiving any payments on which you should have accounted for VAT or

- recovering input tax in relation to the land and buildings as a result of the option, disregarding any input tax that you would have been able to recover under normal partial exemption rules and

- the land or building has not been acquired or disposed of as a transfer of a going concern.

If we are satisfied that you have not put the option into practical effect we will confirm the revocation in writing.

Once the initial three-month period has passed, or you have put the option to tax to practical effect, you cannot ask us for permission to revoke your option to tax until 20 years or more have passed.

9. Input tax

9.1 Rules on reclaiming input tax

Once you have opted to tax your entitlement to recover any input tax you incur will depend on the liability of the supplies you make:

If you make...	then you will normally be...
taxable supplies of the land or buildings	able to recover any input tax relating to those supplies
wholly exempt supplies of the land or those building (see section 3)	unable to recover any input tax relating to supplies
supplies that are both taxable and exempt, for example you may have opted to tax a building that is to be used for both commercial and residential purposes	able to recover only the input tax relating to the taxable supply. Notice 706 Partial exemption explains how to work out how much input tax relates to taxable supplies.

9.2 What about input tax I incurred before I opted to tax?

You can recover any input tax relating to supplies of land or buildings if the supplies are taxable in their own right. For example, a freehold sale of a commercial building within three years of its completion is always standard-rated.

Other than above, you cannot recover input tax relating to supplies of land or buildings made before your option to tax takes effect because these supplies, or any supplies you intended to make, would be exempt from VAT. Input tax relating to these supplies is exempt input tax.

Once you have opted to tax there are two circumstances in which you can recover this exempt input tax:

- if you made no exempt supplies of the land or buildings before you opted to tax you may be able to recover the exempt input tax under the partial exemption 'payback' rule. You can find more information about the payback rule in *Notice 706 Partial exemption* and

- if you made exempt supplies of the land or building before opting to tax you may be able to recover exempt input tax under the permission procedure explained in section 5.

9.3 What about speculative and abortive costs?

As a developer you may spend time and effort investigating potential projects, such as looking for sites and assessing their suitability, having no firm intention to make a particular supply. The input tax on the costs you incur is 'residual', as explained in *Notice 706 Partial exemption*.

Some potential projects are not followed through, and in the end no supplies are actually made. When you decide to abort the project, related input tax should be left as residual.

When you decide to proceed with a project you will have a clear intention as to what supplies you will make. It is normally at this point that you decide whether to opt to tax. You should then adjust the input tax accordingly under the 'payback' and 'clawback' rules. You will find information on these rules in *Notice 706 Partial exemption*. Input tax on the ongoing costs should be attributed to the expected taxable or exempt supplies.

9.4 What about the VAT I incurred prior to my registration?

You may find that you become registered for VAT as a result of opting to tax. Special rules apply to all newly registered persons under which they may be entitled to claim relief for VAT incurred on supplies they obtained before registration. Relief is restricted on supplies of services to those received not more than six months before your registration. This restriction may lead to inequitable treatment compared with a business carrying out similar activities, but who was already VAT registered when the tax was incurred. If you consider you have suffered because of this you should write to your local VAT office and explain your circumstances.

In all cases relief for VAT incurred before registration is restricted to tax which can be directly attributed to a taxable activity. If you incurred tax before registration that was attributable both to exempt supplies before registration as well as taxable supplies after registration, the relief will be restricted proportionately.

9.5 Capital goods scheme

If you acquire land or buildings which are considered to be capital items for the purposes of this scheme, you must review their use in your business over a series of intervals, normally lasting ten years. If there is a change in the extent to which they are used for making taxable supplies you must make an input tax adjustment to take account of this. You will find more information about how the scheme works in the *Notice 706/2 Capital goods scheme*.

10. Time of supply (tax point)

10.1 Normal tax point rules

The normal tax point rules apply to all supplies of land or buildings. These rules are explained in detail in *Notice 700 The VAT Guide*.

If you make leasehold supplies and have opted to tax, a tax point will normally occur when you either issue a tax invoice or receive a payment, whichever is the earlier.

If you are selling the freehold of land or a building a basic tax point will normally occur at the time of legal completion under the terms of the contract, when the freehold is conveyed to the purchaser. The equivalent under Scottish land law is the time of delivery of the disposition. Any payments you receive after the basic tax point do not create a tax point. If you issue a VAT invoice within 14 days after the basic tax point, then the date of issue of that invoice becomes the tax point. If you issue a VAT invoice or receive a payment before the basic tax point, then an actual tax point will be created by whichever happens first, to the extent of the amount invoiced or payment received.

10.2 Does a deposit create a tax point?

Often on the sale of land or buildings, the purchaser pays a deposit at exchange of contracts, followed by payment of the balance on the completion date. An independent stakeholder usually holds the deposit until completion, and the seller receives no payment until that time.

In these circumstances, the deposit payment will not create a tax point. It follows that if the deposit is paid directly to the seller or their agent, the payment does create a tax point. In both cases, an earlier tax point arises if a tax invoice is issued before the seller receives any payment.

10.3 What if I receive arrears of rent following my option to tax?

In a tenanted building, a tax point might not occur until you receive payment. In these circumstances, if you opt to tax after the rent becomes due but before it is paid, you must account for output tax on the rental receipt. This is the case even if the payment covers a period before your option to tax took effect.

11. Transfer of a business as a going concern

11.1 What does 'transferring a business as a going concern' mean?

Notice 700/9 Transfer of a business as a going concern explains the VAT position if you are selling your business or part of it. In certain circumstances special VAT rules apply and the sale of the assets of a business, or part of it, will not be treated as a supply for VAT purposes. The sales affected will be those where a business is sold as a going concern, or where the sale is of part of the business capable of separate operation.

11.2 What if I am transferring land or buildings as part of a transfer of a going concern?

If you have opted to tax the land or buildings and:

- you meet all the conditions specified in *Notice 700/9* **and**
- the purchaser has opted to tax

the transfer of the land or buildings as part of a transfer of a going concern is not a taxable supply. The purchaser must notify the option to tax to us before or on the relevant date and the option must apply from that time. By 'notified' we mean that the purchaser has properly addressed, pre-paid and posted the letter to us. The relevant date is the time of the supply; which is normally the date of the transfer, but will also include receipt of a deposit if that is paid in advance of the date of the transfer (unless the deposit is paid to an independent stakeholder). Further information on tax points can be found in section 10.

However, if the purchaser has not opted to tax and:

- you are transferring land or buildings which are new (less than three years old) or unfinished buildings or civil engineering work which would normally be standard-rated **or**
- you are transferring land or buildings which you have opted to tax

then the conditions for a transfer of a going concern will not have been met in respect of the land or buildings. You will have to charge VAT on the sale of the land or building.

The following table will help you to decide whether the conditions for a transfer of a going concern have been met, depending on the options to tax notified by the seller and purchaser. Remember, you must still meet the conditions in *Notice 700/9*:

Commercial land or building, ordinarily exempt		
Has seller opted to tax?	*Has purchaser opted to tax?*	*Transfer of a going concern provisions met?*
Yes	Yes	Yes
Yes	No	No
No	No	Yes
No	Yes	Yes

New building (less than 3 years old), ordinarily standard-rated		
Has seller opted to tax?	*Has purchaser opted to tax?*	*Transfer of a going concern provisions met?*
Yes	Yes	Yes
Yes	No	No
No	No	No
No	Yes	Yes

11.3 What about the input tax I incur on transfer expenses?

A transfer of a going concern is not a supply for VAT purposes. The input tax incurred on transfer expenses is attributable to the taxable supplies made by the transferor or the transferee.

11.3.1 Transferor

If you have disposed of assets by way of a transfer of a going concern, and the transfer expenses you incurred have a direct and immediate link with the part of the business you have transferred, then the input tax you incurred on those expenses is attributable to the supplies made by that part of the business. If that part of the business only made taxable supplies you can reclaim the input tax in full. If that part of the business only made exempt supplies you cannot recover any of the input tax. If that part of the business made both taxable and exempt supplies, you should treat the input tax as 'residual' and a proportion can be recovered under your existing partial exemption method. Please see *Notice 706 Partial exemption* for more information. If you feel that your current method of apportionment does not produce a fair and reasonable result then we will consider another method, but it is up to you to propose one. We will only approve an alternative method if we are satisfied that it gives a fair and reasonable result in its entirety.

11.3.2 Transferee

If you have acquired assets by way of a transfer of a going concern, and you use those assets exclusively to make taxable supplies, you can reclaim all the input tax you incurred on obtaining those assets. If you use the assets exclusively to make exempt supplies, you cannot recover any of the input tax. If you use the assets to make both taxable and exempt supplies, you should treat the input tax as 'residual' and a proportion can be recovered under your existing partial exemption method. Please see *Notice 706 Partial exemption* for more information. If you feel that your current method of apportionment does not produce a fair and reasonable result then we will consider another method, but it is up to you to propose one. We will only approve an alternative method if we are satisfied that it gives a fair and reasonable result in its entirety.

11.4 What if the land or buildings are in the capital goods scheme?

If you are transferring land or buildings which are capital items for purposes of the capital goods scheme, you should make the purchaser aware of any capital goods scheme adjustments you have made and provide sufficient information to enable the purchaser to carry out any future adjustments under the scheme that might be necessary.

If you have acquired land or buildings that are capital items, you are responsible for continuing the capital goods scheme, and making any further adjustments of input tax required under the scheme, until the intervals are complete.

Further detailed information regarding the operation of the scheme can be found in *Notice 706/2 Capital goods scheme*.

12. Deregistration

12.1 What happens to my option to tax if I deregister?

Your option to tax is not cancelled if you deregister. If you deregister due to a fall in turnover, and then at a later date your income increases above the VAT threshold, the option to tax will still have effect and you must apply to register again.

You may deregister because you are selling your business as a transfer of a going concern. If that is the case, and you are disposing of land or buildings that are capital items for the purposes of the capital goods scheme as part of the transfer, you should inform the purchaser of any adjustments you have made under the scheme.

If the opted land or building is an asset on hand at deregistration you may have to account for output tax in respect of it. For more information please see *Notice 700/11 Cancelling your registration*.

13. Anti-avoidance measures

13.1 Why do Customs need the anti-avoidance measures?

Some organisations, commonly exempt or partially exempt businesses, are not entitled to recover all of the input tax they incur on the purchase of land or buildings, or on major construction projects. As a result, some of these organisations enter into arrangements designed to either increase the amount of input tax they can claim, or to spread the VAT cost of the purchase or construction over a number of years.

To counter this avoidance we introduced a test. The test is applied each time a grant is made. If the test is met the option to tax will not have effect (it will be 'disapplied') in respect of the supplies that arise from that particular grant.

If you are an organisation that normally receives credit for most of the input tax you incur, for example you are fully taxable, then you are unlikely to be affected by the anti-avoidance measures detailed in this section.

13.2 What is the test?

The test is as follows:

If, at the time of the grant of land or buildings (the development):

> • it is the intention or expectation of the grantor, or the person responsible for financing the grantor's development, or anybody connected to either of them, to occupy the development and

> • the person occupying the development will be doing so, or will expect to do so, for other than eligible purposes and

> • the development is, or is expected to become, a capital item for the purposes of the capital goods scheme

> • then the option to tax will not have effect in respect of supplies that arise from that particular grant.

The following paragraphs will explain what the test means and how it is to be applied to each grant.

13.3 When was the test introduced?

The test was introduced on 19 March 1997 and only affects supplies made from that date. The anti-avoidance measure does not apply to any grants made before 26 November 1996. And it does not apply to grants made between 26 November 1996 and 30 November 1999, if the terms of the grant were agreed in writing before 26 November 1996.

Between 19 March 1997 and 9 March 1999 the anti-avoidance measure only affected grants where the development was a capital item at the time of the grant. From 10 March 1999 we extended the anti-avoidance measure to include situations where, although at the time of the grant the development was not a capital item, it was intended or expected that it would become one at a future date. Part of the extended measure required businesses that had made grants between 19 March 1997 and 9 March 1999 to re-visit those grants, and where appropriate, to treat the date of the grant as 10 March 1999.

13.4 What is a grant and who is the grantor?

The word 'grant' refers to the act that transfers the land or building, such as a freehold sale of land or a building, the leasing or licensing of land or a building, or the assignment or surrender of that lease or licence.

The grantor is the person who sells, leases or lets any of the land or buildings and can be anywhere in the 'chain' of people who have an interest in the land or buildings concerned. For example, a freeholder may sell land to another party who constructs a new commercial building on the land to let to another business, who will occupy the building for its own use. In this case there are two grantors: the seller of the land and the business which constructs and leases the new commercial building. It follows that if the occupying business goes on to sub-let part of the building to another business, there would then be three grantors. **The test should be applied to each grant made**.

13.5 How do Customs establish a person's intention or expectation?

The option to tax has no effect in relation to the supplies arising from the grant if either the grantor, or the person responsible for financing the grantor for that particular development, knows or expects that either one of them, or any party connected to them, will occupy the building for other than eligible purposes. **There does not have to be an intention to avoid VAT for the grant to be caught by the test.**

We will consider commercial documents and other evidence such as minutes of meetings, business plans and finance requests to establish the intention and expectation of the businesses that are involved in the particular development.

13.6 What do Customs mean by finance?

For the purpose of the anti-avoidance measure we regard finance as:

- directly or indirectly providing all or part of the funds for the development
- directly or indirectly obtaining those funds from another person
- directly or indirectly providing the funds for discharging all or part of the owner's borrowing for the development or
- directly or indirectly procuring that such a liability will be discharged by another.

Finance could take many different forms, such as loans, guaranteeing a loan, share issues or premium deals.

13.7 When do Customs consider someone to be responsible for financing a development?

For the purposes of the anti-avoidance measure a person is only deemed to have been responsible for financing a development if **two** key conditions are met:

(a) at the time the finance is provided, or the agreement to provide the finance is entered into, the person providing the finance must intend or expect that he or the grantor, or somebody connected to either of them, will occupy the particular development for other than eligible purposes **and**

(b) the funds must be for the purpose of financing the purchase, construction or refurbishment of that development.

If either of these conditions is not met, a person will not be deemed to be responsible for financing the development, even if he has provided the funds to meet part or all of the cost of the development.

13.8 When do Customs consider a person to be connected with another?

We use the test in section 839 of the Income and Corporation Taxes Act 1988 to determine whether people are connected. Examples of connected persons are:

- your husband or wife

- your relatives

- your husband's or wife's relatives

- your business partners and their husbands, wives and relatives

- a company that you control, either by yourself or with any of the persons listed above or

- the trustees of a settlement of which you are a settlor, or of which a person who is still alive and who is connected with you is a settlor.

Relative means a brother, sister, ancestor or lineal descendant. It does not include nephews, nieces, uncles and aunts.

13.9 What do Customs mean by occupied?

A business occupies a building or land if it has any physical presence in that building or land. That physical presence could be by way of a person or of business assets or goods. For example, a business may have a representative in another business' office, or store its goods in a warehouse. A business does not need to be utilising all of the land or buildings for all of the time in order for it to be considered as occupying it.

13.10 What are eligible purposes?

The anti-avoidance measure examines whether the grantor or the person responsible for financing the development intend that the development will be occupied for other than eligible purposes. For someone to be in occupation of the development for eligible purposes they must be occupying it for the purpose of making mainly taxable supplies, or for other supplies which entitle them to credit for their input tax. 'Mainly' means substantially more than half.

Some organisations are always treated as occupying a development for eligible purposes and these include National Health Service Trusts and Government departments. Occupation by local authorities or other bodies, such as police and fire authorities, are treated as eligible provided it is for taxable or non-business purposes.

The following are examples of businesses and organisations that may occupy a development for other than eligible purposes:

- businesses, such as insurance companies and banks, making exempt supplies

- organisations, such as charities, who undertake non-business activities would **not** generally be in occupation for eligible purposes and

- someone who is not, or is not required to be, VAT registered.

13.11 What land or buildings are covered by the capital goods scheme?

The anti-avoidance measure only applies to land and buildings that are, or will become, capital items for the purpose of the capital goods scheme. Generally, a capital item comes within the scheme when it is either bought, or first used. Examples of land and buildings covered by the capital goods scheme are:

- land, a building or part of a building, where the value of the interest supplied to the person buying or leasing it is £250,000 or more

- a building constructed by the owner where the total value of goods and services received in connection with the construction is £250,000 or more

- a building which the owner alters, or an extension or annex which he constructs, where additional floor area of at least 10% is created and the value of the goods and services received in connection with the works is £250,000 or more

- a building which the owner refurbishes or fits out where the value of the capital expenditure on the services received and the goods affixed to the building in connection with the works is £250,000 or more or

- any of the above acquired from the owner during the capital goods scheme adjustment period by way of a transfer of a going concern (see section 11 for more information).

You will find more information about capital items and how the scheme works in *Notice 706/2 Capital goods scheme*.

13.12 What do Customs mean by supplies arising from a grant?

The supplies arising from a grant are commonly the sale premium or rental income received. These are generally treated as made when either invoices are issued or payments are received, but please see section 10 for more details on the time of supply. Payments can include non-monetary considerations received for supplies carried out, such as barter agreements where often no money changes hands between the parties involved for their relevant supplies.

APPENDIX 10: HMRC NOTICE 700/9/02 – TRANSFER OF BUSINESS AS A GOING CONCERN

1. Introduction

1.1 What is this notice about?

This notice explains the VAT treatment of transferring a business as a going concern and is intended to help you ensure that the correct amount of VAT is accounted for and paid.

You should read this notice if you are selling or otherwise transferring a business, or part of a business. It will also be of interest to you if you are acquiring a business. In certain circumstances special VAT rules apply and the sale will not be treated as a supply for VAT purposes, so no VAT should be charged. The sales affected will be those where a business is sold as a going concern or where the sale is of part of a business which can be operated separately.

This notice has been rewritten to improve readability. The following paragraphs give additional guidance which did not appear in the previous edition; 1.5, 2.3.4, 2.3.5, 2.3.7, 2.4.1, 3.2.1, 3.2.2, 3.3, 3.4, 3.6, 7.3, 10.1. The following paragraphs give new information about; notifying a relevant date, 2.4.1, about deduction of VAT on transfer expenses, 2.8 and about VAT groups and transfers, section 4, which did not appear in the previous edition. This new information is included as a result of court decisions.

This notice and others mentioned are available both on paper and on our Internet website at www.hmce.gov.uk.

1.2 What is a Transfer of a Going Concern (TOGC)?

The assets of a business may be transferred in a number of situations. If there has been no transfer of assets there is nothing to which the TOGC provisions can apply. Below are examples of common transfers but the list is not exhaustive:

- the assets may be bought by another person and the existing business may cease to trade

- the existing owner may die or retire and the business assets be taken over by another person

- part of an existing business may be sold to another person and

- the assets may be transferred to a new legal entity, for example, a sole proprietor may take on a partner, or form a limited company.

1.3 What is not a TOGC?

There is no transfer of a business as a going concern through changes in the constitution of a partnership.

If you are registered for VAT but you have not yet made taxable supplies, the transfer of your business might not be the transfer of a going concern. However, where sufficient preparatory work has been undertaken prior to making taxable supplies there may be a business capable of being transferred as a going concern. Section 7 gives examples of transfers of property, some of which are transfers of businesses as a going concern. See also paragraph 1.4 on the transfer of shares.

1.4 Business assets

The assets of a business can include stock in trade, machinery, goodwill, premises and fixtures and fittings. In all these cases the assets are transferred from one person to another and so may be covered by the TOGC provisions.

When there is the transfer of shares in a limited company from one person to another, the assets still belong to the limited company. Thus there is no change in the ownership of the assets so no supplies to which the TOGC provisions could apply.

1.5 Why have the special rules?

The TOGC provisions have two main purposes to:

 • help businesses by improving their cash flow and avoid the need to separately value assets which may be liable at different rates or are exempt and which have been sold as a whole and

 • protect Government revenue by removing a charge to tax and entitlement to input tax where the output tax may not be paid to Customs. For example, where a business charges tax, which is claimed as input tax by the new business but never declared or paid by the old business.

2. Special rules

2.1 What is this section about?

This section deals with when special rules apply to a transfer of a business so that the transfer of some, or all of the assets, is not a taxable supply.

2.2 Why it is important to get the tax treatment right

If **all** the conditions in paragraph 2.3 are met, special rules apply and VAT must not be charged or accounted for on the assets transferred (except, in certain circumstances, on the premises ie land and/or property used in the business. Details of the circumstances in which you must charge tax on the premises are set out in paragraph 2.4).

If VAT is charged when it should not have been the:

 • new owner will not be able to reclaim this amount as input tax, because there was no taxable supply and

 • seller will have to cancel any tax invoice issued and provide the new owner with a refund of the VAT charged. Normally this will be by issue of a credit note or document giving similar effect.

The TOGC rules are **compulsory**. You cannot choose to 'opt out'. So, it is very important that you establish from the outset whether the business is being sold as a going concern.

The relevant law is reproduced at section 6.

2.3 When TOGCs are not taxable supplies

If you meet **all** of the conditions listed below, the transfer of the assets of the business, other than premises, is not a taxable supply and you must **not** charge VAT. Paragraph 2.4 explains whether you need to charge tax on the transfer of the premises.

2.3.1 Business activities

The effect of the transfer must be to put the new owner in possession of a business which can be operated as such. The term 'business' means a business activity recognised as such in VAT law. For example, some of the activities of charities or local authorities are not considered to be business (see *Notice 700 The VAT Guide* for more information). A sale of capital assets is not in itself a transfer of a business as a going concern. However, if the effect of the sale is to put the purchaser in possession of a business, it is a transfer of a going concern, even if the assets are transferred on different dates.

The business, or part business, must be a going concern at the time of the transfer. It can still be a going concern even though it is unprofitable, or is trading under the control of a liquidator or administrative receiver, or a trustee in bankruptcy, or an administrator appointed under the Insolvency Act 1986.

2.3.2 Assets

The assets you are transferring must be intended for use by the new owner in carrying on the same kind of business. If the new owner is to use the assets to carry on a different kind of business you must charge VAT in the normal way. See section 8 for examples.

2.3.3 Consecutive transfers of business

There must not be a series of immediately consecutive transfers of the business. Where A sells its assets to B who immediately sells those assets on to C, because B has not carried on the business the TOGC provisions do not apply to any of the transactions. This means that the sales take their normal VAT liability (taxable or exempt). Such immediate transfers often occur in property transactions where A contracts to sell property to B, and B 'sub-sells' the property to C with both contracts being completed by a single transfer from A to C. Different rules apply in Scotland, however, to the transfer of a property rental business. Under Scottish law the disposition of the 'dominium utile' may been seen to be direct from A to C, and the TOGC provisions may apply, subject to meeting the other conditions in this paragraph and paragraph 2.4.

2.3.4 VAT registration

Where the seller is registered for VAT, the buyer must be registered or at the date of the transfer be required to be registered for VAT because all of the conditions for compulsory registration are met, or be accepted for voluntary registration. This condition is not met if the buyer is not registered and is not required to be registered for VAT. This could be either because:

(a) at the date the transfer takes place, the buyer does not expect the value of their taxable supplies in the next 12 months to be above the deregistration limit, for example the buyer intends to reduce trading by introducing shorter working hours; or

(b) the seller was not required to be registered but was registered voluntarily at the date of the transfer. Thus, at that date, the buyer is not required to register because the value of their taxable supplies in the 12 month period then ended is not above the registration limit.

In such circumstances, unless the buyer is accepted for voluntary registration, the conditions for the transfer to be treated as a TOGC are not met and the sale takes its normal liability. Further details about registration can be found in *Notice 700/1 Should I be registered for VAT?* The supplement to *Notice 700/1 Should I be registered for VAT?* gives details of registration limits.

2.3.5 Seller not VAT registered

There can be a TOGC where the seller is not registered for VAT. For example, because the seller is trading below the registration limit or making wholly exempt supplies. A TOGC is possible in both these circumstances. Thus the sale of an unregistered business which includes trading stock, the value of which might otherwise take the trader over the registration limit, will not do so because it can be treated as not being a supply.

However, where the transfer of assets is a relevant supply for VAT registration purposes, the unregistered person will have to register and account for VAT on the transfer of assets. Further information about relevant supplies can be found in *Notice 700/1 Should I be registered for VAT?*

2.3.6 No significant break in trading

There must be no significant break in the normal trading pattern before or immediately after the transfer. A short period of closure that does not significantly disrupt the existing trading pattern, for example, for redecoration, will not prevent the business from being transferred as a going concern.

2.3.7 Transfer of part of your business

If you are transferring only part of your business, that part must be able to operate alone. It does not matter whether it will, in fact, be operated separately from any other businesses the new owner carries on.

The assets of the part of the business you transfer must have been used to make supplies, they must not merely be used for the overheads of your business (see also paragraph 8.2).

2.3.8 Transfers involving land and property

If the transfer of the land or property would normally be a taxable supply, both the buyer and the seller may need to meet certain conditions for it to be included as part of the TOGC. This is explained in more detail at paragraph 2.4 below.

2.4 Should VAT be charged when land or buildings are transferred as part of a TOGC?

A transfer of a going concern will often involve the transfer of land and buildings. There are extra rules to determine whether VAT should be charged on the transfer of land and buildings – even if the rest of the transfer does qualify for TOGC treatment.

If all the conditions in paragraph 2.3 are met and the purchaser has complied with the following requirements, the transfer of land and buildings can be part of a TOGC.

If the seller is transferring land or buildings:

- on which he has elected to waive exemption or

- which are new (less than three years old) or unfinished buildings or civil engineering works which would ordinarily be standard-rated

and the purchaser has;

- notified to Customs his election to tax the land or buildings by the relevant date and

- with effect from 18 March 2004, has notified the seller by the relevant date that their election has not been disapplied then

the transfer of the land or buildings can be included in the TOGC.

However, if the seller is transferring land or buildings on which there is no election to tax, and the supply is not otherwise standard rated, in other words, if the supply is zero rated or exempt then:

- the purchaser is not required to elect to tax and

- there ceases to be a requirement to notify that their option has not been disapplied.

The seller is responsible for applying the correct VAT treatment and may be required to support their decision. If the transaction is to be treated as a TOGC the seller must be satisfied that the purchaser's election to tax is in place by the relevant date. They may therefore consider asking the purchaser for evidence of this, such as a copy of the notification letter. The seller must have the purchaser's notification of the non-disapplication of the election to tax and may find it prudent to obtain this in writing.

2.4.1 Election to waive exemption

The election to waive exemption by the purchaser, referred to above, must be notified to Customs in writing no later than the relevant date and must apply from that time. You should note that the relevant date is the time of the supply. For VAT purposes the time of supply is normally the date of the transfer, but will also include receipt of a deposit that may otherwise have created a tax point. A tax point is not created by the receipt of a deposit by a third party acting as an independent stakeholder (as opposed to an agent of the vendor) until the money is released to the vendor. Further information on tax points this can be found in *Notice 700 The VAT Guide*.

Where the written notification of the election is sent to us by mail, the notification must be properly addressed, pre-paid and posted on or before the relevant date. Notice 742A Opting to tax land and buildings fully explains the option to tax/election to waive exemption.

2.4.2 Disapplication of the purchaser 's option to tax - the anti-avoidance measure

An election to waive exemption (or option to tax) can be disapplied as a result of an anti-avoidance measure. Where an option is disapplied this means it will cease to have effect on certain supplies. The anti avoidance measure only has effect where land and buildings are occupied for something other than fully taxable business purposes and where the land or building is a capital item for the purposes of Capital Goods Scheme (see *Notices 706 Partial exemption* and *706/2 Capital goods scheme*). The measure is explained fully in *Notice 742A Opting to tax land and buildings* section13.

Changes were made to the measure from 18 March 2004. From the same date the TOGC rules were also amended. Under the new rules transfers of new buildings and civil engineering works (less than three years old) and land and buildings on which the vendor has exercised an option to tax, can only be included within a TOGC where:

> 1. the purchaser confirms that an option to tax has been made and notified by the relevant date, and

> 2. the purchaser makes a declaration to the transferor that his option will not be disapplied by the anti-avoidance provisions (see *Notice 742A*).

Where the purchaser fails to do either of the above the transfer will fall outside of the TOGC provisions and the supply will be subject to VAT. However, the transfer of other business assets may still qualify to be treated as a TOGC.

2.4.3 The following table will help you decide on whether land and buildings can be included in a TOGC

Commercial land or building, ordinarily exempt

Has seller opted to tax (building over 3 years old)?	Has the purchaser opted to tax?	Has the purchaser's option to tax been disapplied?	Transfer of a going concern provisions met?
Yes	Yes	Yes	No
Yes	No	N/A	No
Yes	Yes	No	Yes
No	No	N/A	Yes
No	Yes	Yes	Yes
No	Yes	No	Yes

New building (less than three years old), ordinarily standard-rated

Has seller opted to tax?	Has the purchaser opted to tax?	Has the purchaser's option to tax been disapplied?	Transfer of a going concern provisions met?
Yes	Yes	Yes	No
Yes	No	N/A	No

New building (less than three years old), ordinarily standard-rated (cont)

Has seller opted to tax?	Has the purchaser opted to tax?	Has the purchaser's option to tax been disapplied?	Transfer of a going concern provisions met?
Yes	Yes	No	Yes
No	No	N/A	No
No	Yes	Yes	No
No	Yes	No	Yes

2.5 What are the rules when a property rental business is transferred?

Section 7 gives examples of circumstances concerning the transfer of land/property where there may (or may not) be a transfer of a business of property rental as a going concern. In those cases where there has been such a transfer, the conditions of paragraphs 2.3 and 2.4 must still be met for there to be a TOGC and the supply of assets ignored for VAT purposes.

An optional statement of practice is available where a property rental business is being transferred to a nominee acquiring title for a named beneficial owner. See section 9.

2.6 Deduction of VAT on expenses incurred on the transfer

Although there is no supply for VAT purposes where there is a transfer of a going concern, this does not prevent the deduction, subject to the usual rules, of input tax on related expenses (for example solicitors' fees and estate agents' costs). There is, however, a distinction between the extent to which the transferor (the seller) and the transferee (the buyer) can deduct that input tax.

2.7 Transferees

From 1 June 1996, if a transferee acquires assets by way of the transfer of a going concern and the assets are to be used exclusively to make taxable supplies, the VAT incurred on the cost of acquiring those assets should be attributed to those taxable supplies and can be recovered in full. Conversely, if the assets of the acquired business are to be used exclusively to make exempt supplies, none of the input tax on the cost of acquiring those assets can be recovered. However, if the assets are to be used in making both taxable and exempt supplies, any input tax incurred is residual input tax and must be apportioned in accordance with the agreed VAT partial exemption method.

2.8 Transferors

The sale of the business as a going concern is not a supply and the input tax incurred on the cost of selling the business cannot be attributed to it by the transferor. These costs are, therefore, treated as a general business overhead having a direct and immediate link with the whole of the transferor's business activity and are to be apportioned by reference to the transferor's agreed partial exemption method. However, from 1 August 2001, where part of a business is transferred as a going concern, and those expenses can be shown to have a direct and immediate link with the transferred part of the business, then those expenses form part of the overheads of that part of the business. Where that part of the business made only taxable supplies then tax is deductible on those expenses. Conversely, where that part of the business made only exempt supplies the tax is not deductible. However, where taxable and exempt supplies were made by that part of the business, then the tax is residual input tax and is attributable to taxable supplies by reference to the transferor's partial exemption method.

In instances, either at 2.7 or 2.8 where the existing partial exemption method fails to achieve a fair and reasonable result, then we would be prepared to approve the use of another method.

3. Rules following a TOGC

3.1 *What is this section about?*

This section explains the rules following a TOGC in relation to:

- capital goods scheme considerations
- de-registration and goods still owned by the original business
- transfer of the previous owner's registration number
- business records
- giving away goods or services owned by the previous business
- intrastat rules.

3.2 *The capital goods scheme and how it interacts with the TOGC provisions*

The scheme applies where the value of taxable (other than zero-rated) supplies received in connection with the acquisition or creation of any of the items listed below is £250,000 or more. In the case of computers and computer equipment the scheme only applies where the value of the supply is £50,000 or more. The scheme applies to the following:

- land
- buildings
- civil engineering works
- refurbishments
- computers and items of computer equipment; and, if relevant
- related self-supplies.

Items that fall within the scheme are called capital items.

3.2.1 *How the scheme works*

Essentially, the scheme requires that adjustments are made to the input tax claimed in relation to a capital item if within a period of ten successive intervals (each interval normally corresponds with your partial exemption tax year) there is a change in the extent to which the item is used to make taxable supplies. This period is called the adjustment period. For computers, items of computer equipment and in cases where the interest supplied in the land and buildings etc has less than ten years to run at the time it is supplied to you, then the adjustment period is only five years.

3.2.2 *Capital item is transferred as part of a transfer of a going concern*

If a capital item is transferred to you as part of a transfer of a going concern then you, as the new owner, assume responsibility for any adjustments of input tax required under the scheme for the remainder of the adjustment period. Purchasers should therefore confirm with the seller whether any of the assets being transferred are covered by the scheme and details of the adjustments already made. It is important to be aware that if the purpose to which the asset has been put changes at or after the transfer, the purchaser may need to repay some of the input tax claimed by the original owner. Similarly, he may be entitled to recover more tax than that originally claimed.

If the seller has been fully taxable since the acquisition of the capital item and the buyer is and remains fully taxable until the expiry of the adjustment period, then no adjustments are required under the scheme. It is only when there is a change in the extent to which the capital item is used in making taxable and exempt supplies, within the adjustment period, that adjustments have to be made.

Further details about how the scheme operates can be found in *Notice 706/2 Capital goods scheme.*

3.3 How should I treat business assets that are not transferred if I am de-registering from VAT?

If you are cancelling your registration and have any goods which you have claimed input tax on and are not transferring with the business, you will normally have to account for VAT on these assets. *Notice 700/11 Cancelling your registration* tells you more about this.

If, when you cancel your registration, you have a capital item covered by the scheme and which is still within its adjustment period you will need to make a final adjustment. *Notice 706/2 Capital goods scheme* tells you more about this.

3.4 Reallocation of the VAT registration number

In certain circumstances the new owner can apply to keep the previous owner's registration number. Full details are given on the application form – Form VAT 68 – available from your local VAT Business Advice Centre. **Form VAT 68 must be signed by both the previous owner and the new owner**.

Both the previous and the new owner must agree to the consequences of reallocation set out on Form VAT 68. These include the transfer of any VAT liability to the new owner and are legally binding on both parties. Such consequences also include the transfer of entitlement to unclaimed bad debt relief on debts incurred by the seller of the business. However, there remains the requirement to repay input tax claimed by the seller on supplies he received and which have subsequently become the subject of a bad debt relief claim made by the supplier. Further details about bad debt relief can be found in *Notice 700/18 Relief from VAT* on bad debts.

If the registration number is reallocated, the previous owner must still follow the procedure set out in *Notice 700/11 Cancelling your registration*.

3.4.1 Special arrangements applying to the previous owner's registration

If any special arrangements apply to the previous owner's registration – for example, self-billing – they must normally end when the business is transferred. In such cases, or if the use of a retail scheme is involved, you should ask your local VAT Business Advice Centre for guidance.

3.5 What should happen to the business records?

Any records you had to keep for VAT purposes when you owned the business (or part business) must be transferred to the new owner. The new owner takes over the obligation to keep and preserve them. If you do not wish to transfer your records you must apply to your local VAT Business Advice Centre who may let you keep them.

Business records have to be kept for six years unless Customs and Excise have agreed a shorter period.

3.6 What if I give away goods or services owned by the previous business?

Under the normal rules, when a business gives away goods or services on which input tax has been recovered, VAT is due on that disposal. One-off business gifts costing £50 or less or free samples are exceptions to this rule. Where goods and services are transferred as part of a TOGC, and a previous business has had entitlement to input tax on those supplies, output tax is still due on any subsequent free supply of those goods or services. Further information on gifts and samples can be found in *VAT Notice 700/35 Business gifts and samples*.

3.7 Intrastat rules

VAT registered businesses are required to complete statistical Supplementary Declarations (SDs) if their intra-EC trade exceeds annually set value thresholds for either dispatches (exports) or acquisitions (imports) of goods.

When the VAT registration of a trader responsible for providing SDs is amended as a result of a change of ownership, name, address, legal status or similar change that does not significantly affect their intra-Community operations, then the new VAT registered trader keeps the legal responsibilities and obligations to continue to provide SDs.

4. VAT groups and Transfers of Going Concerns

4.1 Transfers of businesses between members of the same VAT group

The formation of a VAT group creates a single person for VAT purposes and as such any supply by a member of a VAT group is considered to be made by the representative member of the group. Therefore any assets transferred by a group member as part of the transfer of a going concern are considered to be transferred by the representative member.

The transfer of assets within a VAT group, like most supplies between the members of a VAT group, is disregarded for VAT purposes.

4.2 Transfers made to persons outside the VAT group

There cannot be a TOGC when the sole activity of the business transferred is the making of supplies from one group member to another. However, if supplies are also being made to businesses outside of the VAT group, a TOGC is possible.

4.3 Transfers made to a VAT Group

Where a business is sold and the buyer is part of a VAT group and uses the new acquisition simply to make supplies to VAT group members, the business has effectively ceased and it cannot be treated as a TOGC. However, if supplies are also being made to businesses outside of the VAT group, a TOGC is possible. For example:

The purchaser of a property rental business is a member of the same VAT group as the existing tenant	Not a TOGC
A VAT group member sells a property currently being rented to another group member to a third party	Not a TOGC
A property rental business is sold where the tenant who is a member of the outgoing landlord's VAT group is only one of a number of tenants	Can be a TOGC
A property rental business is sold where the tenant who is a member of the purchaser's VAT group is only one of a number of tenants	Can be a TOGC

5. Members of a partly exempt VAT group

5.1 What is this section about?

This section provides information on the requirements for a new owner who is a member of a partly exempt VAT group acquiring a business as a going concern.

5.2 General rules for partly exempt VAT groups

If you are a member of a partly exempt VAT group and you acquire business assets as part of a transfer of a business as a going concern, you must treat these assets as being both supplied to the group and supplied by the group – ie a self-supply is triggered. In practice this means that the representative member must account for output tax in relation to the supply by the group and recover the input tax incurred in relation to the supply to the group in accordance with the partial exemption method in operation. However, the input tax cannot be attributed to the self-supply itself.

5.2.1 Exclusions

The self-supply will not be triggered in relation to:

 • any assets which were assets of the previous owner more than three years before the date of the transfer

- goodwill (eg unidentifiable goodwill, use of a trade mark or trading name, the sole right to trade in a particular area, etc)

- any assets which are zero-rated or exempt (for example zero-rated or exempt freehold or leasehold interests in land) or

- items which fall within the capital goods scheme. For further details of items covered by the capital goods scheme see paragraph 3.2 and *Notice 706/2 Capital goods scheme*.

The above self-supply made by the representative member must not be taken into account when working out how much input tax the VAT group is entitled to recover.

5.3 What is the value for VAT purposes of the supply made to and by the representative member?

The value of the supply by, and to the representative member, is its open market value. If the previous owner is unconnected with your group, this will normally be the consideration you paid for the assets on which tax is due. If VAT is not due on some of the assets, the consideration must be apportioned fairly between the standard-rated assets and other assets. The paragraph on mixed supplies in *Notice 700 The VAT Guide* tells you how to do this.

5.4 Can this VAT due be reduced in any circumstances?

Customs can reduce the VAT chargeable in relation to the self-supply if you can produce satisfactory evidence to show that the previous owner did not recover all of the input tax incurred on the original purchase (for example, if he was partly exempt or the input tax was 'blocked' eg on the purchase of a car).

In a case where the transferor's partial exemption recovery rate (during the partial exemption tax year in which the assets were purchased) is equal to or less than the transferee's recovery rate (during the partial exemption tax year in which the assets were acquired) the VAT charge will be reduced to nil, although no tax will be refunded.

If you consider that you have evidence to show that the tax due should be reduced you should consult the National Advice Service.

6. UK VAT law concerning transfers of going concerns

6.1 Extract from the Value Added Tax (Special Provisions) Order 1995 – Statutory Instrument 1995 No 1268

'5 (1) Subject to paragraph (2) below, there shall be treated as neither a supply of goods nor a supply of services the following supplies by a person of assets of his business –

(a) their supply to a person to whom he transfers his business as a going concern where –

(i) the assets are to be used by the transferee in carrying on the same kind of business, whether or not as part of any existing business, as that carried on by the transferor, and

(ii) in a case where the transferor is a taxable person, the transferee is already, or immediately becomes as a result of the transfer, a taxable person or a person defined as such in section 3(1) of the Manx Act;

(b) their supply to a person to whom he transfers part of his business as a going concern where –

(i) that part is capable of separate operation,

(ii) the assets are to be used by the transferee in carrying on the same kind of business, whether or not as part of any existing business, as that carried on by the transferor in relation to that part, and

(iii) in a case where the transferor is a taxable person, the transferee is already or immediately becomes as a result of the transfer, a taxable person or a person defined as such in section 3(1) of the Manx Act.

(2) A supply of assets shall not be treated as neither a supply of goods nor a supply of services by virtue of paragraph (1) above to the extent that it consists of-

(a) a grant which would, but for an election which the transferor has made, fall within item 1 of Group 1 of Schedule 9 to the Act; or

(b) a grant of a fee simple which falls within paragraph (a) of item 1 of Group 1 of Schedule 9 to the Act,

unless the transferee has made an election in relation to the land concerned which has effect on the relevant date and has given any written notification of the election required by paragraph 3(6) of Schedule 10 to the Act , no later than the relevant date.

(3) In paragraph (2) of this article –

"election" means an election having effect under paragraph 2 of Schedule 10 to the Act;

"relevant date" means the date upon which the grant would have been treated as having been made or, if there is more than one such date, the earliest of them;

"transferor" and "transferee" include a relevant associate of either respectively as defined in paragraph 3(7) of Schedule 10 to the Act.

(a) Schedule 10 was amended by the Value Added Tax (Buildings and Land) Order 1995 (S.I. 1995/279)'

6.2 Extracts from the Value Added Tax Act 1994

'**44 (1)** Subject to subsections (2) to (4) below, subsection (5) below applies where –

(a) a business, or part of a business, carried on by a taxable person is transferred as a going concern to a body corporate treated as a member of a group under section 43;

(b) on the transfer of the business or part, chargeable assets of the business are transferred to the body corporate; and

(c) the transfer of the assets is treated by virtue of section 5(3)(c) as neither a supply of goods nor a supply of services.

(2) Subsection (5) below shall not apply if the representative member of the group is entitled to credit for the whole of the input tax on supplies to it and importations by it –

(a) during the prescribed accounting period in which the assets are transferred, and

(b) during any longer period to which regulations under section 26(3)(b) relate and in which the assets are transferred.

(3) Subsection (5) below shall not apply if the Commissioners are satisfied that the assets were assets of the taxable person transferring them more than 3 years before the day on which they are transferred.

(4) Subsection (5) below shall not apply to the extent that the chargeable assets consist of capital items in respect of which regulations made under section 26(3) and (4), and in force when the assets are transferred, provide for adjustment to the deduction of input tax.

(5) The chargeable assets shall be treated for the purposes of this Act as being, on the day on which they are transferred, both supplied to the representative member of the group for the purpose of its business and supplied by that member in the course or furtherance of its business.

(6) A supply treated under subsection (5) above as made by a representative member shall not be taken into account as a supply made by him when determining the allowance of input tax in his case under section 26.

(7) The value of a supply treated under subsection (5) above as made to or by a representative member shall be taken to be the open market value of the chargeable assets.

(8) For the purposes of this section, the open market value of any chargeable assets shall be taken to be the price that would be paid on a sale (on which no VAT is payable) between a buyer and a seller who are not in such a relationship as to affect the price.

(9) The Commissioners may reduce the VAT chargeable by virtue of subsection (5) above in a case where they are satisfied that the person by whom the chargeable assets are transferred has not received credit for the full amount of input tax arising on the supply to or acquisition, or importation by him of the chargeable assets.

(10) For the purposes of this section, assets are chargeable assets if their supply in the United Kingdom by a taxable person in the course or furtherance of his business would be a taxable supply (and not a zero-rated supply).'

'**49 (1)** Where a business carried on by a taxable person is transferred to another person as a going concern, then –

> **(a)** for the purpose of determining whether the transferee is liable to be registered under this Act he shall be treated as having carried on the business before as well as after the transfer and supplies by the transferor shall be treated accordingly; and

> **(b)** any records relating to the business which, under paragraph 6 of Schedule 11, are required to be preserved for any period after the transfer shall be preserved by the transferee instead of by the transferor, unless the Commissioners, at the request of the transferor, otherwise direct.

(2) Without prejudice to subsection (1) above, the Commissioners may by regulations make provision for securing continuity in the application of this Act in cases where a business carried on by a taxable person is transferred to another person as a going concern and the transferee is registered under this Act in substitution for the transferor.

(3) Regulations under subsection (2) above may, in particular, provide –

> **(a)** for liabilities and duties under this Act (excluding sections 59 to 70) of the transferor to become, to such extent as may be provided by the regulations, liabilities and duties of the transferee; and

> **(b)** for any right of either of them to repayment or credit in respect of tax to be satisfied by making a repayment or allowing a credit to the other;

but no such provision as is mentioned in paragraph (a) or (b) of this subsection shall have effect in relation to any transferor and transferee unless an application in that behalf has been made by them under the regulations.'

7. Transferring a property business as a going concern

7.1 *What is this section about?*

This section provides guidance on when a property can be transferred as a going concern.

7.2 *Examples of when a business can be transferred as a going concern*

If you:

> • own the freehold of a property which you let to a tenant and sell the freehold with the benefit of the existing lease, a business of property rental is transferred to the purchaser. This is a business transferred as a going concern even if the property is only partly tenanted. Similarly, if you own the lease of a property (which is subject to a sub-lease) and

you assign your lease with the benefit of the sub-lease, this is a business transferred as a going concern

• own a building which is being let out where there is an initial rent free period, even if the building is sold during the rent free period, you are carrying on a business of property rental

• granted a lease in respect of a building but the tenants are not yet in occupation, you are carrying on a property rental business

• own a property and have found a tenant but not actually entered into a lease agreement when you transfer the property to a third party (with the benefit of the prospective tenancy but before a lease has been signed), there is sufficient evidence of intended economic activity for there to be a property rental business capable of being transferred

• are a property developer selling a site as a package (to a single buyer) which is a mixture of let and unlet, finished or unfinished properties, and the sale of the site would otherwise have been standard rated, then subject to the purchaser electing to waive exemption for the whole site, the whole site can be regarded as a business transferred as a going concern.

7.3 Examples where there is not a transfer of a going concern

If you:

• are a property developer and have built a building and you allow someone to occupy temporarily (without any right to occupy after any proposed sale) or you are 'actively marketing' it in search of a tenant, there is no property rental business being carried on

• own the freehold of a property and grant a lease, even a 999-year lease, you are not transferring a business as a going concern -you are retaining your asset (the freehold) and creating a new asset (a lease). Similarly, if you own a headlease and grant a sub-lease you are not transferring your business as a going concern.

• sell a property where the lease you granted is surrendered immediately before the sale, your property rental business ceases and so cannot be transferred as a going concern - even if tenants under a sublease remain in occupation

• sell a property to the existing tenant who leases the whole premises from you, this cannot be a transfer of a going concern because the tenant cannot carry on the same business of property rental

• have granted a lease in respect of a building and the tenant is running a business from the premises. The tenant then sells the assets of his business as a going concern and surrenders his lease to you. You grant the new owner of the business a lease in respect of the building. This is not a transfer by you of a property rental business.

8. Same and different kinds of business

8.1 Trading activities after a business is transferred

When selling your business assets, you must check that the purchaser will also be carrying on the same kind of business before the sale can be ignored for VAT purposes under the TOGC rules.

Common areas of difficulty include companies which have more than one trading activity. For example, a brewery is in business selling beers, wines and spirits to the public via their managed house outlets. It is also in business renting properties to tenants (where the tenants are selling to the public). So, for example, if a brewery was leasing a pub to tenants, and then sold the business to someone who was to run the pub themselves, then it would not be a TOGC: the brewery had a business of renting the property, the new owner has a business of running a pub.

You must therefore check whether the person buying your assets is going to operate the business in the same way as you.

8.2 Examples of different types of business

If you:

- grant franchises to operate trading sites, as opposed to operating the actual trading activity of the business, the transferee is not carrying on the same kind of business as you or

- sell your business to a customer who will only use 'your' product to support his existing business and will not be making any supplies of 'your' product to any third parties, the purchaser will not be carrying on the same kind of business.

8.3 Examples of the same kind of business

If you sell:

- a restaurant and/or bar but the purchaser is to immediately alter the style of the business, the same kind of business is still being carried on, eg an Italian restaurant becoming a Mexican restaurant is still a restaurant

- your business to someone who intends to restructure it such that it will not be the same but they actually continue with your business, even if for a very short period of time, they will have carried on the same kind of business.

9. Property letting business – statement of practice

9.1 What is this section about?

See also paragraph 2.5.

This section reproduces the contents of Business Brief 10/96 dated 5 June 1996.

This statement of practice about nominee purchasers acquiring legal title is optional and may only be applied by persons transferring an interest in land to a person who is a nominee for a named beneficial owner. The option is not available if the nominee is acting for an undisclosed beneficial owner.

Where the legal title in land is to be held by a nominee for a named beneficial owner, Customs and Excise will, for the purpose of establishing the transfer of a property letting business as a going concern, from 1 June 1996, consider the named beneficial owner of the land and not the nominee acquiring legal title to be the transferee.

The new optional practice allows a person transferring an interest in land to a nominee for a named beneficial owner, with the agreement of that nominee and beneficial owner, to treat the named beneficial owner as the transferee for the purposes of establishing whether there has been a transfer of a going concern. This Business Brief contains an example format that the parties can use to record agreement if they so wish.

Persons transferring an interest in land to a person who is a nominee for a named beneficial owner will be expected to check the VAT registration and where necessary the VAT elections made by the beneficial owner.

Examples of where a nominee might exist to hold the legal title in property for a beneficial owner are:- where the legal title is held by four or fewer persons on trust for a partnership (this example does not arise in Scottish law); where the legal title is held on trust for an unincorporated association; and where the legal title is held on trust for a pension fund.

9.2 Background

Customs and Excise have reviewed their policy whereby the passing of title in property between legal owners solely determined whether Article 5 of the VAT (Special Provisions) Order 1995 (SI 1995 No 1268) applied in the circumstances above.

Strictly, a transfer of a going concern cannot occur where the transferee is a nominee for a beneficial owner because the beneficial owner will be the person carrying on the business, not the nominee. The optional treatment above does not disturb any transactions prior to 1 June

1996, but from that date allows a more relaxed approach to be adopted. It is deregulatory and should reduce business costs in the circumstances described.

The option does not need to apply to transactions where the nominee is the transferor of the legal title. In these cases, Paragraph 8 of Schedule 10 to the VAT Act 1994 deems the beneficial owner to be the transferor.

The above principles, which are based upon English land law, may also be applied to similar transactions in Scotland and Northern Ireland as necessary.

9.3 Suggested Format of Notice of Agreement

The following Notice of Agreement is optional and other clear written evidence of agreement will be accepted by Customs and Excise. The transferor, transferee beneficial owner and nominee should each retain a copy of any written evidence.

9.3.1 Notice of Agreement to adopt Statement of Practice

Property: (Address)

Transferor/vendor: (X)

Nominee/purchaser: (Y)

Future Beneficial Owner: (Z)

X, Y and Z confirm that they have agreed to adopt the optional practice set out in Customs' Business Brief 10/96 in relation to the purchase of the Property pursuant to an agreement dated (…) between X and Y.

Following the transfer of the Property Y will hold the legal title as nominee for Z, the beneficial owner.

SIGNED for and on behalf of X:

SIGNED for and on behalf of Y:

SIGNED for and on behalf of Z:

DATE:

10. Further help and advice

10.1 Advice

If you need further help or advice or more copies of Customs and Excise Notices, please contact your local Customs and Excise or VAT Business Advice Centre, as appropriate. You will find this in the phone book under 'Customs and Excise'. Our notices and other information are available on the Internet (http://www.hmce.gov.uk).

Whilst our officers will do their best to help you, you should remember that they will not be responsible for advice given, unless:

- all the factors relating to the query were described and

- in the case of queries which cannot be answered by reference to a notice or leaflet, both your request for advice and the reply are given in writing.

- You specify what aspect of the arrangements give rise to your doubts

Notice 700/51 VAT Enquiries Guide gives information about making enquiries and the standard of service you can expect from Customs & Excise.

Help and advice about how to keep your VAT affairs in order can also be obtained from members of the tax accountancy profession. However, there is no requirement to employ an accountant and if you choose to do so, responsibility for the accuracy of your VAT affairs remains with you, the registered person.

Appendix 11: HMRC Business Brief 10/96 (extract)

5 June 1996

Statement of practice on transfer of a property letting business as a going concern

This statement of practice about nominee purchasers acquiring legal title is optional and may only be applied by persons transferring an interest in land to a person who is a nominee for a named beneficial owner. The option is not available if the nominee is acting for an undisclosed beneficial owner.

Where the legal title in land is to be held by a nominee for a named beneficial owner, Customs and Excise will, for the purpose of establishing the transfer of a property letting business as a going concern, from 1 June 1996, consider the named beneficial owner of the land and not the nominee acquiring legal title to be the transferee.

The new optional practice allows a person transferring an interest in land to a nominee for a named beneficial owner, with the agreement of that nominee and beneficial owner, to treat the named beneficial owner as the transferee for the purposes of establishing whether there has been a transfer of a going concern. This Business Brief contains an example format that the parties can use to record agreement if they so wish.

Persons transferring an interest in land to a person who is a nominee for a named beneficial owner will be expected to check the VAT registration and where necessary the VAT elections made by the beneficial owner.

Examples of where a nominee might exist to hold the legal title in property for a beneficial owner are: where the legal title is held by four or fewer persons on trust for a partnership; where the legal title is held on trust for an unincorporated association; and where the legal title is held on trust for a pension fund.

Background

Customs and Excise have reviewed their policy whereby the passing of title in property between legal owners solely determined whether Article 5 of the VAT (Special Provisions) Order 1995 (SI 1995 No 1268) applied in the circumstances above.

Strictly, a transfer of a going concern cannot occur where the transferee is a nominee for a beneficial owner because the beneficial owner will be the person carrying on the business, not the nominee. The optional treatment above does not disturb any transactions prior to 1 June 1996, but from that date allows a more relaxed approach to be adopted. It is deregulatory and should reduce business costs in the circumstances described.

The option does not need to apply to transactions where the nominee is the transferor of the legal title. In these cases, Paragraph 8 of Schedule 10 to the VAT Act 1994 deems the beneficial owner to be the transferor.

The above principles, which are based upon English land law, may also be applied to similar transactions in Scotland and Northern Ireland as necessary.

Suggested format of Notice of Agreement

The following Notice of Agreement is optional and other clear written evidence of agreement will be accepted by Customs and Excise. The transferor, transferee beneficial owner and nominee should each retain a copy of any written evidence.

Notice of agreement to adopt Statement of Practice

Property: (Address)

Transferor/vendor: (X)

Nominee/purchaser: (Y)

Future Beneficial Owner: (Z)

X, Y and Z confirm that they have agreed to adopt the optional practice set out in Customs' Business Brief 10/96 in relation to the purchase of the Property pursuant to an agreement dated (…) between X and Y.

Following the transfer of the Property Y will hold the legal title as nominee for Z, the beneficial owner.

SIGNED for and on behalf of X:

SIGNED for and on behalf of Y:

SIGNED for and on behalf of Z:

DATE:

For further information traders and their advisers should contact their local VAT Advice Centre listed under Customs and Excise in the telephone book.

APPENDIX 12: HMRC BUSINESS BRIEF 5/97 (EXTRACT)

5 March 1997

VAT on building regulation fees in England and Wales

From 13 January the possibility of competition exists across the whole range of building control work and VAT is therefore chargeable at the standard rate on all building control fees as from that date.

New Approved Inspectors have been authorised by the Department of the Environment to provide building regulation services for commercial and mixed developments, as well as the residential and mixed developments for which NHBC (Building Control Services) Ltd was already authorised.

The revised liability rulings apply to building regulation applications received on or after 13 January 1997. Applications received prior to this date should be treated as non-business by local authorities irrespective of when the work is actually carried out or invoices issued. This is because a local authority monopoly existed at the time the application was made and there is, therefore, no competition in respect of the supply of these particular services.

We can also confirm that repayments of VAT paid in error in the past on building regulation fees will continue to be made. These are not caught by the three-year capping provisions.

This supplements and amends the guidance contained in Business Briefs 23/95 and 26/95. For further information traders and their advisers should contact their local VAT Business Advice Centre listed under Customs and Excise in the telephone book.

© Crown copyright

Appendix 13: HMRC Business Brief 26/98 (Extract)

18 December 1998

VAT groups and transfers of going concerns (TOGCs)

This business brief clarifies Customs' policy on whether there can be a transfer of a property rental business as a going concern where the landlord and the tenant or the purchaser and the tenant are members of the same VAT group.

Background

In *Kingfisher Plc* 1993 the High Court found that members of a VAT group are to be considered a single taxable person for VAT purposes. The status of individual members of VAT groups has also been recently considered by the House of Lords in *Thorn Materials Supply Ltd* 1998 which came to the same conclusion. A question raised by those decisions is whether there can be a TOGC when the sole business activity constitutes supplies from one group member to another. With property rental between group members, if the rental supply is disregarded under section 43(1)(a) VATA 1994, it is simply as though the taxable person (the group) is occupying the property itself. Therefore, where a group member landlord sells a property which is tenanted by another group member, it is doubtful that a business exists which is making relevant supplies capable of transfer as a going concern. Conversely, where a landlord sells a property which is tenanted by a company that is a member of the new landlord's VAT group, the business ceases after the transfer because the tenant and the new landlord effectively become one taxable person.

Customs policy is as follows.

The following situations will not be considered to be TOGCs:

1. Where the purchaser of the property rental business is a member of the same VAT group as the existing tenant.

2. Where a member of a VAT group sells a property, which is being rented to another member of the group, to a third party.

The following situation will be considered to be a TOGC:

3. Where the tenant who is a member of the landlord's VAT group is only one of a number of tenants. The presence of a tenant or tenants outside the group means that the whole transaction can still be treated as a TOGC.

Implementation date

This policy will take effect from 1 January 1999. Transactions prior to this date will not be affected. If transfers of the type described at 1 and 2 take place after 1 January 1999 they can still be treated as TOGCs if a deposit or other part-payment of the purchase price is received by the seller before that date. An amendment will be made to Public *Notice 700/9*.

For further information businesses and their advisers should contact their local VAT Business Advice Centre listed under Customs and Excise in the telephone book.

© Crown copyright

Appendix 14: HMRC Business Brief 16/99 (Extract)

20 July 1999

VAT: businesses transferred as a going concern – property

Introduction

This Business Brief clarifies Customs and Excise's policy following the VAT and Duties Tribunal decision in the case of the *Higher Education Statistics Agency* (LON 98/296).

The Higher Education Statistics Agency (HESA), is part of a VAT group which purchased properties with the intention of continuing the leases. The properties, bought at auction, were subject to an Option to Tax by the seller.

Customs refused to allow treatment of the transaction as the transfer of a business as a going concern (TOGC) as HESA did not notify them of their option to tax a property by the relevant date, ie upon payment of the deposit at auction. VAT was therefore chargeable by the seller of the property. HESA appealed against the refusal of TOGC status for the transaction, arguing the relevant date was not the date of payment of the deposit but the date of completion of the sale (some four weeks later – by which time the option to tax was in place).

The Chairman of the Tribunal considered the arguments in the case finely balanced but decided in favour of Customs. The Higher Education Statistics Agency has appealed to the High Court against the Tribunal's decision.

VAT treatment of assets of businesses transferred as a going concern

Generally no VAT should be charged on sales of assets where a business is transferred as a going concern. However before a sale of a property on which the option to tax has been exercised can be treated as a TOGC certain conditions must be met. Unless the purchaser has opted to tax the property and notified Customs in writing by the relevant date, the vendor must charge VAT on its sale.

Customs policy as stated in public *Notice 700/9 Transfer of a business as a going concern* is that the relevant date by which purchaser must notify their option to Customs is on or before the time that the property is supplied. The 'time of the supply' includes receipt of a deposit which may otherwise have created a tax point.

Customs' reaction to the decision

It has been submitted to Customs that the Tribunal decision suggests that the relevant date for the purposes of the TOGC provisions could be the date upon which an equitable interest in the property is transferred to the purchaser, rather than the time when the property is supplied. There is nothing explicit in the Tribunal decision which suggests this and Customs therefore believe the Tribunal's decision does not affect the current policy as set out in *Notice 700/9*.

The decision does, however, suggest that there is a need for Customs to re-examine the definition of the 'relevant date' within the TOGC provisions. This is already included in a review on the TOGC provisions planned for this year and Customs will seek the views of businesses as part of this review.

For further information traders and their advisers should contact their local VAT Business Advice Centre listed under Customs and Excise in the phone book.

Appendix 15: HMRC Business Brief 8/01 (extract)

2 July 2001

Opting to tax buildings to be converted to dwellings

This Business Brief is about how Customs and Excise will implement a Tribunal decision on how the option to tax buildings applies to those buildings which will be converted into dwellings. (The VAT and Duties Tribunal decision in the case of *SEH Holdings Ltd*, LON/98/1362.)

Tribunal decision

An option to tax cannot apply to a building or part of a building intended for use as a dwelling. The question for the Tribunal was whether it could apply to the sale of a building (in this case a pub) that would eventually be converted into dwellings. However the sale was to someone who was not carrying out the conversion work but had the intention to sell the building to someone else another party on the same day.

The Tribunal concluded that the option to tax did apply to the sale of the building. They decided that the person selling the building has only to consider the intended use of the building by the immediate purchaser, and that their intention has to be made known to the person selling the building at the time of the sale. This provides certainty for the person selling the building.

Customs policy

In the light of the Tribunal's decision, Customs policy is that where the immediate purchaser of a building (which the vendor had opted to tax) does not intend to use the building himself as a dwelling nor to convert the building into dwellings for sale or rent, the vendor must account for VAT on the sale of the building.

As the previously published guidance by Customs on this type of transaction was not clear, we will not insist on this policy being applied to previous transactions. However, traders should apply this new policy to transactions taking place on or after 1 August 2001.

There is no change to policy in cases where the immediate purchaser of an opted building does intend to use the building as a dwelling or to convert it to dwellings for sale or rent. In these circumstances, the sale of the building remains exempt unless vendor and purchaser have agreed that the sale should be taxable.

Auction sales

Customs are aware that there may be particular problems at auctions because the vendor is not normally aware of the purchaser prior to the auction day. The vendor may have difficulty in finding out what the purchaser intends to do with the building, at the time he has to decide whether to charge VAT or not if he has opted to tax the building. Similarly a purchaser who intends to convert a non-residential property into dwellings, and sell them zero-rated, may also find it difficult to agree with the vendor in writing, prior to the auction date, that the option to tax should still apply to the sale of the building.

Customs are currently reviewing this area of policy and will include the problems of auction sales. In the meantime we suggest that the purchaser should discuss any problem he is facing with the vendor or his representatives prior to the completion date so that they can agree to apply the correct VAT liability.

Customs recognise that in applying the decision strictly, there may be certain circumstances when the VAT charged becomes an additional cost and that this may discourage some developers from converting commercial property into dwellings. Consequently any business, which needs further advice on applying the decision, should contact their local VAT Office.

Transfer of part of a business as a going concern

This Business Brief sets out Customs' policy on the deduction of input tax incurred on expenses relating to the transfer of part of a business as a going concern. It implements the European Court of Justice decision of 22 February 2001 concerning *Abbey National Plc* (C-408/98).

Background

The Court found that costs incurred on services used for the purpose of transferring assets as a going concern formed part of a taxpayer's overheads. It found that the VAT on these costs had a direct and immediate link with the whole of its business activities. The implication being that where those business activities give rise to both taxable and exempt supplies, then the VAT incurred is only partly deductible.

However, the Court went on to consider instances where the services have a direct and immediate link with the clearly defined part of a business being transferred. It found that where this part of the business makes only taxable supplies then the VAT incurred would be deductible. Customs are changing policy to implement this part of the Court's decision.

Wider implications

Taxpayers who transfer part of their business as a going concern may be affected by this new policy. Customs take the view that VAT incurred on services that wholly relate to the transfer of part of a business, should be treated as an overhead of that part of the business.

Where that part of the business makes only taxable supplies, then the VAT incurred is deductible. Conversely, where only exempt supplies are made then the VAT incurred is not deductible. In instances where both taxable and exempt supplies are made then the VAT incurred is partly deductible, determined by reference to the partial exemption method in place. If the partial exemption method in place fails to achieve a fair and reasonable result Customs may be prepared to approve an alternative method.

Implementing the change

Customs are applying the decision to transfers taking place on or after 1 August 2001. Businesses may, if they wish, apply the new policy from an earlier date. Any business wishing to do so must apply the new treatment consistently from the date it makes the retrospective change. Claims will be subject to the normal three-year limit on refunds and claimants will need to produce the necessary records for the claim to be verified.

For further advice and information, traders and their representatives should contact their local VAT office or phone the national advice line on 0845 010 9000.

© Crown copyright

Appendix 16: HMRC Business Brief 11/01 (extract)

21 August 2001

Transfer of a business as a going concern and notification of option to tax

This Business Brief reports a change in the procedure for notification of an option to tax, where a property is purchased as part of the transfer of a going concern. The change follows the March 2001 decision of the VAT and Duties Tribunal in *Chalegrove Properties Ltd* LON/99/0851.

Background

Under certain circumstances, the buyer has to give written notification to Customs by the relevant date of his option to tax, as part of the conditions of the transfer. It was our view that we should have received this written notification on or before the relevant date. However, the Tribunal did not agree. We accept the Tribunal's view.

Guidance

Where the written notification of the buyer's option is made by letter, it is sufficient for the purpose of notification under Article 5 of Statutory Instrument 1995/1268, that the buyer has, on the relevant date, properly addressed, pre-paid and posted the letter. You may wish to retain evidence of posting. This guidance will apply to future transactions and can also apply to transactions having occurred within three years of the date of any claim (subject to the usual capping rules).

© Crown copyright

Appendix 17: HMRC Business Brief 14/04 (extract)

14 May 2004

2. VAT – partial exemption – attributing input tax to intended supplies of property

This Business Brief article reports a change in policy on evidence of an intention to make taxable supplies of property. It also clarifies policy on attributing input tax to intended supplies of property and when subsequent adjustments need to be made. This takes account of the decision of the VAT and Duties Tribunal in the case of *Beaverbank Properties* (Beaverbank) and of the House of Lords in the case of *Royal and Sun Alliance* (RSA).

This Business Brief withdraws VAT Information Sheet 08/01 regarding the attribution of input tax on speculative supplies of property.

Background

A taxpayer can deduct VAT on costs attributed to taxable supplies that it intends to make in future. Equally, if the intention is to make exempt supplies, then attributed VAT cannot normally be deducted.

Where an intention changes before costs are used the original VAT attribution may need to be adjusted. If the intention changes from exempt to taxable, then a taxpayer may be entitled to claim the VAT previously attributed to the exempt supply. This is known as a payback claim. Conversely, if the intention changes from taxable to exempt then VAT previously deducted may need to be repaid. This is known as a clawback adjustment. Further information is available in *VAT Notice 706 Partial exemption.*

Certain supplies of land and property that are exempt can be made taxable by making and notifying an option to tax (option). Doing so can allow VAT on costs to be deducted where it otherwise could not. Further information is available in *VAT Notice 742A Opting to tax land and buildings.*

Evidence of an intention to make taxable supplies of property

Some land and property supplies are always taxable whereas other supplies are exempt unless an effective option is in place. Prior to the *Beaverbank* case Customs maintained that, where an option was needed to make supplies taxable, then a taxpayer could only have an intention to make taxable supplies once an option was in place.

Customs now accept that a taxpayer can have an intention to make taxable supplies before an option is in place, even though the taxable supplies cannot occur until after the option is made. However, clear documentary evidence of taxable intention is essential.

Suitable evidence includes documents involving third parties that consistently show a firm commitment to make taxable supplies. For example, a document accepting a bank loan on the basis that taxable supplies will be made. However, in most cases, the best evidence of taxable intention remains an effective option to tax.

A firm commitment to make taxable supplies is essential before there can be a taxable intention where the normal liability of planned supplies is exempt. In particular, where property is to be let and the taxpayer is keeping his options open as to whether to opt or not, a taxable intention does not exist.

Customs recognise that property developers often look at many sites in connection with a taxable project and that it may be onerous to immediately opt them all. As projects progress through acquiring an interest in the land and doing necessary work to active marketing, the weight of evidence needed to substantiate a continuing taxable intention without an option will increase. At the same time any commercial reasons to put off opting will decrease. Where a taxpayer is actively marketing a property Customs view the lack of an option as strong evidence that the taxpayer is merely keeping his options open as to whether to opt and that a taxable intention does not exist.

Changes of intention

VAT on costs related to subletting property must be attributed to planned exempt supplies unless there is absolutely no doubt that only taxable supplies will be made. VAT incurred on rents paid (and on other day-to-day costs) that have been attributed to exempt supplies cannot be adjusted once an option is put in place. This is because a payback claim can only be made if costs are put to an alternative taxable use. Costs such as rent for expired periods are not available for use in making taxable supplies because they have effectively been used up in trying to make exempt supplies.

VAT on costs incurred prior to the option that are not used up before the option is made will be available for adjustment assuming all other conditions are met. Equally, VAT on day-to-day costs incurred following the making of an effective option can be attributed to taxable supplies.

Speculative supplies of property (unclear intention)

Some land and property businesses incur VAT on costs without knowing what supplies will be made. For example, costs related to acquiring land for property development when it is not yet clear what type of project, if any, will take place. In these situations it is not possible for VAT to be directly attributed to either taxable or exempt supplies.

Provided the costs are incurred for business purposes, the VAT can be treated as residual VAT relating to the business as a whole. Residual VAT can be deducted to the extent allowed by the taxpayer's partial exemption method.

If a project is aborted, and costs incurred wasted, no adjustments are made to the deduction of VAT on those costs. But, if a project is firmed up or costs are used in different projects in which taxable or exempt intentions are known, then payback or clawback may apply.

Impact of RSA

Following the comments of Lord Hoffmann in *RSA* there has been speculation that the lack of a clear intention of what supplies would eventually be made in speculative property projects prevents the later application of payback or clawback. Customs view the apportionment of residual input tax incurred in speculative projects under partial exemption methods as attribution to taxable and exempt intentions and thus view the input tax as eligible for later adjustment if all other conditions are met.

Claims as a result of the changed policy on intentions

Some taxpayers may consider that they have wrongly attributed input tax in the past based on Customs declared policy. Claims may be submitted for under-claimed input tax subject to the appropriate time limits. For all claims, suitable documentary evidence of intention must be held as discussed above.

(i) If the net value of adjustments is £2,000 or less, the business may amend its VAT account and include the value of the adjustment on its current VAT return.

(ii) If the net value of adjustments is more than £2,000, a separate claim for payment must be submitted to the local VAT office.

Appendix 17: HMRC Business Brief 14/04 (extract)

Recovery of over-claimed tax as a result of RSA

Some taxpayers may have made claims to Customs or prepared their VAT accounts based on the decisions of the High Court or the Court of Appeal in this case. Customs will be seeking to recover any input tax, deducted by taxpayers, which is not now due to the taxpayer. Taxpayers who:

- made claims following the High Court/Court of Appeal decisions or

- relied on the High Court/Court of Appeal decisions when completing their VAT returns and now know that tax has been over-claimed on returns

should make a voluntary disclosure to their local VAT office so that recovery, with interest where appropriate, can be arranged as soon as possible. If a voluntary disclosure is not made and Customs discover the error, the taxpayer may be liable to a mis-declaration penalty.

Further information

For further information please contact the Customs' National Advice Service on 0845 010 9000.

Appendix 18: HMRC Business Brief 21/04 (Extract)

10 August 2004

1. VAT: VAT position of share issues and partnership contributions following the European Court of Justice decision in *KapHag Renditefonds*

This Business Brief clarifies Customs' position on two issues arising from the decision of the European Court of Justice in the German case of *KapHag Renditefonds v Finanzamt Charlottenburg* (Case C-442/01):

> A Whether the issue of shares constitutes a supply for VAT purposes; and

> B The VAT position of contributions to partnerships.

The case of *KapHag* concerned the admission of a new partner into a partnership on payment of a capital contribution. The European Court held that no supply was being made by either the individual partners or the partnership to the incoming partner in return for the capital contribution.

A – Whether the issue of shares constitutes a supply

The *KapHag* decision has been cited as authority for the view that an issue of shares by a company is similarly not a supply for VAT purposes. It is claimed that an issue of shares therefore falls outside the terms of Item 6 of Group 5 of Schedule 9 to the Value Added Tax Act 1994. That Item exempts from VAT:

> 'The issue, transfer or receipt of, or any dealing with, any security or secondary security…'

It is Customs' view that the formation or variation of a partnership arrangement is wholly distinguishable from the position where a company issues shares in return for consideration. *KapHag* was concerned solely with the issues surrounding a partnership. The VAT treatment of share issues has been considered by the Court of Appeal in *Trinity Mirror Plc* ([2001] STC 192) where it was held that an issue of shares by a company did constitute a supply of services for VAT purposes and these fall to be exempt under Item 6 of Group 5 of Schedule 9 to the Act. In most circumstances there will then be a restriction of input tax under the partial exemption rules. Further information is available from *VAT Notice 706 Partial exemption*.

B – Contributions to partnerships

Partnerships to which this section applies include 'normal' partnerships of individuals or corporate bodies, limited partnerships whose members are individuals or corporate bodies, overseas limited partnerships that are registered as 'normal' partnerships or corporate bodies and limited liability partnerships.

Background

In *KapHag*, the incoming partner was contributing cash in return for admission into the partnership but it will often be the case that the contribution is in the form of other assets. For example, a new partner's contribution may comprise land or interests in land. The European Court's decision tacitly accepted the Advocate-General's Opinion that the same principles would apply whether the contribution consisted of cash or other assets. Whatever the nature of the assets comprising the contribution, there is no reciprocal supply from the partnership.

However, where the assets are not cash, the making of the partnership contribution may have other VAT consequences.

The Advocate-General was satisfied that there was 'no doubt that the new partner is effecting an act of disposal of his assets, for which the admission to the partnership is not the consideration' (paragraph 33 of the Opinion). Such a disposal can therefore have VAT consequences when the partner contributing the assets is a VAT registered person. These consequences will vary depending on the nature of the assets being contributed.

KapHag establishes that nothing is provided by the partnership in return for the assets contributed, therefore any such disposal by the incoming partner is made for no consideration. The VAT Act provides that certain things are subject to VAT even when they are provided or done for no consideration. Customs' view is that all those provisions will still apply where there is no consideration when there is a contribution to partnership assets. A VAT registered person may therefore have to account for tax if he contributes assets to the partnership in the circumstances described in the Act. The VAT consequences can be considered under several main heads:

(i) Contribution to partnership comprising services;

(ii) Contribution to partnership comprising goods other than land;

(iii) Contribution to partnership comprising land or interests in land;

(iv) Whether contribution to partnership can constitute the transfer of a going concern;

(v) How the partnership can reclaim the output tax accounted for by an incoming partner on his contribution as its input tax;

(vi) Capital Goods Scheme consequences; and

(vii) Transfer of assets out of a partnership.

(i) Contribution to partnership comprising services

A partnership contribution may comprise services rather than goods – examples of this could be a trademark or trading logo or the use of an asset the ownership of which is retained by the incoming partner. Two legislative provisions set out the circumstances in which such a contribution may be regarded as a taxable supply, paragraph 5(4) of Schedule 4 to the VAT Act and the Value Added Tax (Supply of Services) Order 1993 (SI 1993/1507).

A supply can arise under paragraph 5(4) where a taxable person applies business goods to private use or makes them available for purposes other than those of his business. The taxable person or his predecessor must have been entitled to input tax under sections 25 and 26 of the VAT Act on the supply of those goods (or anything comprised in them) to him.

The Supply of Services Order similarly provides that a supply arises where a taxable person applies bought-in services to private or non-business use for no consideration where he has been entitled to input tax credit under sections 25 and 26. The value of such a supply cannot exceed the taxable person's input tax entitlement.

Where the above criteria are satisfied, a VAT registered incoming partner will have to account for tax on the supply of services that he is regarded as making in the disposal of the services from his existing business. The partnership may be able to recover this as its input tax where the contributed services are to be used for its business. The procedure for doing this is described at (v) below.

(ii) Contribution to partnership comprising goods other than land

If a partnership contribution comprises goods other than land that a taxable person (the transferor) held as assets, then a deemed supply will be generated as a result of Paragraph 5(1) of Schedule 4 to the VAT Act. This deemed supply does not require there to be consideration when the goods are transferred. It does however only apply where the taxable person disposing of the goods, or their predecessor, if for example they obtained the goods by way of a TOGC, was entitled to full or partial credit for the VAT charged when the goods were supplied to him. Where such a deemed supply arises, the incoming partner will have to account for VAT. The partnership may be able to recover this as its input tax where the contributed assets are to be used for its business. The procedure for doing this is described at (v) below.

(iii) Contribution to partnership comprising land or interests in land

The VAT treatment of land or interests in land also depends upon whether the incoming partner or his predecessor was entitled to deduct input tax in relation to the property that he is contributing to the partnership. For example, if he had opted to tax the property, or it was inherently taxable like new freehold commercial property, there may be a deemed supply as described at (ii) above. The incoming partner will then have to account for VAT on this supply. As with other contributed goods, the partnership may be entitled to recover this as input tax where the property is to be used for the partnership's business. The procedure for doing this is described at (v) below.

Please note all submitted notifications of an option to tax need to be signed by 'an authorised signatory' as described in paragraph 7.1 of *VAT Notice 742A Opting to tax land and buildings*.

(iv) Whether contribution to partnership can constitute the transfer of a going concern

It is possible that when assets are transferred by way of a partnership contribution that this could qualify to be treated as a transfer of a going concern (section 49 of the VAT Act and Article 5 of the VAT (Special Provisions) Order 1995 (SI 1995/1268)). If the contribution meets the conditions to be treated as a transfer of a going concern no VAT will be due from the transferor.

(v) How the partnership can reclaim the output tax accounted for by an incoming partner on his contribution as its input tax

When an incoming partner contributes goods and/or services (on which VAT is due as described above) and the partnership uses them for its business purposes, the partnership can recover the VAT as input tax subject to the normal rules. The incoming partner cannot issue a tax invoice, but in order to provide the partnership with acceptable evidence to support a claim for recovery of input tax, he may use his normal invoicing documentation overwritten with the following statement:

> 'Certificate for Tax on Partnership Contribution
>
> No payment is necessary for these goods/services. Output tax has been accounted for on the supply.'

The incoming partner must show full details of the goods and/or services on the documentation and the amount of VAT shown must be the amount of output tax accounted for to Customs and Excise.

(vi) Capital Goods Scheme consequences

Where the capital contribution is in the form of an interest in land or a computer, it may be an existing capital item of the incoming partner under the Capital Goods Scheme (CGS). If the transfer to the partnership constitutes a supply which is a disposal of an existing CGS item, then this will wind up the existing CGS item and a disposal adjustment may be due. If the transfer constitutes a TOGC then this will end the current interval for the incoming partner and the partnership will then be responsible for making adjustments for any remaining intervals.

As transfers of assets capital contributions will always constitute either a supply or a TOGC, any existing CGS items will always either be subject to a disposal adjustment or continuing CGS adjustments.

Even if the asset transferred as a capital contribution is not a CGS item in the hands of the incoming partner, it may create a new CGS item for the partnership when its transfer constitutes a supply. If this happens the partnership will need to make adjustments in subsequent intervals in the normal way.

The CGS is further explained in *VAT Notice 706/2 Capital Goods Scheme*.

(vii) Transfer of assets out of a partnership

KapHag was only concerned with assets moving into a partnership in the form of a partnership contribution. It did not cover the reverse situation, where partnership assets are paid out to an outgoing partner or otherwise disposed of by the partnership for no consideration. Where a transfer of assets out of a partnership for no consideration occurs, one of the following sets of circumstances will apply.

(a) If the incoming partner accounted for output tax when he contributed the assets to the partnership and the partnership was entitled to recover all or part of this as its input tax, there will be a subsequent supply by the partnership when the same assets are transferred out unless the transfer out now satisfies the TOGC criteria.

(b) If no output tax was accounted for when the assets were contributed to the partnership because they constituted a TOGC, the transfer out of the same assets will be a deemed supply upon which the partnership will have to account for tax unless the TOGC criteria are again satisfied.

(c) The partnership may be transferring out more assets than those originally contributed to it. Although the original contribution to the partnership may not have been a TOGC, the subsequent transfer out may now satisfy the TOGC criteria. If it does, no VAT will be due from the partnership.

(d) The original contribution to the partnership may have been a TOGC but the partnership may now be transferring out less of the assets than were originally contributed. Unless the assets being transferred out still meet the TOGC criteria in their own right, there may be a deemed supply upon which the partnership will have to account for the appropriate tax. As explained at (ii) and (iii) above, the entitlement of the partnership or its predecessor to deduct input tax in relation to the items that are the subject of the transfer out will determine whether or not there is a supply.

Application of section 45 of the VAT Act 1994

In the past, there was uncertainty as to whether it was section 45(1) of the VAT Act that led to there being no supply from a partnership to an incoming partner. That section provides for the registration of partnerships in the following terms:

'45(1) The registration under this Act of persons –

(a) carrying on a business in partnership, or

(b) carrying on in partnership any other activities in the course or furtherance of which they acquire goods from other member States,

may be in the name of the firm; and no account shall be taken, in determining for any purpose of this Act whether goods or services are supplied to or by such persons or are acquired by such persons from another member State, of any change in the partnership.'

Partnerships in England and Wales have no legal identity. A new partner joining a partnership, or old one leaving it, would result in a new partnership rather than change the composition of the existing one. Without s45(1), deregistration and registration would be necessary every time a partner joined or left. The purpose of s45(1) is to ensure continuity by providing that a business carried on in a firm's name is treated as a continuing business irrespective of changes in its composition. The situation addressed by s45(1) is therefore entirely different to that considered in *KapHag*.

Further information

Further information on this change is available from Customs' National Advice Service on 0845 010 9000. This number should also be used for general enquiries.

Appendix 19: HMRC Business Brief 30/04

19 November 2004

VAT and partnership 'shares'

Background

Business Brief 21/04 clarified Customs' policy on share issues and partnership contributions following the European Court of Justice (ECJ) decision in *KapHag Renditefonds* (C-442/01). That Business Brief did not deal with the VAT position of transfers of partnership interests ('shares'). This Business Brief explains the VAT treatment of transactions involving the transfer of a partner's 'share'.

Is the disposal of a 'share' in a partnership a supply?

KapHag established that a partnership entity or the existing partners are making no supply when a new partner is admitted in return for making a capital contribution. The question arises whether the subsequent disposal by the partner of that 'share' in the partnership is a supply for VAT purposes. It is important to bear in mind that this 'share' is distinct from the assets that were contributed by the partner when they joined the partnership. Therefore, even though the selling price of the 'share' may be determined by the value of those assets, they are not the subject of the later sale, which has its own liability for VAT purposes.

Although the ECJ has not considered this type of transaction with respect to partnership 'shares', there have been a number of cases where it has given a decision in respect of transactions involving shares in companies. The cases of *Polysar* (C-60/90), *Harnas and Helm* (C-80/95), *Wellcome Trust* (C-155/94) and *Régie Dauphinoise* (C-306/94) have established that the mere acquisition and holding of shares in a company is not to be regarded as an economic activity. However, it has stated that transactions in shares or interests in companies and associations may constitute economic activity in three situations:

(a) Where the transactions constitute the direct, permanent and necessary extension of an economic activity.

(b) Where the transactions are effected in order to secure a direct or indirect involvement in the management of a company in which the holding is acquired.

(c) Where the transactions are effected as part of a commercial share-dealing activity.

Customs considers that the same principles apply to transactions involving partnership 'shares'. This means that in some circumstances the disposal of a partnership 'share' will not constitute a supply and in others it will.

Circumstances in which the disposal of a partnership 'share' will not constitute a supply

This list is not exhaustive. The most common situations in which the disposal of a partnership 'share' by a partner will not be a supply are likely to be:

1. *The 'share' is disposed of for no consideration* – A 'share' in a partnership comprises services rather than goods. When services are transferred, assigned or otherwise disposed of for no consideration, they do not constitute any supply for VAT purposes.

2. *The 'share' being sold was acquired simply as an investment* – Where a partner has acquired his 'share' merely to secure a share in any future profits and has had no involvement in running the partnership, the subsequent sale or assignment of that 'share' for consideration will not be an economic activity. This will not constitute any supply for VAT purposes.

Circumstances in which the disposal of a partnership 'share' will constitute a supply

Again, this list is not exhaustive. The most common situations in which the disposal of a partnership 'share' by a partner will be a supply are likely to be:

1. *Where the partnership 'share' was acquired and disposed of as a direct extension of the partner's economic activities* – Where a partner is a taxable person in their own right, the partnership 'share' may have been acquired in the course or furtherance of their own economic activities. If that is the case, the subsequent transfer or assignment of that 'share' for a consideration will also be economic activity of that taxable person. For example, the partner may have a business asset to be sold and, rather than selling the asset directly, may have contributed that asset into a partnership and sold the resultant partnership 'share' instead. The sale of that partnership 'share' will constitute a supply for VAT purposes.

2. *Where the partnership 'share' was acquired in order to obtain an active role in the business of the partnership* – Where a partner is a taxable person in their own right and had acquired the partnership 'share' in order to actively participate in, or control, the business of the partnership, then the sale of that 'share' can be economic activity on the partner's part. The sale of the 'share' will constitute a supply for VAT purposes.

3. *Where the partnership 'share' was acquired as part of a commercial partnership 'share-dealing' activity* – A partner who is a taxable person may have a business of dealing in partnership 'shares'. This will be economic activity on the partner's part. Sales or assignments of the partnership 'shares' that were acquired in the course of this activity that are for a consideration will constitute supplies for VAT purposes.

For the avoidance of any doubt, you should note that supplies of partnership 'shares' in the above circumstances cannot be disregarded by virtue of section 45(1) of the VAT Act 1994. As Business Brief 21/04 explained, the purpose of s45(1) is to ensure continuity by providing that changes in the composition of a partnership do not create the need for a partnership to deregister and re-register for VAT every time the partners change. It also makes it unnecessary to take account of any changes in the composition of the partnership when determining what supplies have been made or received by the partnership business. The section has no effect upon any supply that one of the partners may be making as a taxable person in their own right.

Liability of supplies of partnership shares

In those circumstances where the disposal of a partnership 'share' is a supply, that supply will be an exempt financial service.

Treatment of VAT on associated purchases

Where the disposal of an existing partnership 'share' is not a supply, the VAT incurred in connection with the disposal will normally not be input tax. Where the disposal is a supply, the related VAT will be input tax, but recovery will normally be fully restricted under the partial exemption rules as the supply is exempt. This is subject to the *de minimis* provisions (see *VAT Notice 706 Partial exemption*).

Application to past transactions

This Business Brief clarifies existing policy and the above principles will be applied to all future transactions. Where a past transaction has been treated differently from the above and resulted in an underdeclaration Customs will take no further action. If a past transaction has been treated differently and resulted in an overdeclaration, businesses may use the voluntary disclosure procedure to reclaim the VAT. Any such claims will be subject to the 'three-year capping rules' and rules relating to the payment of statutory interest.

Further information

For further help and advice please contact Customs' National Advice Service on 0845 010 9000.

Appendix 20: HMRC Business Brief 32/04 (Extract)

2 December 2004

1. VAT – the future of the option to tax: consultation document

Further to the Pre-Budget Report announcement, this Business Brief provides details of a three-month consultation entitled 'The future of the option to tax'. This consultation primarily seeks views on the conditions under which businesses will be able to revoke their option to tax, but it also addresses other associated issues some of which have a wider application on the option to tax.

Background

Until 1989 the construction and sale, together with some leases, of non-residential property were zero-rated for VAT. Following infraction proceedings, the European Court of Justice found this to be contrary to the EC Sixth VAT Directive, therefore VAT became chargeable on such supplies. This meant that the supply of the freehold of a building to a landlord, who rented property for onward exempt leasing, was no longer VAT-free. In order to reduce the VAT impact on business, the Government introduced the option to tax on supplies of commercial property with effect from 1 August 1989. This allowed the landlords to deduct the input tax up front and charge VAT on their supplies of rent over the life of the lease.

In 1995 the law was amended to allow revocation of an option to tax after 20 years, subject to the written consent of Customs having been obtained first.

Purpose of consultation

The first options to tax will become eligible for revocation in August 2009. In order to take into account business practices and needs, the Government is seeking the views and suggestions of property owners to assist in establishing the conditions under which written permission to revoke the option will be given.

As well as looking at issues relating to revocations, the consultation document also deals with a number of associated issues including: the possibility of early revocations; one option covering all properties held (global options); opted properties transferred between members of VAT groups; demolition of opted buildings and how the option applies to extended or linked buildings. These associated issues need to be addressed to ensure the smooth application of any future revocations, but in some cases may have wider application.

Obtaining copies of the Consultation Document

The consultation document can be obtained from Customs web site at http://www.hmce.gov.uk.

Questions about the consultation and requests for printed copies of the document should be referred to:

- Iain Burt on 0207 865 4842, e-mail iain.burt@hmce.gsi.gov.uk; or
- Katherine Thompson on 0208 929 0711, e-mail katherine.thompson@hmce.gsi.gov.uk

All responses must be received by 2 March 2005. They can be sent via e-mail to vrc.review@hmce.gsi.gov.uk, or posted to:

James Ormanczyk
VAT: The Future of the Option to Tax
HM Customs and Excise
Land and Property Team
Third Floor
1 Parliament Street
London
SW1A 2BQ

Further information

For further help and advice please contact Customs' National Advice Service on 0845 010 9000.

© Crown copyright

Appendix 21: HMRC Business Brief 12/05 (extract)

15 June 2005

5. VAT: Landlord inducements to tenants entering leases

This Business Brief article provides revised guidance on the VAT status of inducement payments by landlords to tenants. It replaces earlier guidance in Business Brief 04/03, dated 27 May 2003.

Business Brief 04/03

Business Brief 04/03 set out Customs' policy following the European Court of Justice (ECJ) and High Court decisions in the case of *Trinity Mirror Plc (formerly Mirror Group Plc)*.

In paragraph 26 of the ECJ's judgment, it was held that a 'tenant who undertakes, even in return for a payment from the landlord, solely to become a tenant and pay the rent does not, so far as that action is concerned, make a supply of services to the landlord'. The High Court subsequently held that paragraph 26 of the ECJ judgment is narrowly drawn, and Business Brief 04/03 sought to give guidance on that.

In line with the High Court ruling, Business Brief 04/03 advised that 'a prospective tenant receiving an inducement payment would make a taxable supply by affording the landlord the advantage of being bound by the lease obligations the tenant has to fulfil'. In effect, this meant any such obligations other than to pay the rent (eg to redecorate the demised area every five years) would be sufficient to make the inducement payment consideration for a taxable supply.

Change of policy

Following representations from and detailed discussions with various bodies, HM Revenue & Customs now accept that lease obligations, to which tenants are normally bound, do **not** constitute supplies for which inducement payments on entering leases are consideration.

HM Revenue & Customs believe that the majority of such payments are therefore likely to be outside the scope of VAT as they are no more than inducements to tenants to take leases and to observe the obligations in them. There will be a taxable supply only where a payment is linked to benefits a tenant provides outside normal lease terms. However, merely putting such a benefit as an obligation in a lease will not mean it ceases to be a taxable transaction.

It is considered that this change of policy now effectively puts inducement payments on a similar VAT footing to rent free periods, in being mainly outside the scope of VAT and only a taxable consideration when directly linked to a specific benefit supplied by a tenant to a landlord.

Examples of **taxable** benefits by tenants that may be supplied in return for such inducements are:

- Carrying out building works to improve the property by undertaking necessary repairs or upgrading the property.

- Carrying out fitting-out or refurbishment works for which the landlord has responsibility and is paying the tenant to undertake.

- Acting as anchor tenant.

HM Revenue & Customs accept that this is a difficult area where the undertakings of landlords and tenants can change a number of times in the course of negotiating a tenancy. HM Revenue & Customs will therefore seek as much documentation as possible before reaching a decision. HM Revenue & Customs will not assume that there has been a supply and agree that less specific indicators do not determine the issue. For example, publicity indicating that Company X is to take a lease in a development does not, in itself, determine that the company is an anchor tenant.

Equally, undertakings to use improved materials as part of continuous repairs under a tenant repairing lease would not constitute a taxable benefit to the landlord under the first example above.

Past transactions

The policy change referred to above may mean that there have been certain cases where tax has been charged wrongly in respect of landlord inducements under the guidelines in Business Brief 04/03.

Tenants who have wrongly declared output tax on inducements received are not obliged to adjust their VAT position. However, if they choose to, then, subject to the three-year capping provisions, they should proceed in accordance with *VAT Notice 700/45 How to correct errors and make adjustments or claims.*

Option 1

In accordance with paragraph 3.4 of *Notice 700/45*, where both the tenant and the landlord are registered for VAT, and provided they both agree, tenants may raise credit notes to their landlords and both parties would then adjust their VAT account.

Option 2

Alternatively where the landlord is not registered for VAT, tenants may choose to make a claim under section 80 of the VAT Act 1994 for overpaid tax. Any such claim would be subject to the three-year capping provisions and the unjust enrichment defence. Sections 5 and 14 of *Notice 700/45* refer.

Note that if past transactions are revisited there may be implications as regards deductible input tax – see below.

In all cases where tenants choose to correct past transactions it will be necessary to:

- review the attribution of any input tax incurred on costs, where that attribution was based on those costs being cost components of the taxable supply now being reversed out, and make any resultant adjustments and
- revisit their partial exemption calculations for the prescribed and longer periods involved as necessary.

Whichever method tenants choose to correct the incorrect treatment of inducements as supplies, landlords must reduce their input tax deductions in respect of the inducements to the extent that they ultimately recovered or were entitled to recover input tax previously. This could also require partial exemption calculations to be revisited if an inputs based method is used or to determine whether de-minimis limits are exceeded.

Further information

For further help and advice please contact HM Revenue & Customs' National Advice Service on 0845 010 9000.

Appendix 22: HMRC Business Brief 16/05 (Extract)

18 August 2005

1. VAT ruling – *Abbey National Plc* – virtual assignments

This Business Brief article provides guidance on how to treat supplies of virtually assigned property and the use of Schedule 10 para 8 VAT Act 1994, following the High Court case of *Abbey National* (CH/2004/APP/0496).

Background

(a) Virtual assignment of property

The main issue in this case concerned property that had been leased to, and occupied by, Abbey National ('Abbey'). Abbey sought to outsource its property holdings, including its lease interests, to a third party, in return for a lump sum. In the case of property leased by Abbey, the leases were not generally legally assigned to the third party, as the landlord's permission had not, or could not, be obtained. However, the intention was to leave the third party in the same economic position as though the leases had been legally assigned to them, so that they could then grant purported leases of those properties back to Abbey. This was referred to as a 'virtual assignment'.

The Tribunal (LON/2003/303) agreed with HM Customs and Excise (now HM Revenue & Customs – HMRC) that a 'virtual assignment' back to Abbey of a property that had originally been virtually assigned to the third party was not a supply that came within Article 13(B)(b) of the Sixth VAT Directive – 'a leasing and letting of immovable property'. The Tribunal therefore agreed that there was a taxable supply of agency and management services to Abbey from the third party, rather than an exempt supply of leasing and letting of immoveable property.

The High Court, in hearing Abbey's appeal, identified a critical issue as being the extent to which Abbey's right of occupation under a virtual assignment (ie where Abbey had not legally transferred its interest to the third party) could still be viewed as a genuine right of occupation granted to it by the third party. The High Court accepted that a genuine right of occupation had been granted by the third party to Abbey even though the third party did not have a right of occupation itself to pass on, as the relevant rights had not initially been created between Abbey and the third party. As a result the virtual assignment back from the third party to Abbey was viewed as coming within Article 13(B)(b) of the Sixth VAT Directive – 'a leasing and letting of immovable property', such a supply being exempt unless an appropriate election to waive exemption had been made. As a result, Abbey were successful in their appeal that a virtual assignment of the relevant properties back to them by a third party was a supply equivalent to 'a leasing and letting of immoveable property'.

The Court of Appeal has given HMRC leave to appeal against this decision of the High Court.

(b) Schedule 10, paragraph 8, VAT Act 1994

A secondary issue in this case was the VAT treatment of those leases that Abbey had virtually assigned to the third party and where the property was occupied by Abbey's sub-tenants. The Tribunal had agreed with Abbey that in these cases there was a deemed supply by virtue of Schedule 10 para 8 of the VAT Act 1994 by the third party to Abbey's sub-tenants, as the consideration for the sub-leases granted by Abbey accrued to that third party, despite the third party not having a legal interest in the property.

HMRC cross-appealed on this issue to the High Court. The view of the Court was that as the agreement between Abbey and the third party incorporated a clear and unambiguous declaration of trust, whereby the rents paid by the sub-tenants accrued in full for the benefit of the third party, Schedule 10, para 8 of the VAT Act 1994 applied and thus the third party should be treated as making the supplies to Abbey's sub-tenants. The Court upheld the Tribunal decision, applying the approach indicated by Lord Slynn in the case of *Nell Gwynn House Maintenance Fund Trustees* [1999] STC 79.

HMRC has not appealed against this aspect of the High Court's decision.

The way forward

(i) Virtual assignments

In HMRC's view, under a virtual assignment agreement (ie where the interest in the property has been assigned to a third party without the landlord's consent and is then purported to be assigned back by the third party) the third party's assignment is not an exempt supply of an interest in land, but a taxable supply of management and agency services. As a result, the third party provider should continue to account for VAT on the taxable supply.

As HMRC is appealing against the decision of the High Court, taxpayers may wish to tax the supplies pending the outcome of that appeal. HMRC will issue assessments to taxpayers who chose to follow the High Court decision and exempt their supplies, but will not enforce these assessments unless it is ultimately successful on appeal. If this is the case, interest and penalties will be applied to the assessments.

If the taxpayer decides to follow the views of HMRC, they may submit voluntary disclosures to protect their position. They need to make it clear on the form or in a covering letter that these claims are not to be repaid until the litigation has concluded. If they do not make such an annotation and the claim is repaid, they will be treated as having followed the decision of the High Court.

Given an option to tax cannot be made retrospectively, whatever course of action taxpayers choose to follow for now, they might like to consider whether to opt to tax in respect of either Abbey or HMRC being ultimately successful before the courts.

(ii) Schedule 10, paragraph 8

Where a legal transfer of an interest in a property is contemplated and:

- the benefit of all of the consideration received from sub-leases accrues to a third party and
- that consideration is held in a trust for the benefit of the third party,

then Schedule 10, paragraph 8 of the VATA 1994 applies. The third party will be deemed to have made the supply to the sub-lessees as the benefit of the consideration from those sub-leases accrues to the third party. Such a deemed supply will be exempt, unless an option to tax has been exercised by the third party.

Equally, by virtue of Schedule 10, paragraph 8(b) to the VATA 1994, any input tax attributable to the original grant made by the legal owner becomes the input tax of the third party from the time the deemed supply to the sub-lessee is made. The legal owner must not, in these circumstances, claim any of the input tax directly attributable to the legal grant made to the sub-lessee. Thus, where the legal owner remains in occupation of part of the building for the purpose of his business, and

- is still required to make taxable payments to the landlord, or
- carry out repairs to the property,

the third party will only be entitled to recover a portion of the VAT that is directly attributable to the deemed supply made by the third party to the sub-lessee. This is subject to the third party having exercised an option to tax. The legal owner will still be entitled to recover any appropriate input tax incurred in the course of any taxable supplies made by him in relation to any continued occupation of the building, or part of a building, of which he is a legal owner.

Further information can be found in Public Notice 700/45 'How to correct VAT errors or make adjustments or claims' and Business Briefs 25/04 and 28/04. These are available on the HMRC website or by contacting the National Advice Service on 0845 010 9000.

SUBJECT INDEX

Indexing is by reference to section numbers.
'TOGCs' = 'transfers of business as going concern'

abuse of law
    designated schemes 12.5
    hallmarked schemes 12.4, 12.5
    how and when disclosure
        made 12.6
    leaseback arrangements 12.5
    major interest in a building,
        first grant 12.5
    notifiable schemes 12.3
    penalties for non-compliance
        with disclosure
        requirements 12.7
    principles 12.2
    schemes to be disclosed 12.3
        VAT-registered
            businesses 12.4
accounting periods 1.8
    charging VAT 1.7
    landlords 6.23
    property transactions 7.1
agricultural land
    election to waive
        exemption 6.3, 6.21
alteration
    approved, meaning of 4.1
    commercial buildings 3.4
    non-commercial buildings 3.5
anti-avoidance rules
    election to waive
        exemption 6.5
    and partnership interests 5.7
apportionment of VAT 3.8
architects, services 3.7

assignments
    leases of commercial
        property 5.3
        reverse 5.5
        'virtual' 5.4
    property transactions 7.4
beneficial owners
    elections to waive
        exemption 10.1
    recent developments 10.3
    TOGCs 10.2
break clauses, leases 5.11
buildings
    capital goods schemes 9.2
    construction of 3.2
        as dwelling 3.5
    'new', definition of 5.2
building materials
    definition of 3.6
    recovery of VAT 3.12
    and zero-rating 3.3, 3.5, 3.6
building regulation fees
    standard-rating 3.13
building services and
    materials 3.3
business activity, definition of . . . 2.5
Business Briefs
    election to waive exemption . . . 6.1
    partnership interests 5.7

capital allowances 14.5
capital gains tax 14.6

capital goods scheme

defined 9.1

land and buildings affected 9.2

short leases 9.5

tax adjustment

calculation 9.4

errors in making 9.1

procedure 9.3

TOGCs 9.6

VAT groups 9.7

caravans, residential and

holiday 3.10

certificate of use

non-commercial buildings 3.5

disposal 4.1

CGT (capital gains tax) 14.6

charging VAT 1.7

civil engineering work

capital goods scheme 9.2

'completed' 5.2

construction 3.2, 3.10

'new' 5.2

commercial buildings

alteration 3.4

'completed', meaning 5.2

construction 3.4

disposals . . . . *see* **disposals of**

commercial property

freehold sales 5.2

landlords 6.23

leases, grant or assignment

of . . . . *see under* **leases**

lenders 6.26

'new'

meaning of 5.1, 5.2

standard-rated

transactions 2.1

non-commercial buildings

distinguished from . . 2.2, *see also*

non-commercial buildings

rental properties . . . . *see* **rental**

properties

standard-rating 3.4, 5.2

TOGCs 2.1

uncompleted 5.1

VAT exemptions 2.1

vendors 6.24

compensation

disposals of commercial

property 5.12

completion

property transactions 7.3

connected persons

and charging VAT 1.7

construction

of building, meaning 3.2

civil engineering work . . . 3.2, 3.10

commercial buildings 3.4

meaning 3.2

for VAT purposes 3.1

new 3.2

non-commercial buildings . . 3.1, 3.5

person constructing,

defined 4.1

property transactions 7.2

and reconstruction 3.2

services supplied in course of . . 3.2

standard-rating 2.1, 3.1

works included in 3.2

construction supplies

standard-rating 2.1

conversion

concept 3.2

non-commercial buildings 3.5

Court of Session 4.1

covenants 14.11

crane over-sailing licence, grant . 14.13

demolition

standard-rating 3.9

demolition supplies
standard-rating 2.1
developers
cash contributions by 13.4
non-commercial property,
disposals 4.2
residential, as vendors 6.25
dilapidations
disposals of commercial
property 5.13
disposals of commercial property
assignments *see under* **assignments**
compensation, statutory 5.12
dilapidations 5.13
freehold sales 5.2
leases . . . . *see under* **leases**
licences to occupy 5.8
normal rule 5.1
partnership interests 5.7
rent apportionments 5.14
rent-free periods 5.6
reverse assignments 5.5
reverse premiums 5.5
disposals of non-commercial
property
approved alterations 4.1
certificate of use 4.1
developers, VAT implications
generally 4.2
dwellings 4.1
listed building, substantial
reconstruction 4.1
long leases 4.1
by person constructing 4.1
by persons other than person
constructing 4.3
refurbishment 4.2
short leases 4.1
planning point 4.2
surrenders of leases 4.4

zero-rating 4.1
DIY housebuilders 3.12
dwellings
constructions of buildings
designed as 3.5
developers, VAT
implications 4.2
non-commercial buildings
other than 3.5
qualifying conditions 2.3
zero-rating considerations,
disposals 4.1, 4.2

election to waive exemption
agreement to elect or
not elect 6.7
agricultural land 6.3, 6.21
anti-avoidance provisions 6.5
by beneficial owner 10.1
cessation 6.12
commercial buildings,
surrender of leases 5.4
coverage 6.8
defined 6.1
disadvantages for purchasers
and tenants 6.22
effect 6.9
example of operation 6.13
exempt supplies 6.17
extent of 6.3
finance provision 6.5
landlords of commercial buildings
and land 6.23
meaning 1.12, 6.1
non-commercial buildings,
surrender of leases 4.4
not applicable when 6.4
notification form 6.16
partial exemption 6.18
persons bound 6.10

persons electing 6.6
procedure 6.16
reasons for 6.2
registration for VAT 1.4
rent, adding VAT to 6.14
revoking 6.11
short leases 4.1
timing 6.15
vendors of commercial buildings
 and land 6.24
zero-rating, as most favourable
 tax treatment 6.18
exchange of contracts **5.10, 7.3**
exempt supplies
defined 1.2
election to waive
 exemption 6.17
and input tax 2.1
exemption, election to waive . . . . . *see*
  election to waive exemption

farmers, flat rate of VAT **1.2**
finance provision, election to waive
 exemption **6.5**
first grant of major interest **4.1**
abuse of law 12.5
fixtures and fittings **14.10**
freehold sales
commercial property 5.2
property transactions 7.3

grant
of crane over-sailing licence . . 14.13
first, major interests 4.1, 12.5
of leases
 commercial property . . . 5.3, 5.4
 for premiums 7.4
 and re-grant 5.4
 for rent 7.5
of licences, for rent 7.5

group registration **1.5**

hallmarked schemes, abuse
 of law **12.4, 12.5**
holiday caravans, exclusion from
 zero-rating **3.10**
housebuilders, DIY **3.12**

in-house construction services
self supply 8.3
value 8.4
input VAT
capital goods schemes,
 adjustments 9.4
developers of non-commercial
 buildings 4.2
election to waive exemption . . . 6.2
 incurred before, recovery . . 6.19
exempt supplies and 2.1
property transactions . . . 1.10, 6.18
recovery 1.9, 6.18
 before election to waive
  exemption 6.19
 transaction costs 11.5
 recovery, election to waive
  exemption 6.18
see also **output VAT**
invoicing
property transactions 14.9
and recovery of VAT 14.14

joint ventures
registration of property
 business 1.5

land, covenants concerning **14.11**
land registry fees **14.4**
landlords . . *see also* **tenancies; tenants**
accounting periods 6.23
costs, payments by tenants . . . 14.9

and election to waive
    exemption 6.23
insurance premiums paid to . . 14.8
rights 14.14
VAT position 14.14
abuse of law 12.5

leases
break clauses 5.11
commercial property
    grant or assignment of 5.3
    surrenders 5.4
grants or assignments
    commercial property 5.3
    property transactions 7.4
new, transfer of business as going
    concern 11.2
non-commercial property
    long and short leases 4.1
    surrenders 4.4
reverse surrenders 5.4
surrenders
    commercial property 5.4
    non-commercial property . . 4.4
    property transactions 7.6
    reverse 5.4
variations 5.4, 7.7
legal owners, disregarded for VAT
    purposes **10.1**
lenders, commercial property . . .**6.26**
licences, grant for rent **7.5**
licences to occupy **5.8**
light, rights of **14.12**
listed building, substantial
    reconstruction of **4.1**
local government facilities **2.5**
long leases **4.1**

major interest
defined 4.1
first grant 4.1

abuse of law 12.5
grant in non-commercial
    building 4.3
management companies, transfers of
    roads etc to **13.5**
mixed development,
    sale of **11.3**

nominees, and transfer of business as
    a going concern **10.2**
non-commercial buildings
alteration 3.5
certificate of use 3.5
change of use 8.6
commercial buildings
    distinguished 2.2,
    see also **commercial buildings**
construction 3.1, 3.5
conversion 3.5
defined 2.2
developers, VAT implications . . 4.2
disposals . . . . *see* **disposals of**
    non-commercial property
dwellings, other than 3.5
grant in 4.3
sub-contractors 3.5
zero-rating 2.1, 3.1, 3.3, 3.5
notices
building materials 3.6
certificate of use, non-commercial
    buildings 4.1
election to waive
    exemption 6.17
non-commercial buildings,
    relevant residential or
        charitable purpose 4.2
relevant residential purpose/
    charitable purpose 4.2
notification form, election to waive
    exemption **6.16**

option to tax *see* **election to waive exemption**

output VAT . . . . *see also* **input VAT**

    capital goods schemes,

        adjustments 9.4

    charging 1.7

    property transactions 7.1

    self-supplies 8.1

owner-occupier, sale to or by **11.3**

partnership interests, disposals of commercial property **5.7**

paying VAT **1.9**

pension funds **10.1**

person constructing, defined **4.1**

place of supply **1.11**

planning agreements

    cash contributions, by

        developers 13.4

    roads and sewers 13.2

    statutory provisions 12.3

    transfers of roads etc to

        management companies . . 13.5

planning point, short leases **4.2**

possession before completion **7.3**

premiums

    grant of leases and

        licences for 7.4

    reverse 5.5

property business

    registration requirements 1.5

property transactions

    accounting periods 7.1

    capital allowances 14.5

    capital gains tax 14.6

    completion 7.3

    construction work 7.2

    covenants concerning land . . 14.11

    crane over-sailing licence 14.13

    exchange of contracts 7.3

exemption from VAT 2.1

fixtures and fittings 14.10

freehold sales 7.3

input tax 1.10, 6.18

insurance premiums, paid

    by tenant 14.8

invoicing 14.9

land registry fees 14.4

landlords

    costs, paid by tenant 14.9

    rights 14.14

    VAT position 14.14

leases

    grant or assignment for

        premiums 7.4

    grant for rent 7.5

    surrender 7.6

    variations 7.7

licences, grant for rent 7.5

light, rights of 14.12

output VAT 7.1

planning 14.14

possession before completion . . 7.3

post-completion 7.3

premiums, grants or assignment of

    leases for 7.4

rent, grants of leases and

    licences for 7.5

rent, default by tenant 14.14

service charges 14.7

stamp duty land tax . . . . *see* **stamp duty land tax**

standard-rated transactions,

    miscellaneous 5.9

purchasers

election to waive exemption,

    disadvantages for 6.22

reconstruction

and construction 3.2

listed building 4.1

recovery of VAT

building materials 3.12

and invoicing 14.14

property transactions 1.10

refurbishment **4.2**

capital goods scheme 9.2

registration requirements **1.4**

relevant charitable purpose

non-commercial buildings,

disposal 4.2

use for 2.5

relevant residential purpose

non-commercial buildings,

disposal 4.2

use for 2.4

rent

adding VAT to 6.14

apportionments, disposals of

commercial property 5.14

grant of leases and

licences for 7.5

tenant, default by 14.14

see also **landlords; tenancies;**

tenants

rent-free periods

commercial property 5.6

transfers of business as going

concern during 11.3

rental properties

transfer of business as a going

concern 11.2

residential buildings *see* **dwellings;**

non-commercial buildings

residential caravans

zero-rating 3.10

reverse assignments, case law **5.5**

reverse premiums, case law **5.5**

reverse surrenders, meaning **5.4**

roads, planning agreements . **3.11, 13.2**

sales and leasebacks

transfer of business as going

concern 11.2

see also **leaseback arrangements**

scope of VAT **1.1**

self-build projects (voluntary

bodies) **3.12**

self-supplies

defined 8.1

impact 8.5

in-house construction

services 8.3

value 8.4

non-commercial buildings, change

of use 8.6

persons affected 8.2

TOGCs and 11.4

service charges **14.7**

sewers, planning

agreements **3.11, 13.2**

short leases

capital goods scheme 9.5

non-commercial buildings 4.1

planning point 4.2

stamp duty land tax

background 14.1

and leases, VAT on 14.2

short 4.2

and partnership interests 5.7

and TOGCs 14.3

standard-rating . . . . *see also* **zero-rating**

apportionment of VAT 3.8

architects, services of 3.7

building regulation fees 3.13

building services and

materials 3.3, 3.6

charging VAT 1.7

commercial buildings

construction and

alteration 3.4

freehold sales 5.2
construction 2.1, 3.1
demolition 3.9
demolition supplies 2.1
miscellaneous property
    transactions 5.9
'new buildings' 2.1
surveyors, services of 3.7
taxable supply 1.2
TOGCs 11.1
sub-contractors, non-commercial
    buildings **3.5**
sub-sales, TOGCs 11.3
supply, place of 1.11
surrender of leases
    commercial property 5.4
    non-commercial property 4.4
    property transactions 7.6
    and re-grant 5.4
    TOGCs 11.2
surveyors, services **3.7**

taxable person
    defined 1.3
    rental properties, TOGCs 11.2
    transfer of business as a going
        concern (TOGC) 11.2
taxable supply
    capital goods scheme, tax
        adjustment 9.4
    defined 1.2
    input tax, recovery 6.18
    self-supplies 8.1
    variations of leases 7.7
    vendors of commercial buildings/
        land 6.24
tenancies
    long leases 4.1
    prospective, sale with
        benefit of 11.3

tenants . . . . *see also* **landlords**
    default by 14.14
    election to waive exemption,
        disadvantages for 6.22
    insurance premiums paid by . . 14.8
    joint, registration of property
        business 1.5
    landlords' costs, payment of . . 14.9
    not yet in occupation, transfer
        of business as going
        concern 11.3
    in VAT group of vendor/
        purchaser 11.3
Town and Country Planning
    Act 1990, s106
    planning agreements 12.3
    undertakings under 3.11
transaction costs, input tax 11.5
transfer of business as a going
    concern (TOGC)
    beneficial owners 10.2
    capital goods schemes 9.6
    commercial buildings 2.1
        rental property 5.1
    incorrect analysis of
        transaction 11.2
    mixed development, sale of . . . 11.3
    new leases 11.2
    and nominees 10.2
    notification by transferee 11.2
    owner-occupier, sale to or by . . 11.3
    property TOGCs, miscellaneous
        examples 11.3
    rent-free period, during 11.3
    rental properties 11.2
    rulings 11.2
    sale and leasebacks 11.2
    and self-supply charges 11.4
    stamp duty land tax 14.3
    standard-rating 11.1

sub-sales 11.3

surrenders 11.2

taxable persons 11.2

tenancies, prospective 11.3

tenant in VAT group of vendor or
    purchaser 11.3

tenants not yet in
    occupation 11.3

VAT groups 11.4

VAT, outside scope of 1.2, 2.1

undertakings

Town and Country Planning Act
    1990 (s106) 3.11

VAT groups

capital goods scheme 9.7

elections by members of 6.20

exempt/partly exempt, self-supply
    charge on TOGC 11.4

registration 1.6, 6.20

and TOGCs 11.4

of vendor or purchaser,
    tenant in 11.3

VAT . . . *see also* **input VAT; output VAT**

apportionment 3.8

charging 1.7

irrecoverable, refurbishment
    work 4.2

paying 1.9

recovery of 1.10

scope 1.1

VAT-registered businesses or persons

abuse of law 12.4

accounting periods 1.8

vendors

commercial buildings 6.24

residential developers as 6.25

tenant in VAT group of 11.3

village halls **2.5**

'**virtual' assignments**

definition/case law 5.4

voluntary bodies

self-building projects by 3.12

zero-rating . . . . *see also* **standard-rating**

advantages 4.1

apportionment of VAT 3.8

building materials 3.3, 3.5, 3.6

disposals 4.1

and election to waive
    exemption 6.18

holiday caravans, exclusion
    from 3.10

long leases 4.1

as most favourable tax
    treatment 1.10, 6.18

non-commercial
    buildings 2.1, 3.1, 3.3, 3.5

recovery of VAT . . . . . *see* **recovery
of VAT**

residential caravans 3.10

short leases 4.2

and taxable supply 1.2

Notes

Notes